Death Ride of the Panzers

DENNIS OLIVER

GERMAN ARMOR AND THE RETREAT IN THE WEST 1944-45

Skyhorse Publishing

Skyhorse Publishing books may be purchased in bulk at special discounts for sales promotion, corporate gifts, fund-raising, or educational purposes. Special editions can also be created to specifications. For details, contact the Special Sales Department, Skyhorse Publishing, 307 West 36th Street, 11th Floor, New York, NY 10018 or info@skyhorsepublishing.com.

Skyhorse® and Skyhorse Publishing® are registered trademarks of Skyhorse Publishing, Inc.®, a Delaware corporation.

Visit our website at www.skyhorsepublishing.com.

10 9 8 7 6 5 4 3 2 1

Library of Congress Cataloging-in-Publication Data is available on file.

Cover design by Rain Saukas
Cover photos and illustration courtesy of Dennis Oliver

ISBN: 978-1-5107-2095-4
Ebook ISBN: 978-1-5107-2096-1

Printed in China

Contents

Acknowledgments

I wish to thank the staff at the National Archives and Records Administration in Maryland and Darren Neely, who helped source most of the photographs reproduced in this book. I would also like to thank Professor Yuri Shepelev of the University of St Petersburg, who was able to access a number of German wartime records held at the Russian Central State Archive, Karl Berne and Valeri Polokov for their advice and assistance, particularly in matters of formation and uniform insignia, Gary Kwan who was able to identify some of the units depicted in photographs from private collections, and Claudio Fernandez who assisted with the original research for the illustrations. Richard Hedrick's research, translation, and interpretation of Kriegsstärkenachweissungen was invaluable. I would also like to acknowledge the research carried out by Martin Block, Ron Owen Hayes, and the late Ron Klages.

Introduction

By early 1944, few in Germany and occupied Europe could have doubted that an Allied landing would be long in coming. Indeed, the design and building of static defense installations, which Hitler had christened the Atlantic Wall, had begun as early as March 1942. They were intended to stretch from the Franco-Spanish border along the Bay of Biscay to Brest, follow the Channel coast and the North Sea to Skagen in Denmark, and begin again at the Norwegian-Swedish frontier near the Oslofjord and continue as far north as the Soviet border. The defenses of the Atlantic Wall would also include the Channel Islands, particularly Alderney, which is closest to Britain. The Wall was to be made up of gun emplacements and bunkers constructed from concrete and steel, barbed wire fences, minefields, concrete walls, and fortified artillery positions. The strongest position was situated on the island of Sotra in Norway, where a complete turret taken from the battleship Gneisenau, with three massive 283mm guns, commanded the approaches to Bergen.

The required administrative effort alone was staggering, with some 600 different designs for bunkers, artillery, and machine-gun emplacements involved. As building progressed and resources became more scarce, weapons captured from the Czech, French, and Russian armies were pressed into service. Their use required additional amendments or alterations to the existing emplacements. The building program was given added impetus by the large-scale raids at St Nazaire, which took place just days after Hitler issued the initial order for the building of the Atlantic Wall, and at Dieppe, where over six thousand Allied troops were landed on four separate beaches. Nevertheless, and despite the claims of German propaganda, the construction of the Atlantic Wall was half-hearted. Far from being viewed as a potential invasion front, France was seen as a soft posting by most German troops.

As the result of an extensive inspection tour instigated by Generalfeldmarschall Gerd von Rundstedt (at the time Oberbefehlshaber West), which lasted from May to October 1943, the shortcomings of the German defenses became all too obvious. A key weakness lay in the extensive length of the Wall, which effectively prohibited any defense in depth; many German commanders felt that the system would at best delay an enemy landing. Importantly, the superbly trained and equipped German infantry units—the same who had thrown back the British and Canadian raiders at St. Nazaire and Dieppe—had been continually called upon to supply replacements for the Russian front. By June 1944, the Atlantic wall defenses were manned by depleted formations, with one in six infantry battalions made up of Eastern volunteers from Russia, Georgia, Armenia, and Ukraine.

Opinion was divided as to whether the coming invasion should be met on the beaches with all available resources, including tanks, or held by the defenses of the Atlantic Wall until the enemy's intentions were clear and then countered by powerful armored reserves held much further inland. An advocate of the former was Generalfeldmarschall Erwin Rommel, who conducted a further investigation of the western defenses in November 1943 at the behest of Hitler. Tasked with upgrading the Atlantic Wall, Rommel was to assume command of Heeresgruppe B, the army group responsible for the Pas de Calais and Normandy, the most likely invasion areas. However, Rundstedt and the commander of Panzergruppe West, General Leo Freiherr Geyr von Schweppenburg, were understandably reluctant to bring their tanks within range of the enemy's naval gunfire. In what may have been a compromise solution, and perhaps making a virtue of necessity, it was proposed that the German defenses should consist of what came to be called Crust, Cushion, and Hammer zones.

The Crust zone was the concrete and steel of the Atlantic Wall. The Crust would delay the Allied invasion forces, inflicting as many casualties as possible, until the armored reserves could be committed. It seems that by this time, only the most optimistic German planners believed that the Atlantic Wall alone would actually stop the invaders. Under Rommel's direction, the Crust was reinforced with millions of mines and obstacles intended to stop or disable Allied landing craft. The Cushion zone was the area immediately inland from the beaches and it was planned that this would be defended by fortified emplacements providing

a real defense in depth. However, as most of the available concrete had been used to create the Crust zone, the Cushion consisted of a system of trenches and bunkers constructed from wood and earth. The Hammer would be Schweppenburg's Panzergruppe West, controlling the bulk of the German armor, based much further inland.

When the invasion came, the assumptions of both sides would be sorely abused in the fighting that followed. Although the Normandy battles were for the most part brutal slogging matches conducted between groups of infantrymen, it would be the Panzer units which would time and again cut off an Allied penetration, hold up an enemy attack and finally, between the villages of Chambois and Trun in the Dives valley, save the bulk of the German Army in the West.

Despite the German preparations, the Allied landings on the beaches of Normandy in the early hours of June 6, 1944, and the subsequent establishment of a secure bridgehead could only be described as a spectacular, if qualified, success. The overly complicated chain of command imposed by Hitler, the lack of intelligence in matters as basic as weather forecasting, and the assumption that resisting the invasion would be no different in concept than the opposition of a river crossing (albeit on a larger scale) meant that the defenders were operating under a severe disadvantage. The

German defenders were caught largely off guard. Those in the forward positions, the Crust, were swamped by naval gunfire or overrun by specialist bunker-busting tanks; although many held on to their positions for far longer than could have been reasonably expected, most were simply crushed by the weight of fire. Many of the battalions made up from Eastern volunteers fled or surrendered at the first opportunity.

Further inland, Generalmajor Heinrich-Hermann von Hülsen, the commander of 21.Panzer-Division and the only armored formation close to the coast, had placed his division's Panzer-Regiment 22 on alert as early as 6:00 am. In the ensuing confusion, the first tanks would not move off for another three hours. As Hülsen's men were preparing their tanks, an ad-hoc Kampfgruppe from 12.SS-Panzer-Division Hitlerjugend, made up principally from the first battalion of SS-Panzer-Regiment 12 and the infantrymen of SS-Panzergrenadier-Regiment 26 and both hastily transferred from Panzergruppe West to Rommel's Heeresgruppe B, moved quickly towards the front. By 10:00 am, they were exchanging fire with Canadian units near the village of Buron, northwest of Caen. The fighting here would last for most of the day, with the men of the Hitlerjugend division denying the Canadians their objective of Carpiquet and its airfield. Realizing the importance of the airfield, the Germans strengthened their positions with machine-gun emplacements and an extensive minefield; it would be more than a month before Carpiquet fell to the Canadians. Finally, at 5:30 pm the units of 21.Panzer-Division mounted a concerted counterattack aimed at the Allied positions at Biéville-Beuville. Although elements of the division's infantry actually managed to reach the coast, fighting their way behind enemy lines into the town of Lion-sur-Mer by 8.00 pm, the supporting tanks of Panzer-Regiment 22 were held up at Périers-sur-le-Dan, almost 3 kilometers to their rear, and the Panzergrenadiers were quickly surrounded.

At day's end, the Allies had landed over 130,000 men with their equipment and supporting armor and had advanced up to 10 kilometers inland in places. Although the Germans had not immediately responded with the decisiveness and aggression for which they were justly famous, the steadfastness of the coastal defenses and the initiative of local commanders meant that strategically important centers were denied to the Allies. Theywould not be taken until a heavy price was extracted in both men and equipment.

CHAPTER ONE

THE BREAKOUT

The Beginning

After gaining a bridgehead on the Normandy coast, the American, British, and Canadian units of the invasion force were able to do little more than consolidate the gains that had been made on the first day. Initially slow to react, the German defense was soon conducted with the skill and tenacity learnt in the uncompromising school of the Russian front. Any Allied gains were promptly met with the inevitable counterattack, often mounted by a hastily scraped together formation. Against this, however, must be measured the numbers of men and the amount of supplies that the Allies had been able to land on the invasion beaches since the afternoon of the initial landings, with some 20,000 tons of equipment being unloaded daily in the American sector alone. In the early days of July 1944, more US Army soldiers were waiting in Britain to be shipped to the front than were actually fighting in Normandy. One effect of the changing supply and manpower situation was the perception, if unofficial, that the British army was very quickly becoming the junior partner in the alliance. Although it was true that the British and Canadians fighting to take Caen had faced the strongest German forces, the breakout from Normandy, when it came, would be left to the Americans. The planned assault was given the codename Cobra and its architect, General Omar Bradley, stressed that the retreating Germans must not be allowed to create a solid defensive line as they had in the Bocage and around Caen, indicating just how traumatic those operations had been for the Allies.

After a false start on Monday, July 24, 1944, Operation Cobra went ahead on the following day, preceded by a massive aerial bombardment. The main weight of the bombing caught the tanks of Generalleutnant Fritz Bayerlein's Panzer-Lehr-Division, which had been concealed in the numerous woods and sunken lanes throughout the area. In his post-war account of the battle, Bayerlein claimed that his division was almost annihilated over the course of the next two days, with some fifty percent of the casualties being inflicted by the American bombers. [1]

The Americans quickly broke through the German defenses and, with the capture of Saint-Lô on the Bayeux-Coutances road, the entire western half of the Normandy front began to crumble. By Friday, July 28, 1944, Bradley's headquarters was receiving reports that resistance was in places nonexistent and where the Germans were able

---

1 *It has been suggested, with some justification, that Bayerlein was overstating the case here. The commander of the second battalion of Panzer-Lehr-Regiment 130, Major Helmut Ritgen, stated that not one of his Pzkw IV tanks had been lost as his battalion was held in reserve. He also stated that very few of the division's Panthers and Jagdpanzers, which had been in the frontline, had been destroyed by the bombing. It is entirely possible that the aerial assault accounted for the deaths of more French civilians than German soldiers and it is certainly true that a large number of American troops were killed and injured by their own bombs.*

to mount local counterattacks, they were poorly organized and often easily brushed aside. On the same day Coutances, about 40 kilometers west of Saint-Lô, was taken, but any further progress was halted when the lead American units ran into elements of 2.SS-Panzer-Division and 17.SS-Panzergrenadier. During the evening of the following day, the two Waffen-SS divisions mounted an attack on the exposed flank of US 2nd Armored Division near the village of Saint-Denis-le-Gast, about 15 kilometers to the south of Coutances, and met with some initial success. However, both formations had been fighting in Normandy for weeks without respite or replacements and were already badly depleted. After causing some early confusion and inflicting a number of casualties, the Germans were forced to withdraw, leaving most of their tanks and heavy equipment behind. On Sunday, July 30, in support of the American breakout, the British launched their own offensive code named Operation Bluecoat. Much of the armored reserves that the Germans had hoped to employ against the Americans, including the powerful II.SS-Panzerkorps, were now diverted to face the British. By the following Tuesday, the strategically important town of Avranches, over 30 kilometers to the south of Saint-Lô, fell to the Americans with an intact bridge across the Seine at nearby Pontaubault. Although the Grenadiers of Gen-

eralleutnant Viktor von Drabich-Wächter's 326.Infanterie-Division managed to hold the road junction of Vire, the Americans reached Mortain on August 3, which was less than 20 kilometers to the south. They occupied the town on the afternoon of the same day, inflicting further heavy casualties on 17.SS-Panzergrenadier-Division in the process.[2] By now those Germans units facing the Americans were fighting to escape.

Even the most optimistic German commanders realized that disaster was imminent and Feldmarschall Günther von Kluge, who had replaced Rundstedt as Oberbefehlshaber West in early July, begged Hitler to be allowed to withdraw to the natural barrier of the Seine. He argued that if the army in the west was encircled and destroyed, the Allies could drive straight into Germany. As US Army units were pouring across

_____

2 326.Infanterie-Division had replaced 2.Panzer-Division in the frontline around Caumont in late July and was severely battered by British armored units over the next week. Although the division's Panzerjäger-Abteilung 326 reported that ten Sturmgeschütz III assault guns were on hand in July, they are not mentioned in the following month and may have been either disabled or in repair. In any case, the division was badly undermanned by the first week of August and would lose much of its remaining strength in the defense of Vire. Losses included Drabich-Wächter, who was killed.

the Pontaubault Bridge, Hitler contacted Kluge by telephone from his home at Berchtesgaden. To the field marshal's utter dismay and astonishment, the Fuhrer not only forbade any retreat but ordered Kluge to immediately begin preparations for an attack in force aimed at Avranches, which theoretically would shatter the over-extended Americans.

Viewed from the map table at Berchtesgaden, Hitler's plan had every chance of success. The length of the American supply lines through Avranches did indeed present an opportunity to deliver a severe setback to the Allies if attacked in strength. The failure of the British and Canadians to take Caen meant that the armored units stationed around the town were no longer required, at least for the present. In addition, the identification of Lieutenant-General George Patton's US 3rd Army in western France, which the Germans had feared would be employed in a secondary invasion in the Pas-de-Calais, meant that the divisions stationed north of the Seine could be released for operations elsewhere.

In reality, however, the armored units facing the British had been bled white in almost two months of continual combat; the formations on the east bank of the Seine were all infantry units that had been slowly drained of men and material to reinforce the divisions fighting in Normandy. Moreover, any attack towards Avranches would have to be undertaken through the same dense Bocage countryside that had proven to be so much an advantage to the German defense. Even if these difficulties were to be surmounted, Kluge's men would be required to operate completely without air cover despite the promises of Reichsmarschall Göring, the commander of the Luftwaffe, that over 1,000 aircraft would be made available for the offensive.[3]

Two important considerations were also at play here. The first was Hitler's lack of confidence in his generals, which often bordered on contempt. The assassination attempt of July 20, 1944 had rocked Hitler, but it had also handed him the excuse to disregard any advice from his commanders that did not fit his perception of the situation. Any suggestion of withdrawal was met with accusations of cowardice and lack

of success was usually put down to treachery. To prove their loyalty to both Hitler and Germany, commanders were required to carrying out their orders to the letter regardless of the odds. Until the end of the war the planning and conduct of operations, often down to battalion level, was to be solely the preserve of the Führer. Secondly, Hitler and most of the German generals believed that the US Army was inferior to the British and that the remaining armored assets would be best employed against the Americans. This perception is difficult to explain and was probably created by the initial performance of US soldiers in North Africa. However, the Americans had learnt very quickly and Bradley's men were a far cry from the amateurish, albeit courageous, units that fought in Tunisia. Perhaps tellingly, Hitler confided to his aides that the counterattack would only succeed if Kluge had faith in the plan, preparing a convenient scapegoat in case of failure and providing a glimpse of his own uncertainty.

In a complete about-turn, perhaps encouraged by the news of reinforcements, Kluge now suggested that the attack go ahead without delay. Somewhat uncharacteristically, Hitler insisted that the attack not commence until August 8, the earliest when all the available units could be assembled, even at the risk of the situation at the front deteriorating further. However, after pro-

tests from both Kluge and his subordinate, SS-Obergruppenführer Paul Hausser, the commander of 7.Armee, it was agreed that the attack should commence at 10:00 pm on Sunday, August 6, 1944. The attack was to be codenamed Operation Lüttich with tactical control exercised by XLVII.Panzerkorps commanded by General Hans Freiherr von Funck, much to the chagrin of Hitler, who wanted General Heinrich Eberbach to lead the offensive.[4]

Many histories describing the battles around Mortain, including the official US Army account, accept that small, isolated American units were able to hold off up to four elite German armored divisions, two infantry divisions, and a number of powerful armored Kampfgruppen until reinforcements were able to resolve the situation. If the German units available to Kluge had been at anywhere near full strength, he would have had at his disposal tens of thousands of men and hundreds of armored vehicles. But the truth is that the German formations were so depleted that at best the

---

3 *Prior to the invasion, the Luftwaffe had just over 3,600 combat aircraft on the Western front. Although this may sound impressive, this total included the single-seat and twin-engined fighters engaged directly in the defense of the Reich and almost 1,000 nightfighters. Dedicated ground attack aircraft accounted for just 265 airplanes. On July 31, the day before the Americans took Avranches, just 231 fighter sorties were mounted over France and the bombers had long been restricted to operating during the short summer nights. It is difficult to understand why Kluge put any faith in Görings promises.*

4 *The Belgian city of Liège is referred to in German as Lüttich. In August 1914 Liège, universally considered one of the strongest fortresses in Europe, was captured by a small infantry force under the command of Eric Ludendorf, until then an unknown brigade commander. At the time Kluge was a young captain on the staff of XXI.Armeekorps.*

divisions were little more than strong brigades. A typical example would be the Kampfgruppe made up from the survivors of 17.SS-Panzergrenadier-Division Götz von Berlichingen. The division had been decimated after resisting the American breakthrough at Saint Lô during the early stages of Operation Cobra and was surrounded at Coutances, where it lost most of its remaining equipment. By early August, the division consisted of a number of small battle groups. The strongest of these was Kampfgruppe Ulrich, made up from a single Panzergrenadier battalion supported by a number of PzKw IV tanks, which had been detached from SS-Panzer-Regiment 2. They were, in all probability, all five combat-ready tanks that the regiment possessed at that time. The strongest unit available to Kluge was 116.Panzer-Division with perhaps sixty Panthers, although the recalcitrance of the divisional commander, General Gerhard Graf von Schwerin, did almost as much to hamper the attack as did the stubborn American resistance. By the afternoon of August 6, just hours before the attack was scheduled to begin, elements of only three Panzer divisions and one Panzergrenadier division had made their way to the Mortain area with parts of 1.SS-Panzer-Division Leibstandarte SS Adolf Hitler, which had been expected to move over 60 kilometers during the hours of darkness, struggling to reach

their assembly points.[5] Late in the evening a dense fog descended on the area. Just after midnight, as some units from the Leibstandarte division were still arriving at their designated jumping-off points, the attack went forward.

The two battle groups of 2.SS-Panzer-Division, under the overall command of Brigadeführer Otto Baum, pushed ahead to Mortain and in total darkness took the town by storm, capturing intact a battalion headquarters of the US 120th Infantry Regiment. Realizing that he must keep moving towards the west if the operation was to have any chance of success, Baum urged his men on, racing down the road from Mortain to Saint-Hilaire-du-Harcouët and securing the high ground north of Milly, threatening the town of Saint-Hilaire. Unknown to Baum, this was the junction of the US 1st and 3rd Armies. His presence there finally prompted the American command to take the attack seriously and despatch a combined arms force from the US 3rd Armored Division into the area.

The rapid advance of Baum's Kampf-

---

5   *In an incredible stroke of bad luck, the Leibstandarte's progress had been brought to a halt after the Panzer crews had managed to down an Allied fighter, only to have it crash directly onto the lead tank, blocking the road and holding the column up for hours.*

gruppe had left in its wake a single battalion of the US 120th Infantry Regiment, which had managed to hold on to Hill 317, located just to the east of Mortain at the edge of a forest. As the fog began to lift, the Americans on Hill 317 realized that they could easily observe every German unit in the area and proceeded to call down artillery fire, which increased in accuracy as the weather cleared. The small garrison on Hill 317 defended their position stubbornly, and despite determined attacks by the Grenadiers of the Götz von Berlichingen, division they managed to hold on and proved to be a thorn in the side of the German offensive throughout the battle.

To the north of Mortain, the first of the two battlegroups made up from elements of 2.Panzer-Division, on the right of the division's front, had thrust deep into the American lines. It had encountered little opposition save for being briefly delayed by a minefield, which accounted for the popular and experienced commander of Panzer-Regiment 3, Major Hans Schneider-Kostalski, who had been coordinating the attack. After the mines were cleared, the tanks continued on to le-Mesnil-Adelée, over 10 kilometers to the north-west of Mortain, brushing aside the US 119th Infantry Regiment and entering the village as the sun was rising. The second battlegroup, although moving off some two hours late, advanced rapidly and took advantage of the thick fog to captur the village of Bellefontaine.

By 5:00 am, the tanks of the right-hand column of 2.Panzer-Division were engaged in a firefight with a US Tank Destroyer battalion in front of Saint-Barthélemy and lost a number of vehicles before the town was eventually taken, although the American claim of forty German tanks destroyed is certainly exaggerated (official German records giving a figure of fourteen). However, the Germans could go no further, running into the lead elements of US 3rd Armored Division, which was being hurriedly moved forward. To make matters worse, the thick curtain of fog had started to lift and many of the German units, which by know had learnt to anticipate the inevitable Allied air-strikes, began to take to take up defensive positions and camouflage their tanks as best they could. The first American fighter-bombers had appeared over Mortain during the early morning, and before midday the skies were filled with Allied aircraft that ranged across the battlefield for more than three hours. Claims of over 100 German tanks destroyed are, however, certainly exaggerated and it is likely that American artillery units accounted for most of the German casualties and material losses. In spite of Görings promise that almost 1,000 Luftwaffe aircraft would support Kluge's offensive, not a single German fighter reached the Mortain area.

The Mortain counterattack had cost Funck's Panzerkorps the better part of its armored strength that could not be replaced and would surely have been more profitably used in the defensive operations of the coming weeks. Although localized skirmishes continued throughout the next day and Funck dutifully prepared for another assault, as ordered by Hitler, the rapidly deteriorating situation all along the front ensured there would be no further offensive operations at Mortain.

The prediction made by the commander of I.SS-Panzerkorps, Oberstgruppenführer Josef 'Sep' Dietrich, that depleting the Caen defenses of an armored reserve in order to prop up Kluge's offensive would lead to the fall of the city proved entirely correct. On August 8, 1944, the same day it was finally decided to abandon the attacks around Mortain, units of US 3rd Army captured Le Mans. Le Mans had been the headquarters of Hausser's 7.Armee and its loss threatened the German units in Normandy with encirclement. The infantry divisions of General Adolf-Friedrich Kuntzen's LXXXI.Armeekorps could do little to stop the Americans and the irreplaceable tanks of 9.Panzer-Division, which had originally been promised to Kluge, were fed into the battle piece by piece.

On the same day US Army units entered Le Mans, the British and Canadian forces around Caen launched a major offensive, codenamed Totalise, aimed at the high ground north of the town of Falaise, about 25 kilometers south of Caen. Despite a massive artillery bombardment and the employment of specially converted personnel carriers, the British and Canadians, in two days of desperate fighting, were able to progress less than halfway to their objective down the Route de Falaise before the advance began to stall. Only by chance were units of Oberführer Kurt Meyer 's 12.SS-Panzer-Division Hitler Jugend in the area, having been ordered to Mortain. By this time, Meyer's division had been reduced to two under-strength battle groups. The first and most powerful was led by Obersturmbannführer Max Wünsche, the commander of SS-Panzer-Regiment 12. In addition to his regiment's third and eighth companies equipped with Panther and Pzkw IV tanks, Wünsche could count on the Tigers of 2.Kompanie, schwere-SS-Panzer-Abteilung 101, and the under-strength first and second battalions of SS-Panzergrenadier-Regiment 26. Meyer also had at his disposal Kampfgruppe Waldmüller, made up of parts of the second battalion of SS-Panzer-Regiment 12 and a company from SS-Panzerjäger-Abteilung 12. With the survivors of 89.Infanterie-division, Meyer's men did much to halt the Allied offensive, denying Potigny to the British and thereby holding onto the Caen-Falaise road.

Renewing the attack on August 10, the

Canadians reached the high ground north of Falaise but, exhausted and facing determined opposition, they were unable to advance any further. The following morning, the Canadian corps commander replaced his armored divisions with infantry formations, effectively admitting that the offensive was at an end. Once again, as they often did in Normandy, the Germans had been able to scrape together just enough men and tanks to hold their line. Meyer's fortuitous initiative, bordering on insubordination, in refusing to move his division to Mortain probably made the crucial difference.

Nothing could, however, alter the fact that the Americans were steadily approaching from the south and, in the end, the pressure from the British and Canadians in the north must succeed in breaking the German front. Indeed, the British commander Montgomery, rather unusually supported by Patton, now suggested that the only option left to the Germans was a general retreat to the east and, in his view, the British should forego the capture of Falaise and instead strike towards the Seine while the Americans block the escape route through the Loire valley.[6]

Hitler, characteristically, had other ideas

and refused to allow a single unit to be withdrawn. In addition, the Führer persisted in his view that the British divisions were the main threat. Hitler ignored the advice of Kluge, who pointed out that the US Army had just kicked Hausser's 7.Armee out of its headquarters at Le Mans and pinned down the tanks of 9.Panzer-Division in the south. When the American offensive resumed, Patton's 3rd Army was able to advance to Alençon by August 12, 1944, and after beating off a strong German counter thrust by the tanks of Panzergruppe Eberbach, found themselves on the outskirts of Argentan by the following day, an advance of over 70 kilometers from their start point.[7]

With the major prize of Argentan in sight, and the defenders in disarray, the local American commander received an order to halt and then, to his astonishment, to withdraw. The reason given was that the British were advancing from the north and were determined to avoid any friendly-fire incidents.

The origins of this extraordinary order have never been satisfactorily explained and debate still rages over the identity of the author. In any case, a large gap of almost 20 kilometers in width was left open between Argentan in the south and Falaise in the north, both of which were still in German hands, which presented the Germans with the opportunity of escape. In addition, the short pause in the fighting allowed Kluge to reorganize his remaining armored reserves for the desperate struggle he knew was about to take place.

Just after midday on August 14, 1944, a new British offensive codenamed Tractable commenced with tanks and infantry advancing behind a dense smoke screen. The plan called for units of Canadian 1st Army, supported by the newly arrived Polish 1st Armored Division, to take Falaise by midnight of the first day and then move on to Trun, almost 20 kilometers to the south-east. From there, an advance to nearby Chambois would enable a link up with the Americans. Unlike previous operations, this assault would take place in daylight.

In one of those unbelievable chance occurrences, which seem to happen all too frequently in war, a Canadian officer carrying a complete set of plans for the coming operation drove into the German lines only hours before the offensive was about to begin. In short order the Allied plans were in the hands of the redoubtable Oberführer Meyer, whose

---

6 *Eisenhower and Bradley rejected Montgomery's plan in favour of the more conservative option of Patton pushing on to Argentan while the British were to take Falaise.*

7 *General Heinrich Eberbach, it will be remembered, was Hitler's choice to lead the Mortain attack. His ad hoc Panzergruppe was one of the last armored reserves left to the Germans and consisted of parts of 1.SS-Panzer-Division and 2.Panzer-Division, the second battalion of Panzer-Regiment 33 of 9.Panzer-Division, and elements of 116.Panzer-Division, although none of the latter's tanks or reconnaissance units were available.*

12.SS-Panzer-Division battle groups had done so much to halt Operation Totalise just days earlier. With every detail of the Allies intentions known to him, Meyer was able to make the most of his meager resources and placed his few remaining tanks and infantry along the Caen-Falaise road, where they were able to intercept the main Canadian drive. Although the smoke screen at first hampered the German defenders, a company of twelve 8.8 cm Pak 43 anti-tank guns were able to inflict severe casualties on the Canadian armored units, destroying a large number of tanks, including that of the killing the brigade commande and killing the entire crew. Despite the mounting casualties, the Canadians continued to attack throughout the remainder of the day, at one point meeting head-on a counterattack made by the Tigers of 2.Kompanie, schwere-SS-Panzer-Abteilung 102.[8]

---

8 *On the morning of August 14, 1944, this company, which had been continually engaged since the first week of July, had only three operational tanks, numbered 212, 231, and 241. Later that day during an attack near Soulangy Tiger 231, commanded by Untersturmführer Loritz, was lost and late in the afternoon Tiger 212 of Untersturmführer Münster was destroyed by Canadian infantrymen. On the following day the remaining vehicle, Tiger 241 commanded by Untersturmführer Martin Schroif, was joined by the tanks of 1.Kompanie and was involved in the fighting around Potigny.*

As darkness fell, parts of two Canadian infantry divisions had reached the high ground north of Falaise but were unable to break through the German defenders and enter the town. Further to the north, the Poles had taken Potigny earlier that afternoon.

Early on the following day, both the Canadian and Polish armored divisions resumed their drive south-east, pushing Meyer's men back towards the town of Falaise. At the same time on the left flank, the two infantry divisions which had gained the heights to the north-east of the town pushed south. At the end of another day's fierce fighting, Sherman tanks of 1st Canadian Army were in Soulangy, just three kilometers from the center of Falaise, but the town still held out and Trun, to the east, was firmly in German hands. However, on August 16, elements of the Canadian 2nd Infantry Division broke into Falaise. Although it would take a two more days to completely secure the town that was now only defended by scattered and isolated groups of German soldiers, the Canadians could regroup their forces for a final push to capture Trun, link up with the Americans, and close the ever-narrowing escape corridor.

At the very moment that Canadian infantrymen were fighting their way into Falaise, Hitler was demanding that Kluge mount another counterattack. Pleading that any offensive action was quite impossible and that the best part of the German army in the west was about to be encircled, Kluge at last persuaded Hitler that a general withdrawal was the only option left and Hitler relented late that afternoon. Not to be denied some measure of revenge, Hitler sacked the Feldmarschall and had him recalled to Germany on the following day. Convinced that he was about face execution and dishonour, Kluge took his own life by swallowing poison on a stopover in Metz. Hitler, who had been unable to contact Kluge for some hours during the morning of August 17 and immediately suspected that he was conspiring with the enemy, was now convinced and greeted the news with the comment that Kluge "probably would have been arrested anyway."

Kluge's replacement as Oberbefehlshaber West was Feldmarshall Walter Model, who had made a reputation for himself in conducting defensive operations in the east, often saving desperate situations, and was greatly admired by Hitler. In contrast to Kluge, Model was given a free hand. His first order was that Hausser's 7.Armee and Panzergruppe Eberbach should retreat immediately through the 20 kilometre wide gap that was still open south of Falaise on the afternoon of August 17, 1944. With the Americans once again advancing, it was crucial to hold open this corridor as long as possible. Obergruppenführer Wilhelm Bittrich's

II.SS-Panzerkorps were to hold off the British and Canadians on the northern edge, while on the southern front the remnants of XLVII.Panzerkorps, which had already been badly battered at Mortain, would hold the Americans.[9]

On August 18, the tanks of 1st Polish Armored Division, which had been organized into three battle groups, set off an a sweeping manoeuvre towards the southeast with the intention of outflanking Model's armored units and linking up with the Americans who had taken Argentan. The Canadians captured Trun on the same day and by August 19 the Poles had reached the outskirts of Chambois, just eight kilometers from Argentan, and driven out the last of the German defenders by nightfall. That same evening they established contact with the units of the US 3rd Army. Everything did not, however, go in the Allies favor. As the Poles were fighting their way into Trun, a Kampfgruppe of 2.Panzer-Division had managed to break through the Canadian front at Saint-Lambert-sur-Dives, almost exactly between Trun and Chambois, and kept the road open for six hours while large numbers of German troops made their escape. Just before sunset the Canadians managed to regain their positions and, although small parties infiltrated the Allied lines during the night and crossed the River Dives to safety, the German's escape route now known as the Falaise Gap was closed for the time being.

On the morning of August 20, 1944, Model ordered the remaining tanks of 2.SS-Panzer-Division and 9.SS-Panzer-Division to attack from outside the pocket towards the Polish positions on Hill 262, the high ground above the village of Coudehard referred to as Mont-Ormel, less than 6 kilometers to the north-east of Argentan.[10]

By noon, another Kampfgruppe made up of elements of 10.SS-Panzer-Division, 12.SS-Panzer-Division, and 116.Panzer-Division joined the battle and broke through the Polish front, once again opening the gap. While the Poles were occupied at Mont-Ormel, a battle group from 9.SS-Panzer-Division prevented the Canadians from coming to their assistance and within a few hours approximately ten thousand Germans were able to escape. The Polish units on the high ground of Mont-Ormel were, however, able to direct a steady rain of artillery fire onto the retreating Germans and Obergruppenführer Hausser, who had arrived on the scene, ordered that the Poles be annihilated. Scraping together the remnants of 2.SS-Panzer-Division and 352.Infanterie-Division, he threw them at the Mont-Ormel positions, inflicting such damage that the defenders could only watch as the survivors of XLVII.Panzerkorps fled through the gap. Exhausted, both sides chose not to continue the fight after nightfall, although sporadic artillery fire continued to harass the retreating Germans.

On the following morning, at 11:00 am, a final attempt was made to overrun the Polish positions at Mont-Ormel. The attack was only narrowly defeated; little more than an hour after the Germans withdrew, the Canadians managed to reinforce the Polish units defending the hill. That afternoon, the survivors of the German divisions which had been attempting to keep the gap open were ordered to retreat towards the Seine. By the evening of Monday, August 21, Canadian armored units had reached the Polish forces at Coudehard, while two Canadian infantry divisions had taken Saint-Lambert-sur-Dives and secured the area north of Chambois. What had become known as the Falaise

---

9   *By this time Bittrich's corps was made up of the 9.Panzer-Division, 3.Fallschirmjäger-Division, and parts of 21.Panzer-Division while XLVII. Panzerkorps, with General von Funck still in command, contained the survivors of 2.Panzer-Division and 116.Panzer-Division.*

10 *By this time 2.SS-Panzer-Division was made up of as few as ten tanks of SS-Panzer-Regiment 2 supported by the remnants of the third battalion of the Der Führer regiment, the remaining assault guns, and parts of the division's reconnaissance battalion.*

Pocket had finally been sealed.[11]

The German losses in this final battle of the Normandy campaign have never been calculated accurately. Estimates of casualties range from 10-15,000 men killed with a further 40-50,000 listed as missing or taken prisoner. Some formations were almost totally destroyed in the fighting, such as 12.SS-Panzer-Division, which could only muster three hundred men and ten tanks by the end of the Normandy battles and what little heavy equipment they managed to save was for the most part lost in the Seine crossings. The sacrifices of the armored units had, however, saved tens of thousands of their comrades who would play an essential part in the defensive battles of the next weeks and months, particularly in the Netherlands.

---

11   *Initially trapped inside the Pocket were the greater parts of 84.Infanterie-Division 276.Infanterie-Division, 277.Infanterie-Division, 326.Infanterie-Division, 353.Infanterie-Division, 363.Infanterie-Division, 2.Panzer-Division, 116.Panzer-Division, 1.SS-Panzer-Division, 10.SS-Panzer-Division, 12.SS-Panzer-Division, and 3.Fallschirmjäger-Division, plus stragglers from most of the German units that served in Normandy. Elements of these units would be able to escape during the battle, in particular the armored formations. Probably the most reliable figures given for material losses were those put forward by the Bombing Analysis Unit of the RAF in 1945, which estimated that 900 tanks and self-propelled guns and more than 14,000 motor vehicles were destroyed in the Pocket and the Gap and the fields and villages between Falaise and the Seine.*

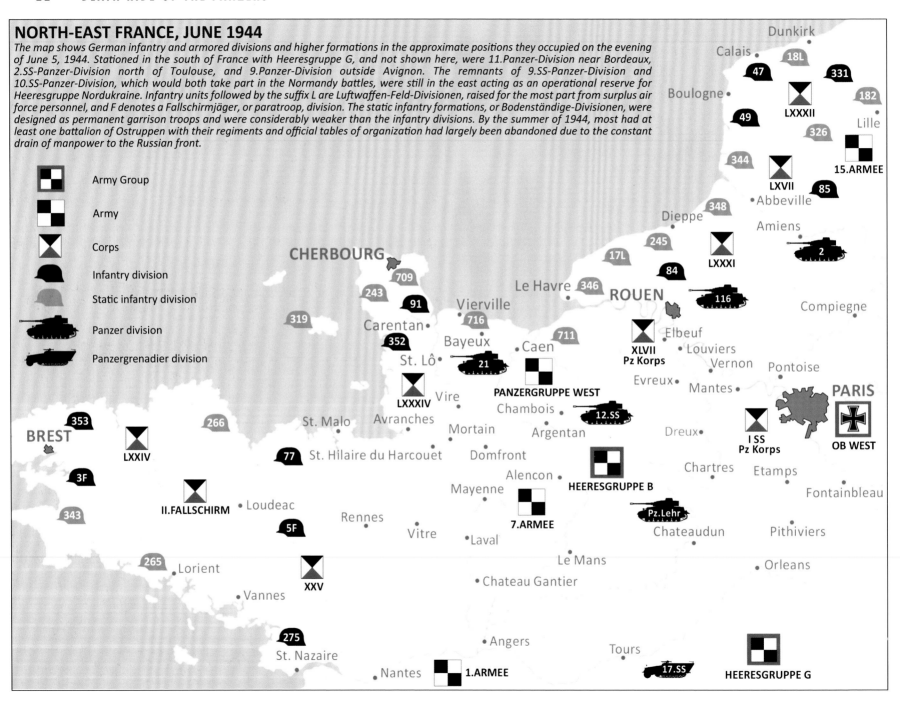

NORTH-EAST FRANCE, JUNE 1944

The map shows German infantry and armored divisions and higher formations in the approximate positions they occupied on the evening of June 5, 1944. Stationed in the south of France with Heeresgruppe G, and not shown here, were 11.Panzer-Division near Bordeaux, 2.SS-Panzer-Division north of Toulouse, and 9.Panzer-Division outside Avignon. The remnants of 9.SS-Panzer-Division and 10.SS-Panzer-Division, which would both take part in the Normandy battles, were still in the east acting as an operational reserve for Heeresgruppe Nordukraine. Infantry units followed by the suffix L are Luftwaffen-Feld-Divisionen, raised for the most part from surplus air force personnel, and F denotes a Fallschirmjäger, or paratroop, division. The static infantry formations, or Bodenständige-Divisionen, were designed as permanent garrison troops and were considerably weaker than the infantry divisions. By the summer of 1944, most had at least one battalion of Ostruppen with their regiments and official tables of organization had largely been abandoned due to the constant drain of manpower to the Russian front.

Army Group

Army

Corps

Infantry division

Static infantry division

Panzer division

Panzergrenadier division

PANZER-REGIMENT, JUNE-JULY 1944

All formations of the German Army were governed according to orders referred to as Allgemeine Heeresmitteilungen, issued on a regular basis by Oberkommando des Heeres, the high command of the army. These orders also fulfilled the functions of a bulletin or gazette, announcing the issue of awards or the confirmation of promotions. When organizational changes were called for, the relevant Allgemeine Heeresmitteilung was accompanied by one or more Kriegstärkenachweisung, today usually abbreviated to K.St.N, which were comprehensive tables of establishment showing the official composition of a unit in detail, listing the exact number of personnel and type of equipment from armored vehicles to small arms. Each Kriegstäärkenachweisung was identified by a title, number, and date. For example, Stabskompanie einer Panzer-Abteilung(frei Gliederung) K.St.N 1150(fG) von 1.4.1944. This particular K.St.N refers to the organization of a Panzer battalion's staff or headquarters company effective from April 1, 1944. The suffix "frei" Gliederung can be literally translated as free organization, but more accurately describes a freeing up of the administrative and resources burden involved in each company administering its own supply and transport needs. Beginning in early 1944, these services were transferred to battalion command level or higher, although the system was not extended to the army as a whole until August of that year. Not all these records survived the war; however, our knowledge of those affecting the armored units of the Wehrmacht is quite extensive. A number of authoritative books, especially the works of the late Tom Jentz, include details of the organizational changes introduced during the 1939-45 period with reference to the relevant K.St.N documents and it would serve no purpose to repeat those here. Rather, in this diagram and most of the others throughout this book, I have chosen to present a snap shot of an actual unit during a specific period, offering a comparison where necessary with the official establishment. I should stress that the information that has come down to us today is sometimes fragmentary or contradictory. Where this is so, I have either tried to make it obvious or omitted it entirely. The regiment shown here is SS-Panzer-Regiment 9, which was attached to 9.SS-Panzer-Division Hohenstaufen and took part in the fighting in Normandy and the attempts to relieve the units trapped in the Falaise Pocket.

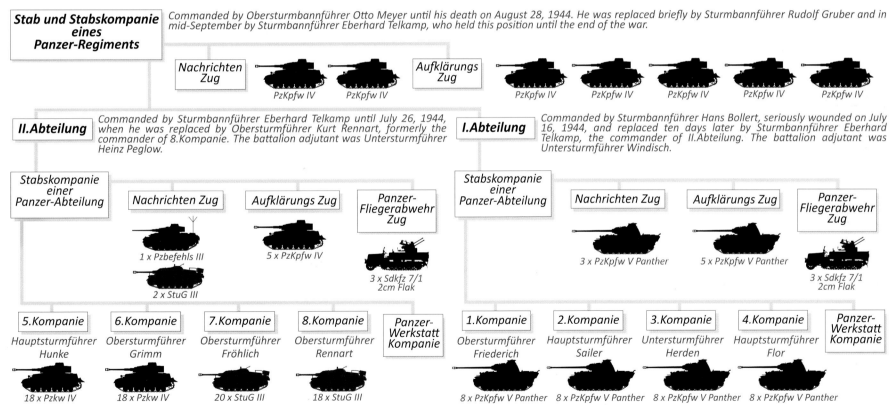

Stab und Stabskompanie eines Panzer-Regiments — Commanded by Obersturmbannführer Otto Meyer until his death on August 28, 1944. He was replaced briefly by Sturmbannführer Rudolf Gruber and in mid-September by Sturmbannführer Eberhard Telkamp, who held this position until the end of the war.

Nachrichten Zug — PzKpfw IV — PzKpfw IV

Aufklärungs Zug — PzKpfw IV — PzKpfw IV — PzKpfw IV — PzKpfw IV — PzKpfw IV

II.Abteilung — Commanded by Sturmbannführer Eberhard Telkamp until July 26, 1944, when he was replaced by Obersturmführer Kurt Rennart, formerly the commander of 8.Kompanie. The battalion adjutant was Untersturmführer Heinz Peglow.

I.Abteilung — Commanded by Sturmbannführer Hans Bollert, seriously wounded on July 16, 1944, and replaced ten days later by Sturmbannführer Eberhard Telkamp, the commander of II.Abteilung. The battalion adjutant was Untersturmführer Windisch.

Stabskompanie einer Panzer-Abteilung

Nachrichten Zug — 1 x Pzbefehls III / 2 x StuG III

Aufklärungs Zug — 5 x PzKpfw IV

Panzer-Fliegerabwehr Zug — 3 x Sdkfz 7/1 2cm Flak

Stabskompanie einer Panzer-Abteilung

Nachrichten Zug — 3 x PzKpfw V Panther

Aufklärungs Zug — 5 x PzKpfw V Panther

Panzer-Fliegerabwehr Zug — 3 x Sdkfz 7/1 2cm Flak

5.Kompanie — Hauptsturmführer Hunke — 18 x Pzkw IV

6.Kompanie — Obersturmführer Grimm — 18 x Pzkw IV

7.Kompanie — Obersturmführer Fröhlich — 20 x StuG III

8.Kompanie — Obersturmführer Rennart — 18 x StuG III

Panzer-Werkstatt Kompanie

1.Kompanie — Obersturmführer Friederich — 8 x PzKpfw V Panther

2.Kompanie — Hauptsturmführer Sailer — 8 x PzKpfw V Panther

3.Kompanie — Untersturmführer Herden — 8 x PzKpfw V Panther

4.Kompanie — Hauptsturmführer Flor — 8 x PzKpfw V Panther

Panzer-Werkstatt Kompanie

The figures given here are accurate for June 6, 1944. At that time, I.Abteilung was in training at Truppenübungsplatz Mailly-le-Camp, east of Paris, and did not come under the division for reporting purposes. Between June 7 and 9, a further thirty-nine Panthers were received, bringing the battalion up to full strength with eight tanks allocated to the battalion headquarters and seventeen in each company. A further three Panthers would have gone to the regimental headquarters. On June 10, 1944, 9.SS-Panzer-Division was ordered to adopt the new "frei Gliederung" structure where the Werkstatt, Flak, and transport units would have been attached to the regimental headquarters. But given the fluid state of the fighting in Normandy, it is probable that very little, if any, re-organization took place.

SCHWERE PANZER-ABTEILUNG 503, JUNE-JULY 1944

Tiger tanks were allocated to independent heavy armor battalions or schwere Panzer-Abteilungen. Two Tiger units of the Waffen-SS and a single Heer battalion took part in the Normandy battles together with Panzer-Kompanie 316 (Funklenk), which used a number of Tigers and Sturmgeschütz III assault guns to coordinate the company's Borgward BIV remotely-controlled demolition vehicles. The battalion depicted here is schwere Panzer-Abteilung 503, which had returned to Germany from the Eastern Front in May 1944 and was reequipped with a full complement of twelve Tiger II with the so-called Porsche turret, all allocated to 1.Kompanie, and thirty-three Tiger I tanks.

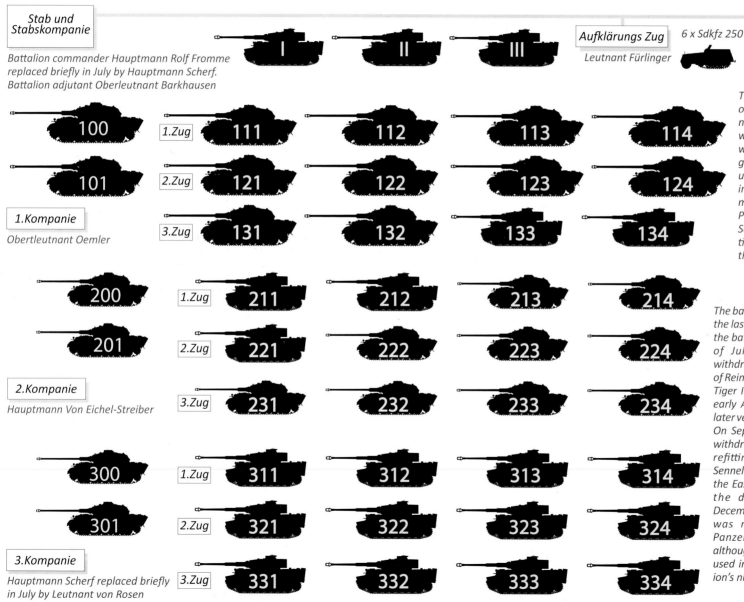

Stab und Stabskompanie

Battalion commander Hauptmann Rolf Fromme replaced briefly in July by Hauptmann Scherf. Battalion adjutant Oberleutnant Barkhausen

Aufklärungs Zug
Leutnant Fürlinger

6 x Sdkfz 250

Panzer-Fliegerabwehr Zug

Leutnant Brodhagen
The Panzer-Fliegerabwehr Zug, or anti-aircraft platoon, would normally have been equipped with Sdkfz 7 halftracks armed with the quad 20mm or 37mm guns. However, I have been unable to locate any definitive information on this. Similarly, many battalions contained a Pionier-Zug equipped with Sdkfz 251/7 halftracks at this time, but it would seem that this battalion did not.

1.Kompanie
Obertleutnant Oemler

1.Zug
2.Zug
3.Zug

2.Kompanie
Hauptmann Von Eichel-Streiber

1.Zug
2.Zug
3.Zug

The battalion arrived in France during the last week of June and took part in the battles for Normandy. At the end of July 1944, 3.Kompanie was withdrawn to Mailly-le-Camp, south of Reims, in order to re-equip with the Tiger II and returned to the front in early August. These tanks were the later version with the Henschel turret. On September 9, the battalion was withdrawn from the front and after refitting at Truppenübungsplatz Sennelager in Germany, was sent to the Eastern front and it took part in the defense of Budapest. On December 21, 1944, the battalion was renamed schwere Heeres-Panzer-Abteilung Feldherrnhalle, although the new title is often seen used in conjunction with the battalion's number.

3.Kompanie
Hauptmann Scherf replaced briefly in July by Leutnant von Rosen

3.Zug

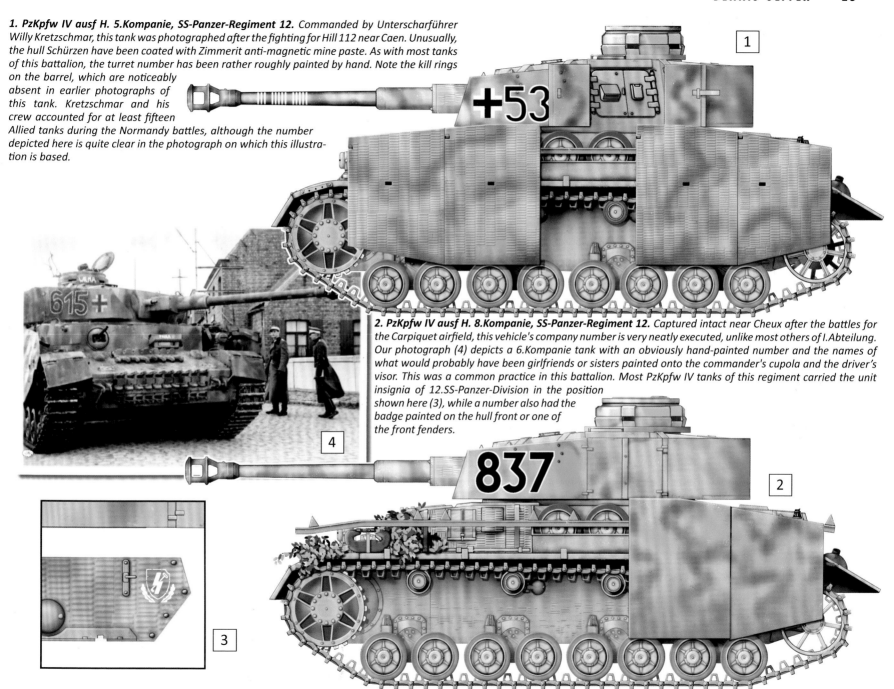

1. PzKpfw IV ausf H. 5.Kompanie, SS-Panzer-Regiment 12. *Commanded by Unterscharführer Willy Kretzschmar, this tank was photographed after the fighting for Hill 112 near Caen. Unusually, the hull Schürzen have been coated with Zimmerit anti-magnetic mine paste. As with most tanks of this battalion, the turret number has been rather roughly painted by hand. Note the kill rings on the barrel, which are noticeably absent in earlier photographs of this tank. Kretzschmar and his crew accounted for at least fifteen* Allied tanks during the Normandy battles, although the number depicted here is quite clear in the photograph on which this illustration is based.

2. PzKpfw IV ausf H. 8.Kompanie, SS-Panzer-Regiment 12. *Captured intact near Cheux after the battles for the Carpiquet airfield, this vehicle's company number is very neatly executed, unlike most others of I.Abteilung. Our photograph (4) depicts a 6.Kompanie tank with an obviously hand-painted number and the names of what would probably have been girlfriends or sisters painted onto the commander's cupola and the driver's visor. This was a common practice in this battalion. Most PzKpfw IV tanks of this regiment carried the unit insignia of 12.SS-Panzer-Division in the position shown here (3), while a number also had the badge painted on the hull front or one of the front fenders.*

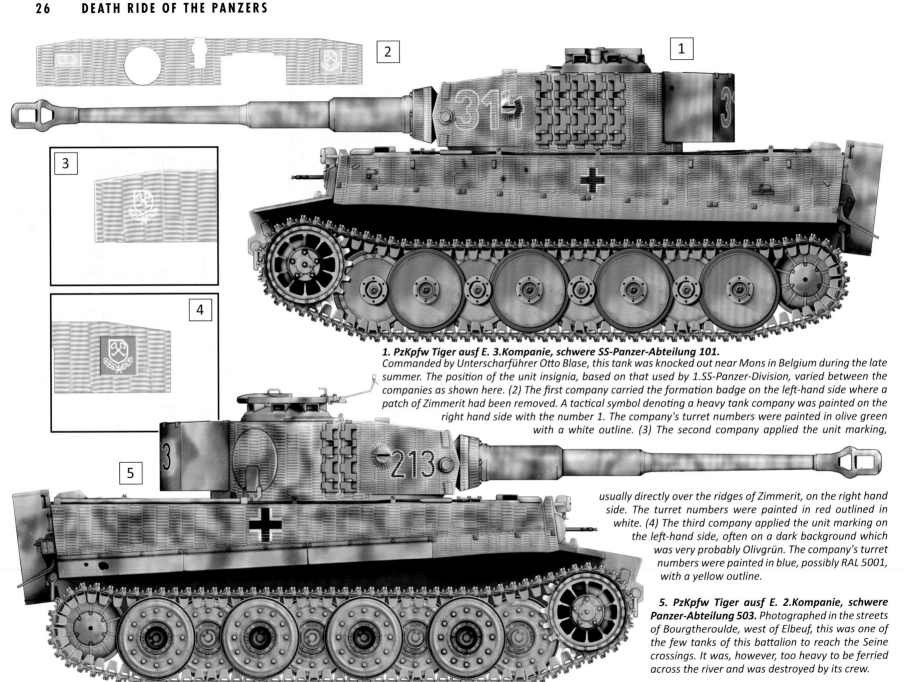

1. PzKpfw Tiger ausf E. 3.Kompanie, schwere SS-Panzer-Abteilung 101.
Commanded by Unterscharführer Otto Blase, this tank was knocked out near Mons in Belgium during the late summer. The position of the unit insignia, based on that used by 1.SS-Panzer-Division, varied between the companies as shown here. (2) The first company carried the formation badge on the left-hand side where a patch of Zimmerit had been removed. A tactical symbol denoting a heavy tank company was painted on the right hand side with the number 1. The company's turret numbers were painted in olive green with a white outline. (3) The second company applied the unit marking, usually directly over the ridges of Zimmerit, on the right hand side. The turret numbers were painted in red outlined in white. (4) The third company applied the unit marking on the left-hand side, often on a dark background which was very probably Olivgrün. The company's turret numbers were painted in blue, possibly RAL 5001, with a yellow outline.

5. PzKpfw Tiger ausf E. 2.Kompanie, schwere Panzer-Abteilung 503. Photographed in the streets of Bourgtheroulde, west of Elbeuf, this was one of the few tanks of this battalion to reach the Seine crossings. It was, however, too heavy to be ferried across the river and was destroyed by its crew.

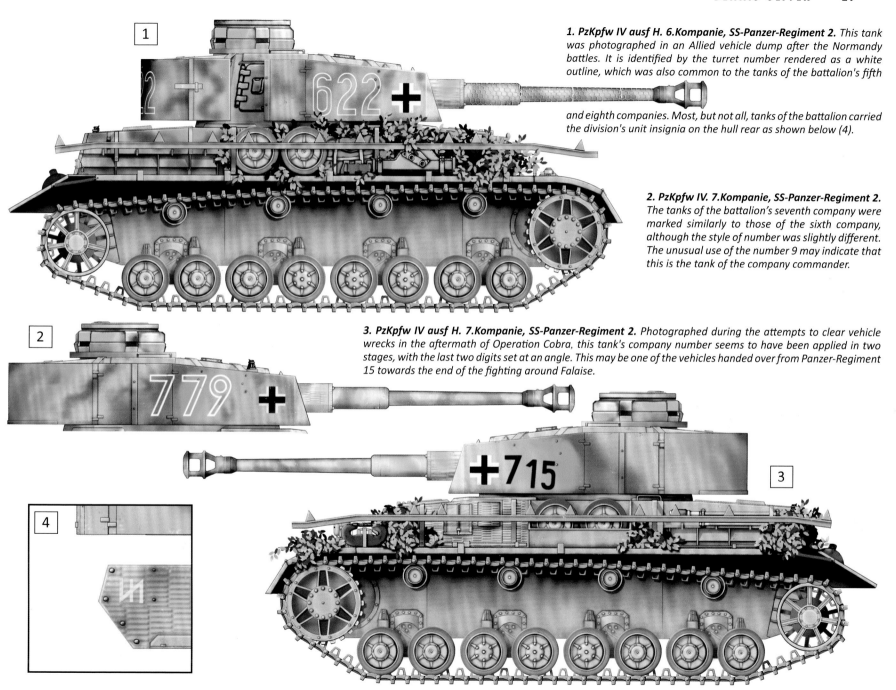

1. PzKpfw IV ausf H. 6.Kompanie, SS-Panzer-Regiment 2. This tank was photographed in an Allied vehicle dump after the Normandy battles. It is identified by the turret number rendered as a white outline, which was also common to the tanks of the battalion's fifth and eighth companies. Most, but not all, tanks of the battalion carried the division's unit insignia on the hull rear as shown below (4).

2. PzKpfw IV. 7.Kompanie, SS-Panzer-Regiment 2. The tanks of the battalion's seventh company were marked similarly to those of the sixth company, although the style of number was slightly different. The unusual use of the number 9 may indicate that this is the tank of the company commander.

3. PzKpfw IV ausf H. 7.Kompanie, SS-Panzer-Regiment 2. Photographed during the attempts to clear vehicle wrecks in the aftermath of Operation Cobra, this tank's company number seems to have been applied in two stages, with the last two digits set at an angle. This may be one of the vehicles handed over from Panzer-Regiment 15 towards the end of the fighting around Falaise.

1. PzKpfw IV ausf H. 6.Kompanie, Panzer-Lehr-Regiment 130. *This tank was knocked out in June during the fighting for Villiers-Bocage and was still in place when the Normandy battles ended. On June 11, 1944, the battalion commander, Prinz Wilhelm Schönburg-Waldenburg was killed in action and from that day the tanks of II.Abteilung carried a rendition of his family crest (2) in the position shown here.*

3. PzKpfw IV ausf H. 5.Kompanie, Panzer -Lehr-Regiment 130. *Photographed in the ruins of Saint-Gilles, west of Saint-LÙ, following the Operation Cobra battles, this tank's company number has been applied directly over the loading label which was painted, in various styles, onto all German army vehicles. A detailed view of the loading label is shown above (4) and indicates the vehicle type, weight and weight class, in this case "S" for "Schwere," or heavy.*

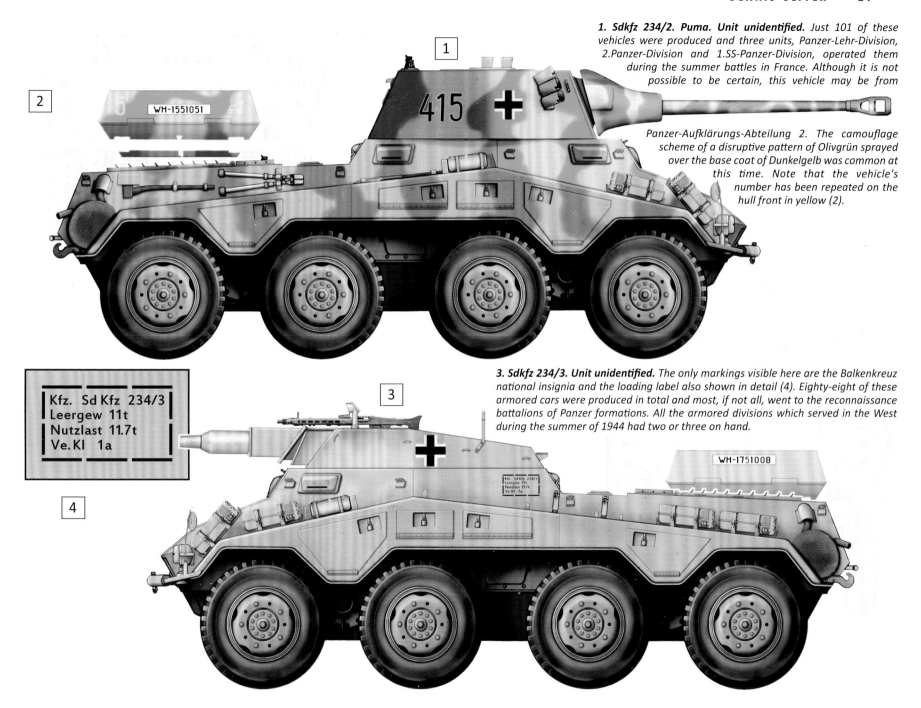

1. Sdkfz 234/2. Puma. Unit unidentified. *Just 101 of these vehicles were produced and three units, Panzer-Lehr-Division, 2.Panzer-Division and 1.SS-Panzer-Division, operated them during the summer battles in France. Although it is not possible to be certain, this vehicle may be from*

Panzer-Aufklärungs-Abteilung 2. The camouflage scheme of a disruptive pattern of Olivgrün sprayed over the base coat of Dunkelgelb was common at this time. Note that the vehicle's number has been repeated on the hull front in yellow (2).

WH-1551051

415

3. Sdkfz 234/3. Unit unidentified. *The only markings visible here are the Balkenkreuz national insignia and the loading label also shown in detail (4). Eighty-eight of these armored cars were produced in total and most, if not all, went to the reconnaissance battalions of Panzer formations. All the armored divisions which served in the West during the summer of 1944 had two or three on hand.*

Kfz. Sd Kfz 234/3
Leergew 11t
Nutzlast 11.7t
Ve.Kl 1a

WH-1751008

1. Sdfkfz 165. 15cm schwere Panzerhaubitze sFH 18/1 auf Geschˌtzwagen III/IV Hummel. Panzer-Artillerie-Regiment 119. *This regiment was attached to 11.Panzer-Division and had just three of these guns on hand after the battles of July and August 1944. The large letter D, painted onto the front of the*

superstructure, denotes a Batterie and the division's famous unit insignia (2) is depicted below that.

3. Sdfkfz 165. 15cm schwere Panzerhaubitze sFH 18/1 auf Geschˌtzwagen III/IV Hummel. SS-Panzer-Artillerie-Regiment 10. *The regiment was attached to 10.SS-Panzer-Division and reported that six of these vehicles were on hand when the division left Russia for the Western Front in June 1944.*

The division's unit insignia (4) was painted onto the superstructure front, with a large Batterie letter, and also at the left rear. Note the Sternantenna D, normally used with the Fu8 command radio, which is also visible in the photograph at right (5). All the regiment's surviving vehicles were destroyed by their crews near Saint-Lambert, east of Falaise, after running out of fuel.

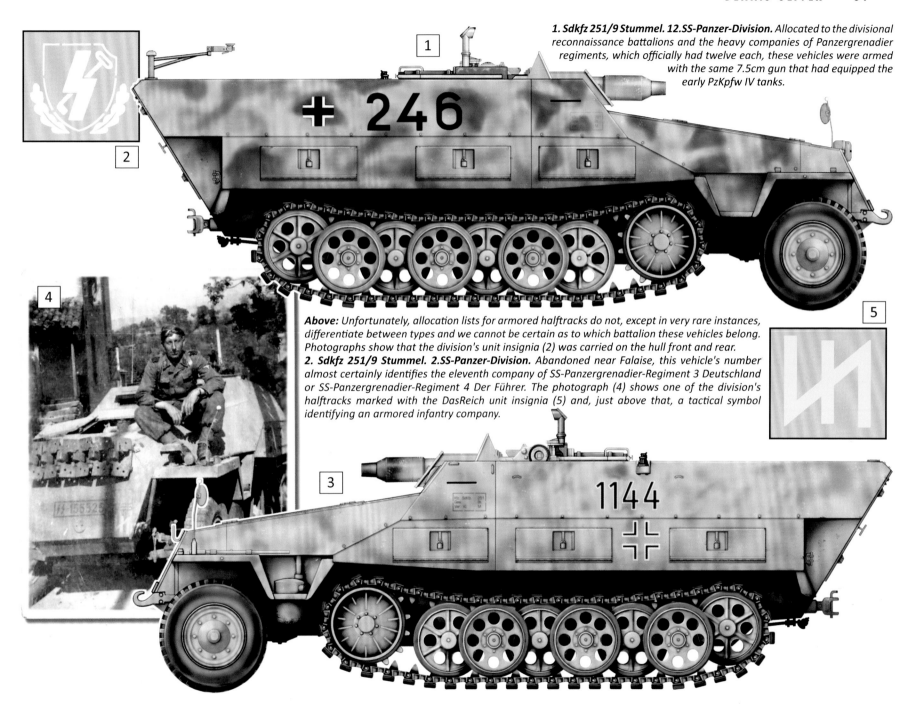

1. Sdkfz 251/9 Stummel. 12.SS-Panzer-Division. *Allocated to the divisional reconnaissance battalions and the heavy companies of Panzergrenadier regiments, which officially had twelve each, these vehicles were armed with the same 7.5cm gun that had equipped the early PzKpfw IV tanks.*

Above: *Unfortunately, allocation lists for armored halftracks do not, except in very rare instances, differentiate between types and we cannot be certain as to which battalion these vehicles belong. Photographs show that the division's unit insignia (2) was carried on the hull front and rear.*
2. Sdkfz 251/9 Stummel. 2.SS-Panzer-Division. *Abandoned near Falaise, this vehicle's number almost certainly identifies the eleventh company of SS-Panzergrenadier-Regiment 3 Deutschland or SS-Panzergrenadier-Regiment 4 Der Führer. The photograph (4) shows one of the division's halftracks marked with the DasReich unit insignia (5) and, just above that, a tactical symbol identifying an armored infantry company.*

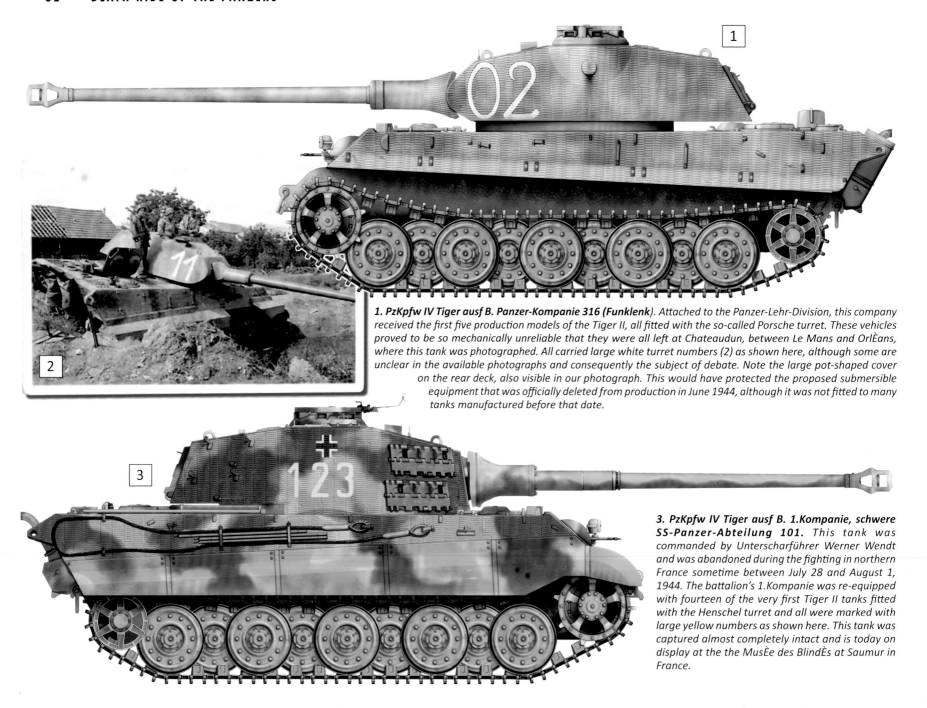

1. PzKpfw IV Tiger ausf B. Panzer-Kompanie 316 (Funklenk). Attached to the Panzer-Lehr-Division, this company received the first five production models of the Tiger II, all fitted with the so-called Porsche turret. These vehicles proved to be so mechanically unreliable that they were all left at Chateaudun, between Le Mans and Orlèans, where this tank was photographed. All carried large white turret numbers (2) as shown here, although some are unclear in the available photographs and consequently the subject of debate. Note the large pot-shaped cover on the rear deck, also visible in our photograph. This would have protected the proposed submersible equipment that was officially deleted from production in June 1944, although it was not fitted to many tanks manufactured before that date.

3. PzKpfw IV Tiger ausf B. 1.Kompanie, schwere SS-Panzer-Abteilung 101. This tank was commanded by Unterscharführer Werner Wendt and was abandoned during the fighting in northern France sometime between July 28 and August 1, 1944. The battalion's 1.Kompanie was re-equipped with fourteen of the very first Tiger II tanks fitted with the Henschel turret and all were marked with large yellow numbers as shown here. This tank was captured almost completely intact and is today on display at the the Musèe des Blindès at Saumur in France.

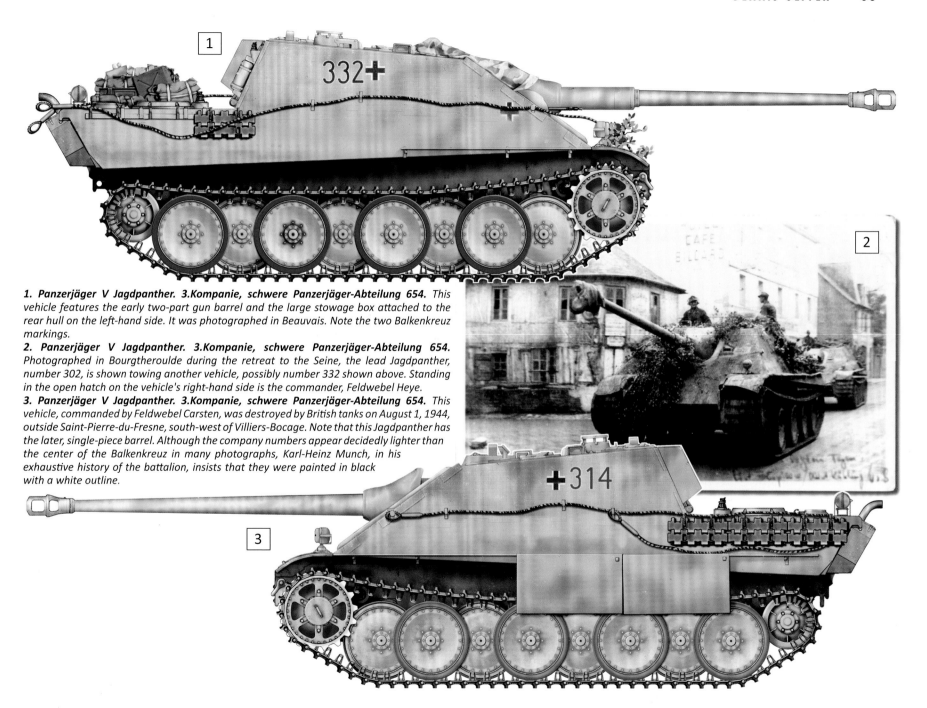

1. Panzerjäger V Jagdpanther. 3.Kompanie, schwere Panzerjäger-Abteilung 654. *This vehicle features the early two-part gun barrel and the large stowage box attached to the rear hull on the left-hand side. It was photographed in Beauvais. Note the two Balkenkreuz markings.*

2. Panzerjäger V Jagdpanther. 3.Kompanie, schwere Panzerjäger-Abteilung 654. *Photographed in Bourgtheroulde during the retreat to the Seine, the lead Jagdpanther, number 302, is shown towing another vehicle, possibly number 332 shown above. Standing in the open hatch on the vehicle's right-hand side is the commander, Feldwebel Heye.*

3. Panzerjäger V Jagdpanther. 3.Kompanie, schwere Panzerjäger-Abteilung 654. *This vehicle, commanded by Feldwebel Carsten, was destroyed by British tanks on August 1, 1944, outside Saint-Pierre-du-Fresne, south-west of Villiers-Bocage. Note that this Jagdpanther has the later, single-piece barrel. Although the company numbers appear decidedly lighter than the center of the Balkenkreuz in many photographs, Karl-Heinz Munch, in his exhaustive history of the battalion, insists that they were painted in black with a white outline.*

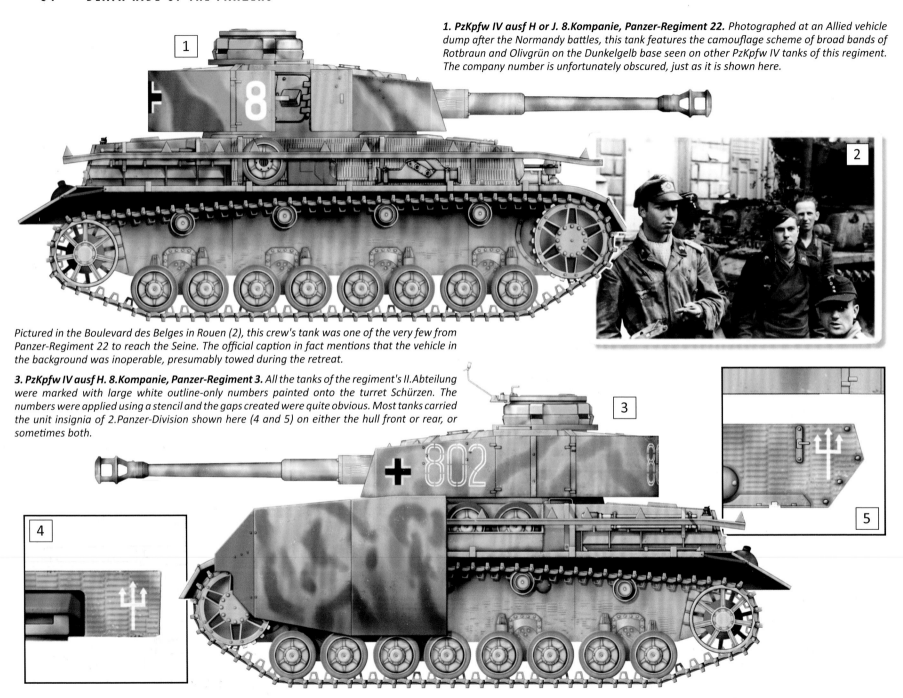

1. PzKpfw IV ausf H or J. 8.Kompanie, Panzer-Regiment 22. Photographed at an Allied vehicle dump after the Normandy battles, this tank features the camouflage scheme of broad bands of Rotbraun and Olivgrün on the Dunkelgelb base seen on other PzKpfw IV tanks of this regiment. The company number is unfortunately obscured, just as it is shown here.

Pictured in the Boulevard des Belges in Rouen (2), this crew's tank was one of the very few from Panzer-Regiment 22 to reach the Seine. The official caption in fact mentions that the vehicle in the background was inoperable, presumably towed during the retreat.

3. PzKpfw IV ausf H. 8.Kompanie, Panzer-Regiment 3. All the tanks of the regiment's II.Abteilung were marked with large white outline-only numbers painted onto the turret Schürzen. The numbers were applied using a stencil and the gaps created were quite obvious. Most tanks carried the unit insignia of 2.Panzer-Division shown here (4 and 5) on either the hull front or rear, or sometimes both.

1. PzKpfw V Panther ausf A. 1.Kompanie, Panzer-Regiment 24. *During the summer of 1944, the regiment's I.Abteilung was attached to 116.Panzer-Division and the tanks were marked with large white numbers, with possibly a very thin dark outline, on the turret sides.*
The last two digits, which identified the individual tank and platoon, were repeated (2) on the turret rear to the left of the access door. The spare fuel containers, carried in specially made brackets, were a field modification which was an identifying feature of this battalion's Panthers (3).

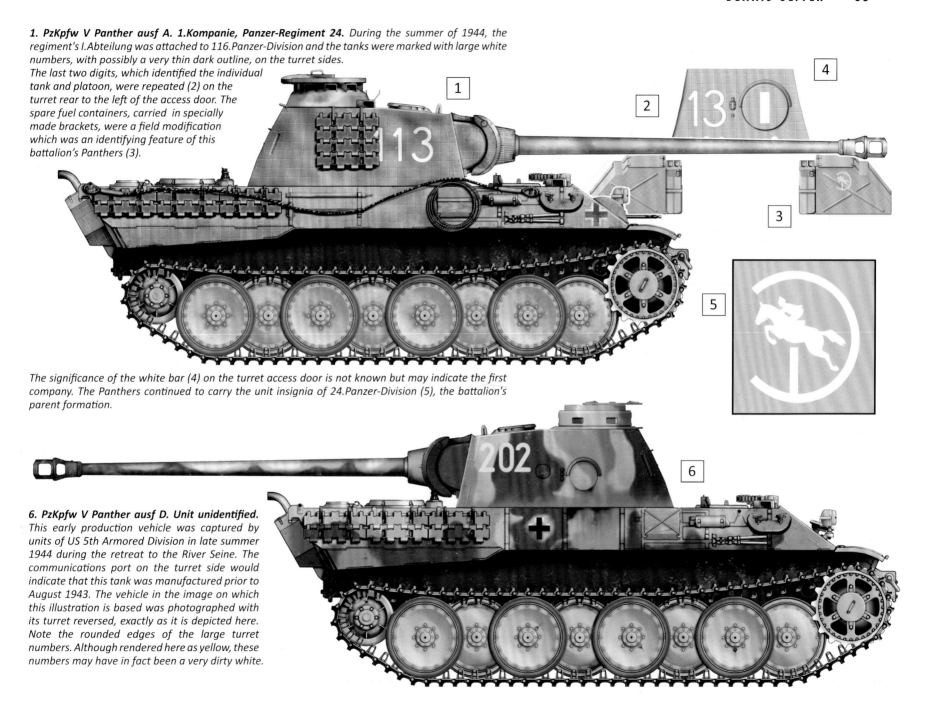

The significance of the white bar (4) on the turret access door is not known but may indicate the first company. The Panthers continued to carry the unit insignia of 24.Panzer-Division (5), the battalion's parent formation.

6. PzKpfw V Panther ausf D. Unit unidentified.
This early production vehicle was captured by units of US 5th Armored Division in late summer 1944 during the retreat to the River Seine. The communications port on the turret side would indicate that this tank was manufactured prior to August 1943. The vehicle in the image on which this illustration is based was photographed with its turret reversed, exactly as it is depicted here. Note the rounded edges of the large turret numbers. Although rendered here as yellow, these numbers may have in fact been a very dirty white.

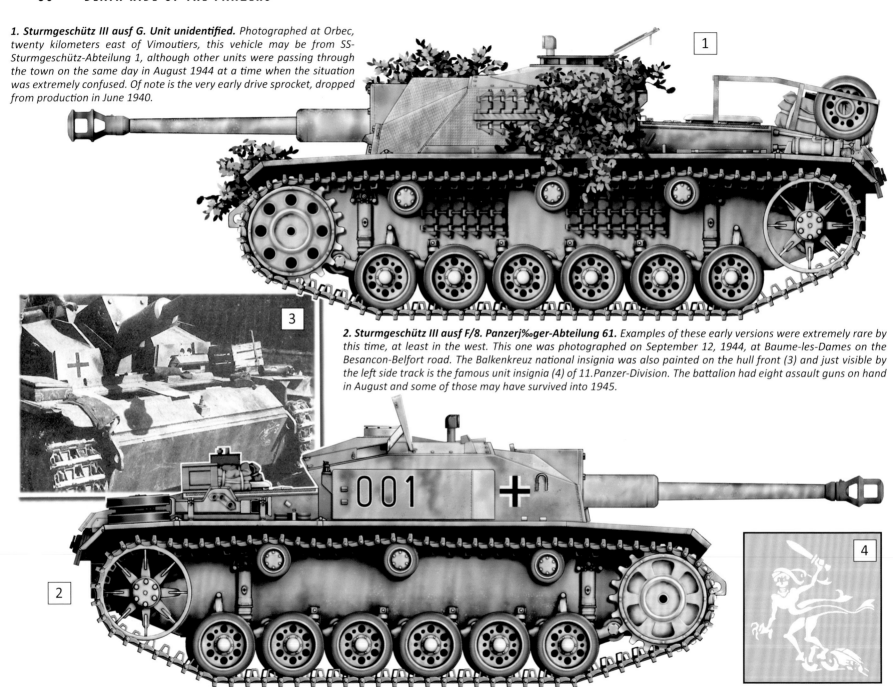

1. Sturmgeschütz III ausf G. Unit unidentified. *Photographed at Orbec, twenty kilometers east of Vimoutiers, this vehicle may be from SS-Sturmgeschütz-Abteilung 1, although other units were passing through the town on the same day in August 1944 at a time when the situation was extremely confused. Of note is the very early drive sprocket, dropped from production in June 1940.*

2. Sturmgeschütz III ausf F/8. Panzerj‰ger-Abteilung 61. *Examples of these early versions were extremely rare by this time, at least in the west. This one was photographed on September 12, 1944, at Baume-les-Dames on the Besancon-Belfort road. The Balkenkreuz national insignia was also painted on the hull front (3) and just visible by the left side track is the famous unit insignia (4) of 11.Panzer-Division. The battalion had eight assault guns on hand in August and some of those may have survived into 1945.*

1.01. Panzer-Regiment 22 of 21.Panzer-Division had six of these elderly PzKpfw IV ausf C tanks armed with the short barreled 75mm gun on hand in June 1944, all concentrated in 8.Kompanie. The camouflage scheme is unusual and appears to be made up of bands of a dark color, probably Olivgrün, over a base coat of Dunkelgelb.

1.02. This PzKpfw IV of Panzer-Regiment 22 was photographed on July 13, 1944 in a hull-down position overlooking the Caen-Lébisey road. The lighter color of the roughly applied camouflage scheme is generally assumed to be local mud applied with a brush, however examination of the original photograph suggests that although a great deal dirt and mud is present, these patches of light color may have been sprayed on and would therefore have to be paint. The style used to depict the company number is typical of the tanks of this regiment and an example is shown in the color illustrations.

1.03. Photographed sometime after on July 18, 1944 following the bombardment that preceded Operation Goodwood, this Tiger I of 3.Kompanie, schwere Panzer-Abteilung 503 was commanded by Oberfeldwebel Sachs. By the end of the first day of Goodwood, the battalion's third company would be reduced to just a single service-able tank.

1.04. British troops inspect a Tiger II of 1.Kompanie, schwere Panzer-Abteilung 503 in Le-Plessis-Grimoult, south of Caen, on August 10, 1944. The company began the campaign with twelve of these tanks with the so-called Porsche turret and two Tiger I tanks, which also equipped the second and third companies. British accounts insist that this tank was knocked out by a round from a 2inch mortar, although it is difficult to believe that such a small projectile could have account for the damage seen here. German records state that it was disabled by a nearby explosion. By the time this photograph was taken, the battalion was down to nine operational Tigers.

1.05. Photographed near Saint-Germain-de-Tallevande on August 15, 1944, this badly damaged Sturmgeschütz III may have belonged to 2.SS-Panzer-Division or 17.SS-Panzergrenadier-Division, both of which were operating near there at the time and had a number of these vehicles on hand.

1.06. A Sturmgeschütz III ausf G said to have been photographed near Tournai-sur-Dives on August 21, 1944. In the original print of this photograph it is possible to see what may be the unit insignia of 9.SS-Panzer-Division Hohenstaufen on the front fender. The second battalion of the division's SS-Panzer-Regiment 9 was equipped with these vehicles. The application of the Zimmerit paste in the so-called waffle pattern is indicative of assault guns manufactured by the firm of Alkett. The absence of a gun travel lock on the hull front would suggest that this vehicle was assembled prior to May 1944.

1.07. This Panther ausf A was photographed in the ruins of Rue Saint Germain in the town of Argentan on August 21, 1944, by which time the fighting was taking placed to the north in the Falaise Pocket. This tank is usually associated with I.Abteilung, Panzer Regiment 24 which was attached to 116.Panzer-Division, however there is some suggestion that it may have in fact belonged to Panzer-Regiment 33 of 9.Panzer-Division. While both divisions were engaged in this area in mid-August, the distinctive hooks on the turret side would suggest that the Panzer-Regiment 33 identification may be correct. While the Panthers of Panzer-Regiment 24 did suspend lengths of track from the turret sides, they were held by rectangular shaped brackets, usually two per side, welded approximately five inches from the edge of the turret roof.

CHAPTER TWO

THE RETREAT

After months of struggling through the close confines of the Bocage country of northern France and battering away at the German defenses around Caen, the Allies had succeeded in breaking the enemy's line and encircling large parts of 7.Armee and 5.Panzerarmee in the Falaise Pocket. The opportunity to build a defensive line along the natural barrier of the Seine, as Feldmarschall Kluge had earlier suggested, had been lost and the river now became an obstacle to the retreating Germans. The Seine, as it meanders through northern France, is over 100 kilometers from the Falaise battlefield at its nearest point and the Allies were now racing to cut off the retreating Germans. Additionally, many of the Seine bridges had been destroyed by aerial bombardment and most of the troops who managed to reach the river would have to cross on ferries. Despite these difficulties, and the fact that most of the retreating units were not coherent formations, the Germans showed few signs of panic and the command staff and technical services performed near miracles in organ-izing a withdrawal under what could only be described as the worst possible conditions.

On August 15, while the Canadians were battling to take the town of Falaise, units of the US Army and Free French forces were landing in southern France. The Allied landings on the Côte D'Azur were opposed by Generaloberst Johannes Blaskowitz's Heeresgruppe G, made up of a number of infantry formations with 11.Panzer-Division, the only armor available to Blaskowitz, held in reserve. The defenses were spread so thinly that Oberkommando der Wehrmacht, the military high command, had seriously considered withdrawal to a defensive line near Dijon, over 300 kilometers from the coast. This idea was quickly dropped in the aftermath of the July 20 plot to assassinate Hitler, following which the relinquishing of any territory was looked upon with suspicion. Nevertheless, Blaskowitz realized that the force under his command could not withstand a determined assault, backed as it would be by sea and air power, and planned for a fighting withdrawal towards the north. The only ar-mored formation allocated to Heeresgruppe G was 11.Panzer-Division, which was under Hitler's direct control and stationed to the west of Avignon and the Rhône river, at least four hour's drive from the nearest coastline. Blaskowitz had expected to be able to count on the tanks of 9.Panzer-Division, which had been rebuilding at Carcassone, west of Narbonne, but this formation was transferred to the Normandy front in early July.

Commanded by Generalleutnant Wend von Wietersheim, 11.Panzer-Division was at about half strength in early August. It had forty-nine Panthers and twenty-six Pzkw IV tanks on hand with Panzer-Regiment 15 and a handful of self-propelled guns with Panzerjäger-Abteilung 51 and the division's two Panzergrenadier regiments. Blaskowitz had made numerous requests that it be moved closer to the area between the port cities of Marseille and Toulon, which he considered the most likely place for an Allied assault. Less than forty-eight hours prior to the first landings, the Führer relented and during the afternoon of August 13, 1944, Wietersheim's tanks prepared to move east. This was complicated by the need to share any available rail transport with two infantry divisions and the destruction of the bridges across the Rhône during the preliminary Allied bombardment on the morning of August 15, which effectively trapped 11.Panzer-Division on the western bank.

It would be the afternoon of August 21 before the first elements of the division crossed the river. By this time, US Army units had advanced to Montélimar, almost 70 kilometers north of Avignon, where they were able to threaten the retreating Germans. The infantry formations in the area, under the command of General Friedrich Wiese's 19.Armee, could do little to halt the Americans and Wiese implored Wietersheim to ferry his tanks across the river by any means available and move with all possible speed to Montélimar. An energetic and experienced commander, Wietersheim directed his armored reconnaissance battalion under Major Karl Bode, which had crossed the river earlier and was intending to feint towards Aix-en-Provence, to now head north to Montélimar. On August 22, Bode's men arrived in the Montélimar area and found that the Americans had occupied the high ground between the Rhône and Roubion Rivers, from which they were able to fire on any German units withdrawing to the north. Skirting the Roubion, Bode at-

tacked the American position from the rear with the support of a scratch infantry force made up from Flieger-Ausbildungs-Regiment 71, a Luftwaffe training unit. However, the armored car and halftracks of Aufklärungs-Abteilung 11 were at a distinct disadvantage against the American tanks, which received reinforcements during the battle, and Bode was forced to withdraw.

On the following day Bode made another attack across the Roubion, but his battalion had been greatly weakened by the previous day's fighting and was driven back by intense artillery fire. Slowly, parts of Wietersheim's division were able to move towards the north and as Bode's men were making a final attempt to drive the Americans from their positions on the high ground above Montélimar, the division's headquarters staff and an armored Gruppe under Major Karl Thieme, a battalion commander of Panzergrenadier-Regiment 110, arrived in the area. On August 24, a detailed copy of the American plans for the following day fell into the German's hands, allowing General Wiese to prepare a pre-emptive strike. All his available forces were concentrated in Korpsgruppe von Wietersheim, which would include the tanks of 11.Panzer-Division with 198.Infantry-Division, a Luftwaffe infantry unit, and an anti-aircraft regiment equipped with 88mm guns. In addition, five super-heavy railroad guns would be availa-

ble if the tracks could be kept open. Wietersheim divided his battle group into four elements, each commanded by veterans of the Russian front that he knew well. On August 25, he launched five separate attacks against the American center while his tanks penetrated both flanks along the lines of the Roubion and Drôme Rivers, temporarily isolating the American position. But Allied reinforcements were continually arriving and, although Wietersheim's men were able to keep the escape routs open, the retreating Germans were almost constantly harassed from the air and by artillery fire. In addition, the Germans had left the main road north at La Coucourde, some 10 kilometers north of Montélimar, completely undefended and the American commander rushed a combined arms team to secure the area and block the road. At midnight Wietersheim, admonished by Weise for such an obvious lapse, personally led a column of his tanks, which charged into the American position and cleared the road, destroying ten American tanks and tank destroyers in the process.

Despite these tactical successes, the situation of Weise's 19.Armee was becoming increasingly desperate. The major ports of the south were all in Allied hands and men and supplies were streaming ashore, allowing the Americans to push not only to the north but also the west in pursuit of the withdrawing Germans. On August 24, the Americans had entered Avignon without a fight and had turned north towards Korpsgruppe von Wietersheim and the retreating formations of 19.Armee, held back only by a lack of fuel. Meanwhile, the remainder of Blaskowitz's army group were fleeing towards the east and were concentrated to the north of Lyon. Under continuous air attack and harassed by Resistance fighters, this force was now in danger of being overtaken by US 3rd Army, which was advancing at a rapid pace from the west and had already crossed the Seine at two points.[1]

With the situation at Montélimar stabilized, at least for the moment, Weise ordered the bulk of 11.Panzer-Division with its commander to move north to Lyon, which would have to be held if Heeresgruppe G was to escape destruction. The divisions of General Baptist Kniess' LXXXV.Armeekorps, which had arrived in the Montélimar area as part of the general retreat, would be given the task of keeping the road to the north open. Between August 26 and 28, Kniess' infantrymen kept up the attacks against the American positions in the Roubion and Drome areas, cleverly keeping the enemy occupied with their flanks and unable to launch an attack in strength on the road, along which the German forces were still moving north.

By the evening of August 27, the remnants of General Otto Richter's 198.Infantrie-Division were the only troops left in Montélimar. Towards midnight Richter gathered his two remaining regiments, with the last of the stragglers that had made their way into the town, and headed north. Unfortunately, they ran head on a major American offensive and Richter and most of his men were forced to surrender.

During the morning of August 29, units of US 3rd and 36th Divisions entered Montélimar and rounded up some 500 prisoners, capturing a further 2,500 in the general area in the following days. However, the bulk of 19.Armee had been allowed to escape and Wietersheim's tanks would now be able to cover the retreat as far as Dijon, where Blaskowitz hoped that Wiese's remaining divisions could form a solid front and await the arrival of the German forces now streaming in from western France. If that could be accomplished, the survivors of Heeresgruppe G would withdraw eastwards the Vosges Mountain and the Belfort Gap. Eager to avoid any repeat of the slogging match of Montélimar, 11.Panzer-Division was ordered to secure Blaskowitz's eastern flank, fight a delaying action but conserving its precious tanks by denying the Americans a set-piece battle, and gradually pull back in the direction to the Belfort Gap.[2]

The situation in the north was no less dire. With the closure of the Falaise Pocket on August 21, 1944, the Canadians had pushed along the coast to Honfleur, on the southern edge of the Seine estuary. Earlier, on August 19, units of US 3rd Army had reached the Seine at Mantes-Gassicourt, almost 60 kilometers north of Paris, and seized a footbridge which German engineers had only partially destroyed. Although of limited use, this bridge posed a serious threat to the German flank and it was only an uncharacteristic lack of aggression on the part of US 3rd Army that saved the Germans from disaster. By August 23, a much more substantial crossing had been captured at Melun; however, this was over 30 kilometers south of the capital. Both these crossings, although unexploited for the moment, were of concern for the Germans: if the west bank of the river from Paris, north to Rouen then on to the coast at Le Havre,

---

1   *With Blaskowitz were two complete infantry divisions, a corps headquarters, and a large number of German civilian staff. The accounts of many German veterans would suggest that the difficulties caused by the Resistance have been greatly exaggerated in some postwar histories.*

2   *The division's Panzer-Regiment 15 had lost heavily in the fighting around Montélimar and on September 1st was able to report that while the headquarters and first battalion could field thirty-seven Panthers, the second battalion had just sixteen Pzkw IV tanks on hand. The battalion's sixth, seventh, and eighth companies had no tanks at all.*

could not be held, the retreating German divisions would find themselves trapped in yet another pocket. Nor would the Germans be allowed to retreat unhindered; what remained of the shattered Panzer divisions of 5.Panzerarmee, now commanded by Oberstgruppenführer Dietrich, would have to provide a screen behind which the infantry formations of Eberbach's 7.Armee could retire.[3]

The report prepared by the staff of 5.Panzerarmee made for depressing reading. The armored divisions available to Dietrich could each muster, on average, about 3,000 men. Even this figure is deceptively optimistic as some divisions had been almost totally destroyed; for example, 12.SS-Panzer-Division was left with just ten tanks and 300 men. The total armored vehicle strength of 5.Panzerarmee in late August was made up of approximately 250 tanks of all types.

Ordering 7.Armee to coordinate the forces that crossed to the eastern bank of the Seine, Model left Dietrich in command of the armored screen on the western side. Model, recognizing the danger of the American bridgehead at Mantes-Gassicourt, ordered that it be destroyed immediately and

that Dietrich prepare to hold Elbeuf at all costs, shielding Rouen and the only bridge left to the Germans.[4]

The main line of resistance of 5.Panzerarmee was organized into two broad sectors. The western sector opposed the British and Canadians and the southern sector faced the Americans; it was the latter that Model felt was crucial. Here the German line was held by the infantry units of General Kuntzen's LXXXI.Armeekorps and the few remaining tanks of 116.Panzer-Division. This force would be too weak to withstand a determined push and Model directed 49. Infanterie-Division and 18.Luftwaffen-Feld-Division to the area with the intention of sealing off the American bridgeheads. In addition, the remnants of 1.SS-Panzer-Division, 12.SS-Panzer-Division, and 2.Panzer-Division were ordered to move to LXXXI.Armeekorps' area on the afternoon of August 21. These formations were, however, so depleted that they were only able to field ten serviceable tanks in total. On the following day, after a massive aerial bombardment, the Americans, led by 130 Sherman tanks, attacked Kuntzen's positions. During the previous evening. 2.Panzer-Division and

9.SS-Panzer-Division had been ordered to move from the area around Lisieux, about 35 kilometers east of Caen where they were facing the British, to reinforce LXXXI.Armeekorps. However, they were still preparing to move when the American attack began and could only muster twenty-five tanks between the two divisions. On Kuntzen's left flank, the infantry of 17.Luftwaffen-Feld-Division simply crumbled and the American tanks did not stop until they reached Louviers, 10 kilometers south-east of Elbeuf, and threatened the Seine crossing sites. Faced with the threat of encirclement, Model had no choice but to take more troops from the western sector, despite the pleas of the local commanders General von Obstfelder and Gruppenführer Bittrich, who felt that the line was already disastrously thin. Model's bold strategy, however, paid off. While the British and Canadians remained inactive, Gruppe Schwerin, which included a number of Tiger II tanks of schwere Panzer-Abteilung 503, managed to reduce the American bridgeheads and even recapture La Roche-Guyon, which had been evacuated on August 18. Nevertheless, Model felt that the attack was not pursued with sufficient speed or aggression and blamed Dietrich, contending that a concerted assault should have pushed the front back to Evreux. Dietrich, who had been on the battlefield, realized the impossibility of the task that he had been given and

3 Josep 'Sep' Dietrich, it will be remembered, had led I.SS-Panzerkorps in Normandy. The former commander of 7.Armee, Oberstgruppenführer Paul Hausser, had been seriously wounded in the Falaise fighting and replaced by General Heinrich Eberbach.

4 By this stage all the Seine bridges had either been destroyed or captured, with the exception of the railway bridge at Rouen. As many as sixty ferries would carry much of the German army across the river.

asked to be relieved of his command. Eventually Model was convinced that the attacking force had been wholly inadequate and later informed Hitler's headquarters that the sternest orders could not alter insurmountable facts.

On August 23, the American units that had pushed Kuntzen's corps aside to take Louviers were able to advance towards Elbeuf. The Germans were now forced to attack, regardless of the enemy's superiority, in order to stave off disaster. The withdrawal of the mobile units from the western sector was given a new urgency, particularly because most movement had to take place at night. For the attack, Gruppe Schwerin was reinforced with 2.SS-Panzer-Division and 21.Panzer-Division, but this force was not enough to push the front any further to the south. When the Americans counterattacked they were able to reach the outskirts of Elbeuf, raising the possibility of an Allied force crossing the river and attacking the ferry points from the rear. The Germans had nothing with which to oppose a strong thrust across the Seine; their last reserve, the remaining tanks of 9.SS-Panzer-Division, were already engaged in the area around Elbeuf. Model could do little other than order 7.Armee to continue the crossings "ceaselessly and at maximum speed." However, at this critical stage, the Americans seemed to hesitate, and on August 25, the tanks of

Gruppe Schwerin managed to push them out of Elbeuf, albeit temporarily. The Allies seemed content to disrupt the crossings by destroying the ferries with air power and artillery. The decisive thrust that Model feared was imminent never materialized and 7.Armee was allowed to escape. Now a way had to be found for 5.Panzerarmee to disengage and cross the river and German command felt that this must be accomplished in a single phase to have any chance of success.

To cover the retreat, the remaining tanks and assault guns were pulled back to a line to protect the crossings at Caudebec-en-Caux, Duclair, Elbeuf, and Rouen. The latter was the major crossing point and this could not escape the notice of the Allied air forces for long. On August 25, with tanks and trucks massed at the quayside, a wave of bombers plastered the town, causing fires which were still blazing the following day. It is perhaps surprising that the Allies did not attack the other crossing points with such vigour; one German account mentioning that on the same day the bombers raided Rouen, the streets of Oissel, just over 5 kilometers to the south, were jammed with an estimated 5,000-7,000 vehicles. On the day Rouen was bombed, the commandant of Paris formally surrendered the city, allowing French and American units to enter the French capital.

By this time the British had crossed the

Seine further to the north and were headed for the Somme, which Model had hoped would provide the next natural barrier to the Allied advance. Still, the Germans fought ferociously to hold what ground they possessed, with the tanks and artillery of 116.Panzer-Division fighting all day on August 26 to drive the Americans back near Bourgtheroulde, just over 5 kilometers west of Elbeuf. That night the last three self-propelled guns of the division's Panzer-Artillerie-Regiment 146, which had been rendered inoperable during an air attack, were withdrawn from the front and towed across the Seine. The German rearguard was being slowly whittled away. A Kampfgruppe made up of the tanks of 116.Panzer-Division and 2.SS-Panzer-Division were ordered to hold Elbeuf for as long as possible, but were outflanked when US 2nd Armored Division entered the town from the south. The tank crews of 116.Panzer-Division fought the Americans to a standstill and withdrew late that night under the cover of heavy rain. Most of the men of 2.SS-Panzer-Division who escaped did so by swimming across the Seine. In the morning, US Army units handed the town over to the Canadians, who had advanced from the north. The survivors of 2.Panzer-Division crossed the river on August 28, while 331.Infantry-Division took over the section of the front to the east of Duclair and Rouen. In the early hours of August 28, the last elements of 9.SS-Panzer-Division crossed the river at Duclair under fire but lost the popular commander of SS-Panzer-Regiment 9, Otto Meyer, who had survived the fighting in Normandy and the Falaise Pocket.[5]

Later that day, the Grenadiers of 331.Infanterie-Division finally pulled back across the river and on the same day the Canadian 3rd and 4th Armored Divisions entered Rouen. During the evening of August 31, a number of daring tank crews from schwere SS-Panzer Abteilung 102 returned to Rouen to destroy the three operational Tiger tanks which they had reluctantly abandoned on the east bank of the Seine. Not content with remaining in the area to watch the explosions, they also destroyed two Panthers that had been claimed by the French Resistance, using Panzerfausts before returning to their own lines in a stolen rowboat. These men were in all likelihood the last Germans to cross the Seine.

Between August 20 and August 24 alone the Germans had managed to ferry some 25,000 vehicles to the east bank of the Seine. Although most of the heavy tanks

were abandoned, and British Intelligence estimated that 95 percent of the men who reached the river after the debacle at Falaise managed to get across, including the rearguards. In addition to the ferries, twenty-four separate crossing sites had been in operation and, despite the railway bridge at Rouen being the best known and possibly the sturdiest, the pontoon bridge at Poses near Pont l'Arche was the busiest, where an estimated 16,000 vehicles crossed in the space of five nights and three days. The bridge was never bombed as it was usually dismantled during the day and no road led to it, which would have attracted the attention of Allied fighter bombers.

Once the retreat beyond the Seine had been completed, Model intended that 7.Armee would cover the withdrawal of what remained of 5.Panzerarmee to Arras, north-east of Amiens and the Somme. Once there, Dietrich was to hand command back to Eberbach. However, on the afternoon of August 31, Eberbach and most of his staff were taken prisoner by a British armored unit, depriving Model of one of his most able and experienced tank commanders. The British drive towards Amiens drove a wedge between 15.Armee and 5.Panzerarmee and destroyed any hopes of establishing a new defensive line on the Somme. Model was forced to retreat again with the British threatening Brussels.

In the south, the units of Heeresgruppe G continued their withdrawal through Lyon, which Blaskowitz, the army group commander, hoped to hold only long enough for his troops to pass through to the north. In answer to an uprising within the city, he directed the divisions of General Erich Petersen's IV. Luftwaffen-Feld-Korps to secure the city until the night of August 31, when Blaskowitz expected the last of his troops to pass through.[6]

He also ordered Wietersheim, the commander of 11.Panzer-Division, to destroy all the bridges across the Rhône and Ain Rivers east of Lyon to deny the Americans the important road junction of Bourg-en-Bresse, 50 kilometers north of Lyon between the Rhone and Saone Rivers. However, before Wietersheim could complete his orders, the Americans managed to capture two bridges across the Ain and reach the village of Méximieux, almost 20 kilometers to the northeast of Lyon on the northern bank of the Rhone. Realizing the danger this presented, Wietersheim sent Major Heinz Bödicker, the commander of the division's Panzer-Pionier-Bataillon 209, with his engineers and a

5 *I have been able to find no less than four different dates for Meyer's death but I am satisfied that the date given here is correct. He should not be confused with Kurt Meyer, the commander of 12.SS-Panzer-Division, who would be captured just one week later.*

6 *Petersen was a paratroop officer who had commanded a division in Russia before being transferred to France. Although technically his corps came under the command of the Lufwaffe, its three infantry divisions were all army formations.*

number of Panther tanks from Panzer-Regiment 15, to drive back the Americans and destroy the Ain bridges at Port-Galland and Chazey-sur-Ain, the latter about 2 kilometers south-east of Méximieux. Advancing from Montluel, just outside Lyon, Bödicker was supported by Kampfgruppe Kilp, which had been ordered to open the road between La Vabonne and Méximieux, which ran north-east from Lyon. Before the 1940 campaign, La Vabonne had been a French army camp and was now held by a company of the US 179th Infantry Regiment and Company Giraud, a French Resistance unit, supported by a number of M10 Tank Destroyers. The German attack began on August 31 after a short artillery barrage and lasted all day, with Kampfgruppe Kilp eventually beaten back as darkness fell. However, the arrival of Kampfgruppe Müller the next morning enabled the Germans to surround the camp and take prisoner the US Army and Resistance fighters.

As the Germans were making their final assault on La Vabonne, the tanks and halftracks of Kampfgruppe Bödicker spilled from the camouflage of the woods between La Boisse and Balan and raced to Chazey-sur-Ain, were they were able to capture the bridge by 6:00 am and very quickly destroy it with explosive charges. Ignoring the Americans in Méximieux for the moment, Bödicker turned his men back towards the remain-

ing bridge at Port-Galland. At the village of Saint-Maurice-de-Gourdans, less than a kilometer from their objective, the Germans ran into a strong roadblock position set up by the first battalion of 179th Infantry Regiment. The defenders were able to call on artillery support from the south bank of the river and after a fierce fight that left most of the village in ruins, Major Bödicker realized his Kampfgruppe was not strong enough to take the bridge and withdrew towards La Vabonne. Making contact with the other battle groups, Bödicker assumed command of all three and decided to move towards Méximieux, which was reached at about noon. Within half an hour the Germans began their first assault. The attack from the south, where most of the tanks are involved, met with little success, but the units attacking the northern edge of the town were able to take the Château de Méximieux, within sight of the American headquarters. Confused fighting continued throughout the night but by 3:00 am Bödicker ordered his men to withdraw. Although the bridge at Port-Galland remained open and Méximieux was firmly in Allied hands, the actions of Kampfgruppe Bödicker had held up the American advance for the best part of two days. Although French units entered Lyon on September 2, the last Germans left the city with a distinct lack of urgency in the early hours of the following day as Resistance fighters battled

with the Milice for control of the city.[7]

An attempt to cut off the withdrawal at Bourg was itself surrounded and severely mauled at Montreal on September 3 by a Kampfgruppe under the command of by Major Karl Bode, who had done so much to hold up the Americans at Montélimar. By this time, however, most of the German force had withdrawn through Mâcon, almost halfway to Dijon.

Although forward elements of US VI Corps, advancing from the south, were able to establish contact with units of Patton's 3rd Army on September 10, they were not able to push forward to the Belfort Gap. By September 14, Heeresgruupe G had been reinforced by a number of armored units[8] and held a line centered on Belfort running from Nancy in the north to the small town of Blamont on the Swiss border.

The German army now presented a con-

---

7   *The Milice française was a collaborationist paramilitary organiation which had hounded the Resistance since its creation in 1943. Its member were, if anything, more brutal than the Gestapo and SD and could expect little mercy from either the Resistants or the French military.*

8   *The OKW situation map shows parts of 15.Panzergrenadier-Division, which had been transferred from Italy, with the newly raised Panzer-Brigaden 111, 112, and 113 in addition to the tanks of 11.Panzer-Division.*

tinuous front through the Schedlt Estuary, across Belgium north of Liege then south to the fortress city of Metz and on to Nancy, where the boundary of General Otto von Knobelsdorff 1.Armee met Blaskowitz's Heeresgruppe G.

During the first week of September, Antwerp and Dieppe had fallen to the British and Canadians and the ports of Le Havre and Boulogne-sur-Mer, which Hitler had declared a Fortress City, were both threatened. On the southern front and in the center, the Americans were closing on Aachen and the Saar. Rearguard actions were often overrun with little difficulty, while German counterattacks were hastily prepared and usually brushed aside with ease, as most of the superbly trained and equipped units that the Wehrmacht possessed when the Normandy campaign began had simply ceased to exist. The ease with which the Allies had advanced through Belgium in the north and towards the borders of the Reich in the center and south, in addition to the staggering losses suffered in the battles across Normandy and Brittany, had convinced many of the Allied commanders that the Germans were spent as a military force. To the reverses in the west must be added the losses incurred on the Eastern front, where the Germans had long been pushed out of Russian territory. However, by early September the situation began to change and the front began to so-

lidify, although at the time this was almost imperceptible. Although the city of Antwerp fell to the Allies on September 4, it was ineffective as a port while the Scheldt Estuary remained in German hands. Most importantly, the failure to capture the approaches to the city allowed over sixty thousand men of General Gustav-Adolf von Zangen's 15.Armee to escape, although much of their heavy equipment was left behind. These men were used to bolster the garrison of the central Netherlands.

On the very day Antwerp was abandoned, Generalfeldmarschall Gerd von Rundstedt was recalled from retirement and reinstated as Oberbefehlshaber West, replacing Model, who had held the post for just eighteen days and was now relegated to the command of Heeresgruppe B. The main responsibility for saving the situation, however, would rest with the brilliant and energetic Model, who wasted no time in formulating a plan which would allow Germany to hold the Western Front.

PANZER-BRIGADE 107, AUGUST 1944

During a conference held on July 2, 1944, to consider the dire situation on the Eastern Front, Hitler suggested that small, highly mobile units would be capable of cutting off and destroying the Russian armored spearheads that were by then penetrating deep into the front of Heeregruppe Mitte. This was exactly what local commanders had been accomplishing for three years with ad-hoc Kampfgruppen or battle groups, often scraped together from badly depleted units and even stragglers. It was a method of fighting at which the Germans had proven themselves masters. That this idea was both unoriginal and had been fermenting in Hitler's mind for some time is suggested by his extremely detailed instructions that these formally-organized Kampfgruppen should number twelve, be made up of an armored infantry battalion, a tank force of approximately thirty to forty vehicles, a company of towed anti-tank guns and a number of mobile anti-aircraft weapons. Further, he insisted that the formations be called brigades and as they would be expected to operate into the winter months, the Jagpanzer 38(t), which was about to enter service, should be fitted with new, wider tracks. The army's first proposal that a number of Panzer divisions then undergoing refit be converted to what were called Panzer-Kampfgruppen. Eventually, an order was issued on July 11, 1944, calling for ten brigades to be formed, numbered from 101 to 110, based Hitler's directions. Each was to contain a Panzer battalion of three companies equipped with PzKpfw V Panther tanks and a fourth company made up of Pz IV/70(V) tank destroyers. The battalion staff would field another three Panthers and four mobile anti-aircraft guns. It was anticipated that the brigades numbered from 101 to 104 would be ready for deployment by August 15, those numbered 105 and 106 by the end of that month, 107 and 108 by the middle of September, and within another two weeks 109 and 110 would take the field. The original order was amended on July 24, changing little except to grant the honor title Feldherrnhalle to Panzer-Brigade 106 and Panzer-Brigade 110. The formation shown here, Panzer-Brigade 107, was formed in late July 1944, from the remnants of 25.Panzergrenadier-Division. The brigade fought in Holland during September and October 1944, where it suffered heavy losses. In November, the surviving personnel and material of the brigade were absorbed by the refurbished 25.Panzergrenadier-Division.

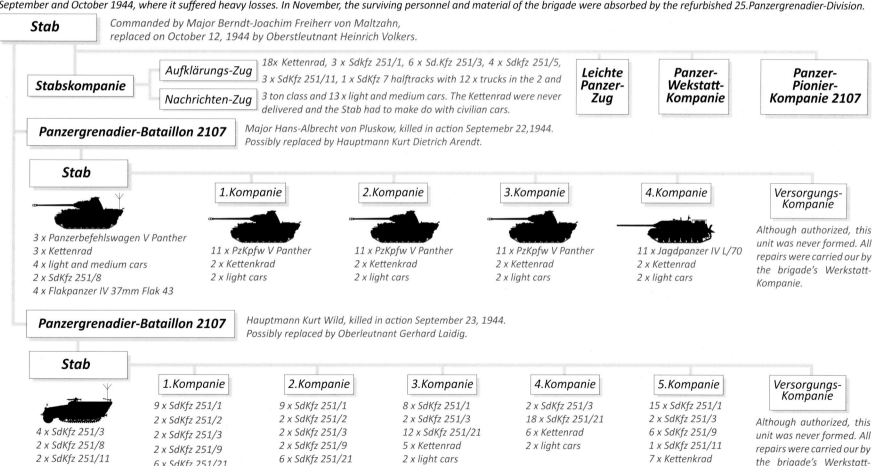

PANZER-BRIGADE 111, SEPTEMBER 1944

It was expected that the second generation of independent Panzer brigades, raised in September 1944 and numbered from 111 to 113, would be far stronger in armor than the brigades raised earlier in the year. However, when the formation depicted here, Panzer-Brigade 111, went into action for the first time near Lunèville in the opening phase of what would become known as the Battle of Arracourt, the brigade headquarters reported that just six PzKpfw IV tanks and nineteen Panthers were on hand and ready for combat. During the battle, the Jagdpanzer IV tank destroyer company, which may have been at full strength, was attached to Panzer-Abteilung 2111. The Panzergrenadier units had none of their allocated halftracks and the few available trucks were used to move the support weapons into position. The brigade was practically annihilated in the fighting around Arracourt, losing most of its personnel, including the commander. Accounts that suggest that the tank strength actually increased during this time are probably including the vehicles of Panzer-Brigade 112, which were taken over before the initial assault.

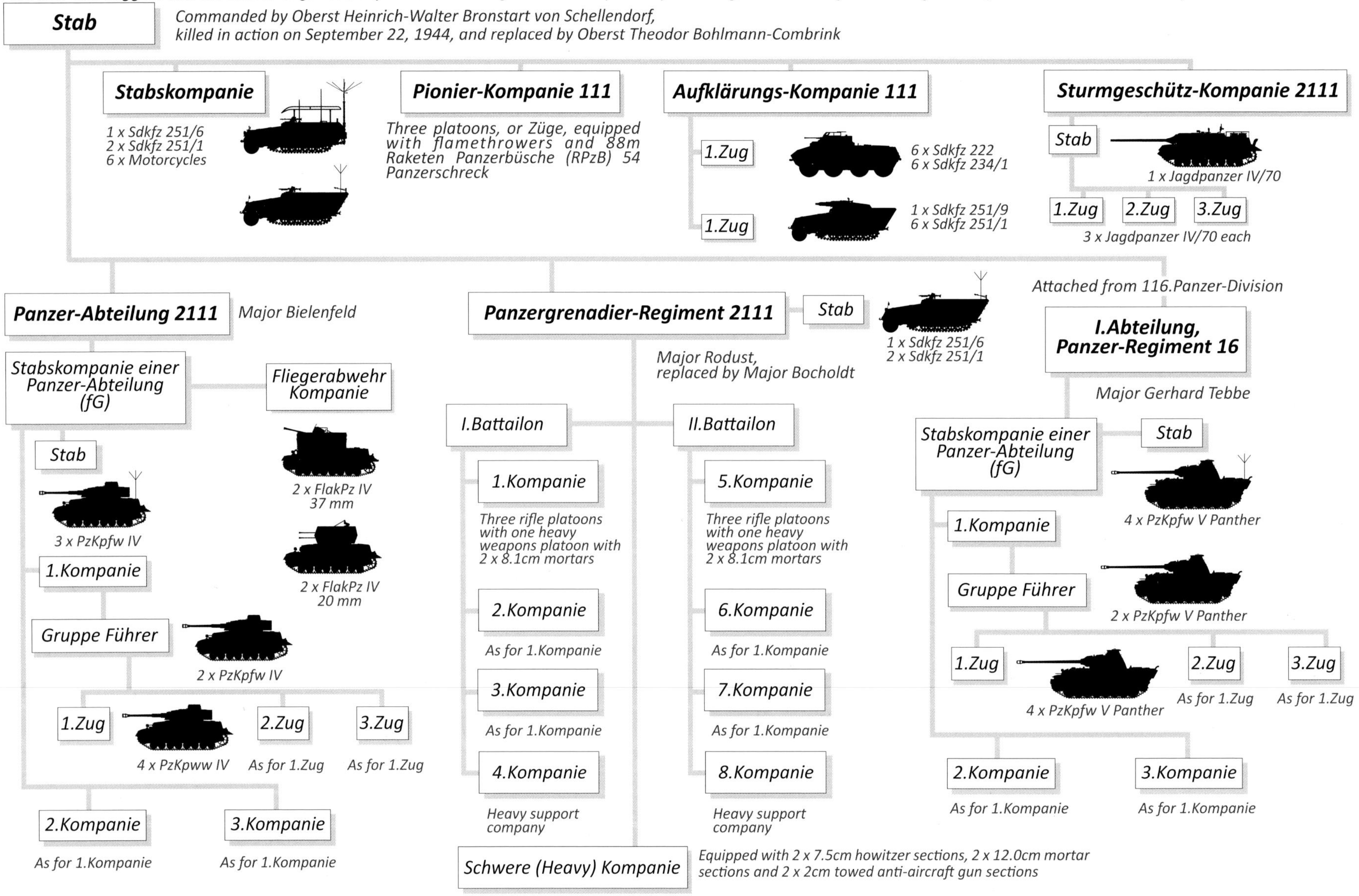

Stab — *Commanded by Oberst Heinrich-Walter Bronstart von Schellendorf, killed in action on September 22, 1944, and replaced by Oberst Theodor Bohlmann-Combrink*

Stabskompanie
1 x Sdkfz 251/6
2 x Sdkfz 251/1
6 x Motorcycles

Pionier-Kompanie 111
Three platoons, or Züge, equipped with flamethrowers and 88m Raketen Panzerbüsche (RPzB) 54 Panzerschreck

Aufklärungs-Kompanie 111
1.Zug — 6 x Sdkfz 222 / 6 x Sdkfz 234/1
1.Zug — 1 x Sdkfz 251/9 / 6 x Sdkfz 251/1

Sturmgeschütz-Kompanie 2111
Stab — 1 x Jagdpanzer IV/70
1.Zug   2.Zug   3.Zug — 3 x Jagdpanzer IV/70 each

Panzer-Abteilung 2111 — *Major Bielenfeld*

Stabskompanie einer Panzer-Abteilung (fG)
Stab — 3 x PzKpfw IV
1.Kompanie
Gruppe Führer — 2 x PzKpfw IV
1.Zug — 4 x PzKpww IV   2.Zug — As for 1.Zug   3.Zug — As for 1.Zug
2.Kompanie — As for 1.Kompanie   3.Kompanie — As for 1.Kompanie

Fliegerabwehr Kompanie
2 x FlakPz IV 37 mm
2 x FlakPz IV 20 mm

Panzergrenadier-Regiment 2111
Stab — 1 x Sdkfz 251/6 / 2 x Sdkfz 251/1
Major Rodust, replaced by Major Bocholdt

I.Battailon
1.Kompanie — Three rifle platoons with one heavy weapons platoon with 2 x 8.1cm mortars
2.Kompanie — As for 1.Kompanie
3.Kompanie — As for 1.Kompanie
4.Kompanie — Heavy support company

II.Battailon
5.Kompanie — Three rifle platoons with one heavy weapons platoon with 2 x 8.1cm mortars
6.Kompanie — As for 1.Kompanie
7.Kompanie — As for 1.Kompanie
8.Kompanie — Heavy support company

Schwere (Heavy) Kompanie — Equipped with 2 x 7.5cm howitzer sections, 2 x 12.0cm mortar sections and 2 x 2cm towed anti-aircraft gun sections

Attached from 116.Panzer-Division

I.Abteilung, Panzer-Regiment 16
Major Gerhard Tebbe

Stabskompanie einer Panzer-Abteilung (fG)
Stab — 4 x PzKpfw V Panther
1.Kompanie
Gruppe Führer — 2 x PzKpfw V Panther
1.Zug — 4 x PzKpfw V Panther   2.Zug — As for 1.Zug   3.Zug — As for 1.Zug
2.Kompanie — As for 1.Kompanie   3.Kompanie — As for 1.Kompanie

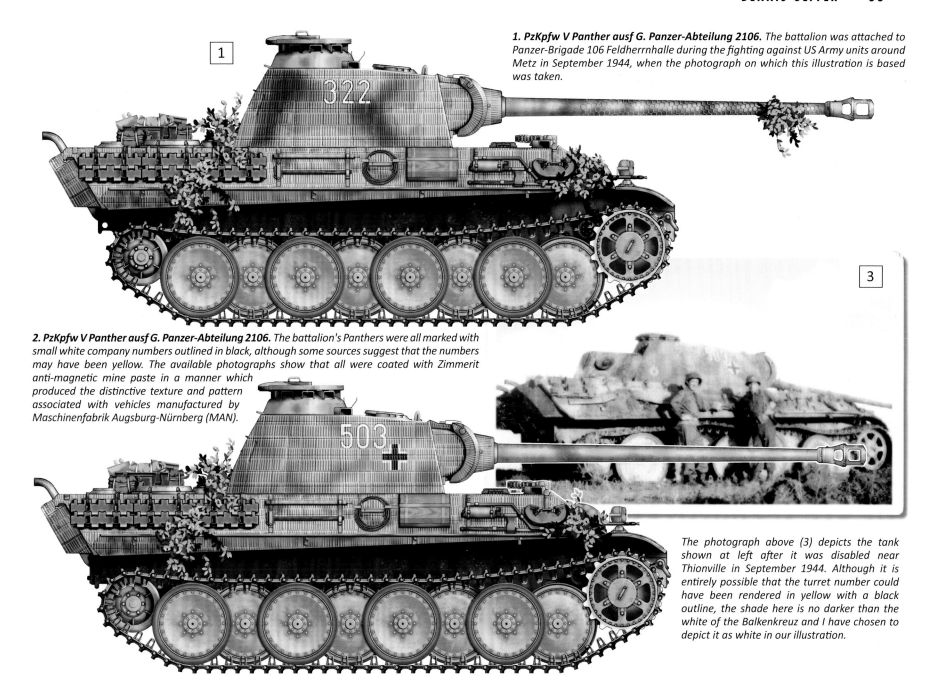

1. PzKpfw V Panther ausf G. Panzer-Abteilung 2106. *The battalion was attached to Panzer-Brigade 106 Feldherrnhalle during the fighting against US Army units around Metz in September 1944, when the photograph on which this illustration is based was taken.*

2. PzKpfw V Panther ausf G. Panzer-Abteilung 2106. *The battalion's Panthers were all marked with small white company numbers outlined in black, although some sources suggest that the numbers may have been yellow. The available photographs show that all were coated with Zimmerit anti-magnetic mine paste in a manner which produced the distinctive texture and pattern associated with vehicles manufactured by Maschinenfabrik Augsburg-Nürnberg (MAN).*

The photograph above (3) depicts the tank shown at left after it was disabled near Thionville in September 1944. Although it is entirely possible that the turret number could have been rendered in yellow with a black outline, the shade here is no darker than the white of the Balkenkreuz and I have chosen to depict it as white in our illustration.

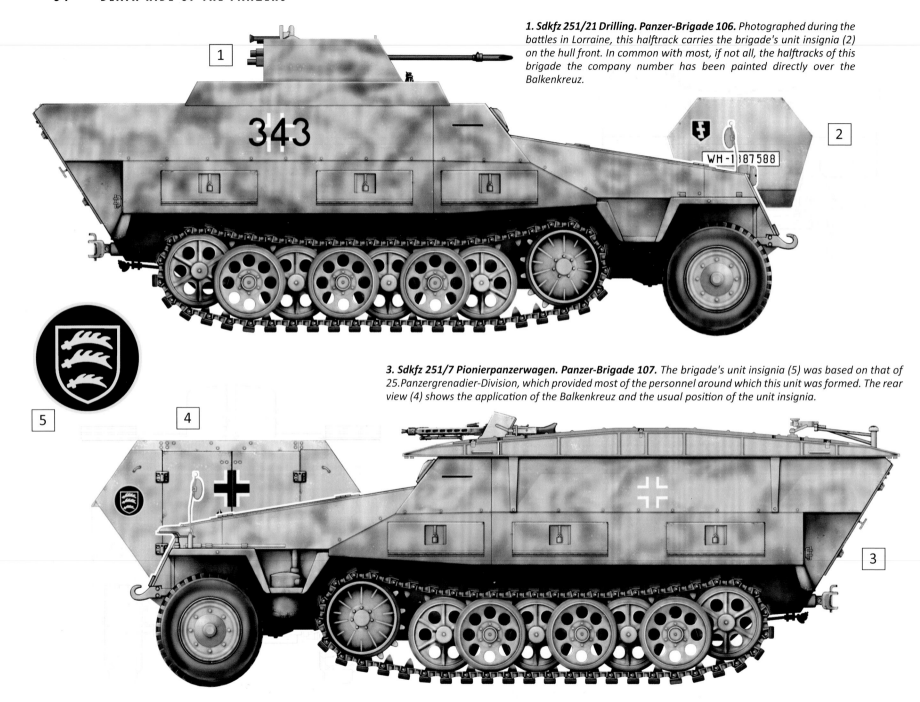

1. Sdkfz 251/21 Drilling. Panzer-Brigade 106. *Photographed during the battles in Lorraine, this halftrack carries the brigade's unit insignia (2) on the hull front. In common with most, if not all, the halftracks of this brigade the company number has been painted directly over the Balkenkreuz.*

3. Sdkfz 251/7 Pionierpanzerwagen. Panzer-Brigade 107. *The brigade's unit insignia (5) was based on that of 25.Panzergrenadier-Division, which provided most of the personnel around which this unit was formed. The rear view (4) shows the application of the Balkenkreuz and the usual position of the unit insignia.*

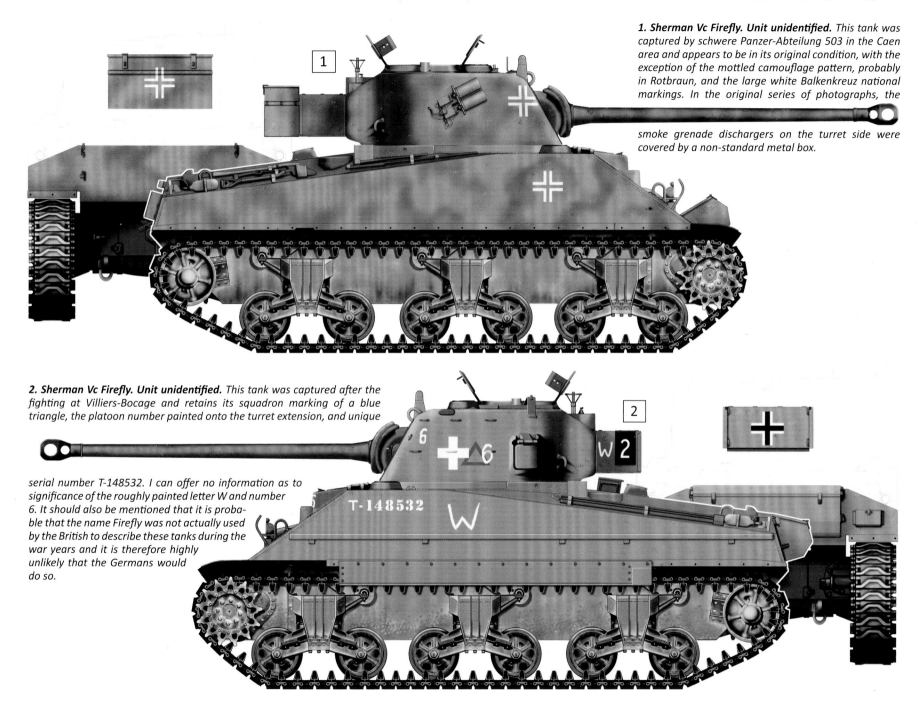

1. Sherman Vc Firefly. Unit unidentified. *This tank was captured by schwere Panzer-Abteilung 503 in the Caen area and appears to be in its original condition, with the exception of the mottled camouflage pattern, probably in Rotbraun, and the large white Balkenkreuz national markings. In the original series of photographs, the*

smoke grenade dischargers on the turret side were covered by a non-standard metal box.

2. Sherman Vc Firefly. Unit unidentified. *This tank was captured after the fighting at Villiers-Bocage and retains its squadron marking of a blue triangle, the platoon number painted onto the turret extension, and unique*

serial number T-148532. I can offer no information as to significance of the roughly painted letter W and number 6. It should also be mentioned that it is probable that the name Firefly was not actually used by the British to describe these tanks during the war years and it is therefore highly unlikely that the Germans would do so.

1. PzKpfw IV ausf J. Unit unidentified. *This tank was photographed near Liege in late 1944 and is devoid of any markings other than the Balkenkreuz national insignia, which is painted onto the turret Schürzen in what is the usual position for these tanks. Both 16.Panzer-Regiment of 116.Panzer-Division and SS-Panzer-Regiment 1 from 1.SS-Panzer-Division lost a number of PzKpfw IV tanks in this area in September and this vehicle may belong to one of those formations. This illustration provides a clear example of the frame to which the hull Schürzen were attached and the four metal supports which held the frame in position. The small triangular fittings along the top edge of the frame corresponded to brackets welded or bolted to the inside face of the individual Schürzen plates.*

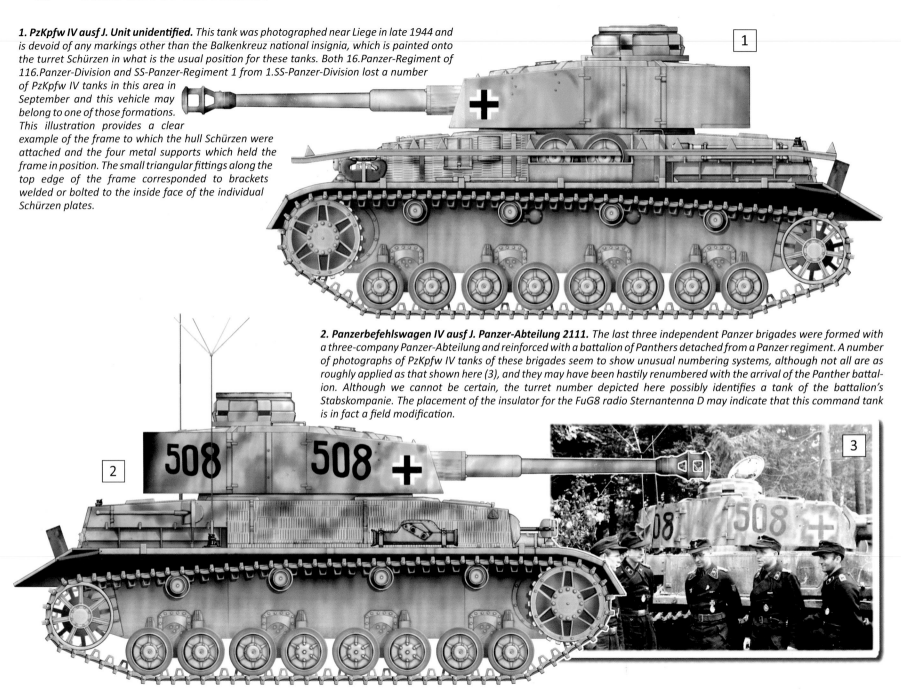

2. Panzerbefehlswagen IV ausf J. Panzer-Abteilung 2111. *The last three independent Panzer brigades were formed with a three-company Panzer-Abteilung and reinforced with a battalion of Panthers detached from a Panzer regiment. A number of photographs of PzKpfw IV tanks of these brigades seem to show unusual numbering systems, although not all are as roughly applied as that shown here (3), and they may have been hastily renumbered with the arrival of the Panther battalion. Although we cannot be certain, the turret number depicted here possibly identifies a tank of the battalion's Stabskompanie. The placement of the insulator for the FuG8 radio Sternantenna D may indicate that this command tank is in fact a field modification.*

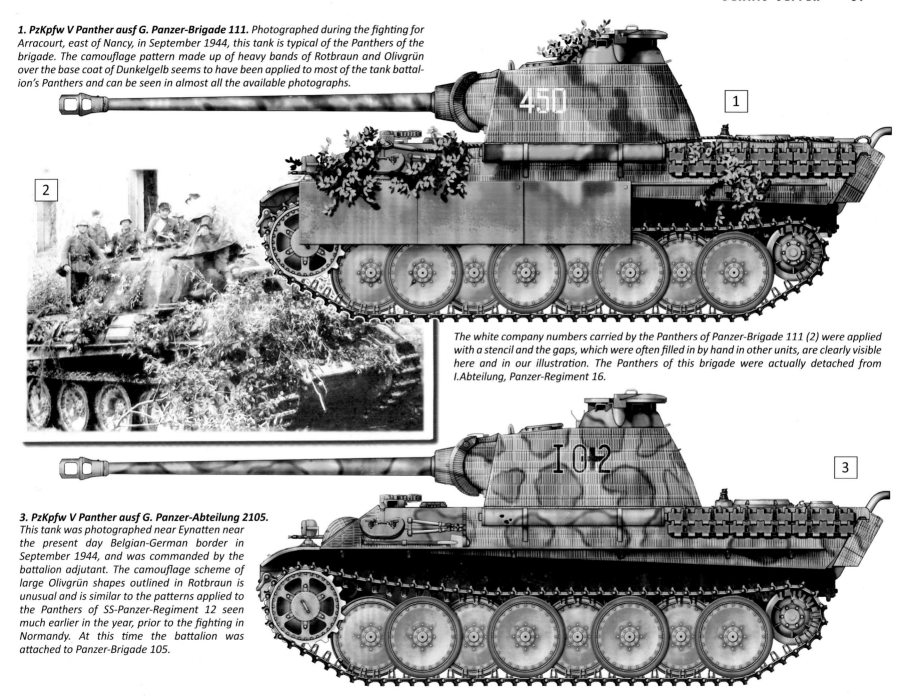

1. PzKpfw V Panther ausf G. Panzer-Brigade 111. *Photographed during the fighting for Arracourt, east of Nancy, in September 1944, this tank is typical of the Panthers of the brigade. The camouflage pattern made up of heavy bands of Rotbraun and Olivgrün over the base coat of Dunkelgelb seems to have been applied to most of the tank battalion's Panthers and can be seen in almost all the available photographs.*

The white company numbers carried by the Panthers of Panzer-Brigade 111 (2) were applied with a stencil and the gaps, which were often filled in by hand in other units, are clearly visible here and in our illustration. The Panthers of this brigade were actually detached from I.Abteilung, Panzer-Regiment 16.

3. PzKpfw V Panther ausf G. Panzer-Abteilung 2105. *This tank was photographed near Eynatten near the present day Belgian-German border in September 1944, and was commanded by the battalion adjutant. The camouflage scheme of large Olivgrün shapes outlined in Rotbraun is unusual and is similar to the patterns applied to the Panthers of SS-Panzer-Regiment 12 seen much earlier in the year, prior to the fighting in Normandy. At this time the battalion was attached to Panzer-Brigade 105.*

1. PzKpfw Tiger ausf E. Schwere Panzer-Kompanie Hummel. *Formed from elements of Panzer-Ersatz und Ausbildungs-Abteilung 500, a training unit, the Tigers of this formation featured a mixture of early and mid-production features, including at least one vehicle with all steel wheels. Although very few photographic references are available to us, due to the large amounts of foliage camouflage with which all these tanks were covered, it appears that all fourteen of the company's Tiger I tanks were numbered following the regulation sequence. The number here, for example, indicates the fourth tank of the second platoon, with the company number for all being one. The two command tanks of Hauptmann Hummel and Leutnant Knaak were numbered 101 and 102, respectively. It would seem that the three platoons used different colors for the turret numbers, although the exact shades are a matter of some debate. All had the Balkenkreuz placed centrally on the hull sides, as shown in our photograph at right (2) and illustration.*

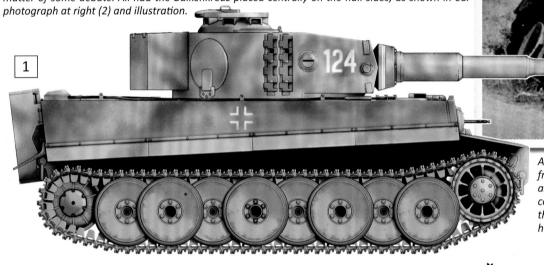

Another identifying feature of this company's tanks, although missing from our photograph, were the spare track links fitted to the hull front as additional armour. These were uniformly applied throughout the company, with three combat tracks welded above each fender and three transport tracks placed between the driver's vision block and the hull machine gun.

3. PzKpfw Tiger ausf B. Schwere Panzer-Abteilung 506. *Like most vehicles fighting around Arnhem, this tank is covered with foliage camouflage. This may be the Tiger II, numbered 203, abandoned along the Heuvelstraat during the attack on Elst, between the Nederrijn and Waal Rivers, in October 1944.*

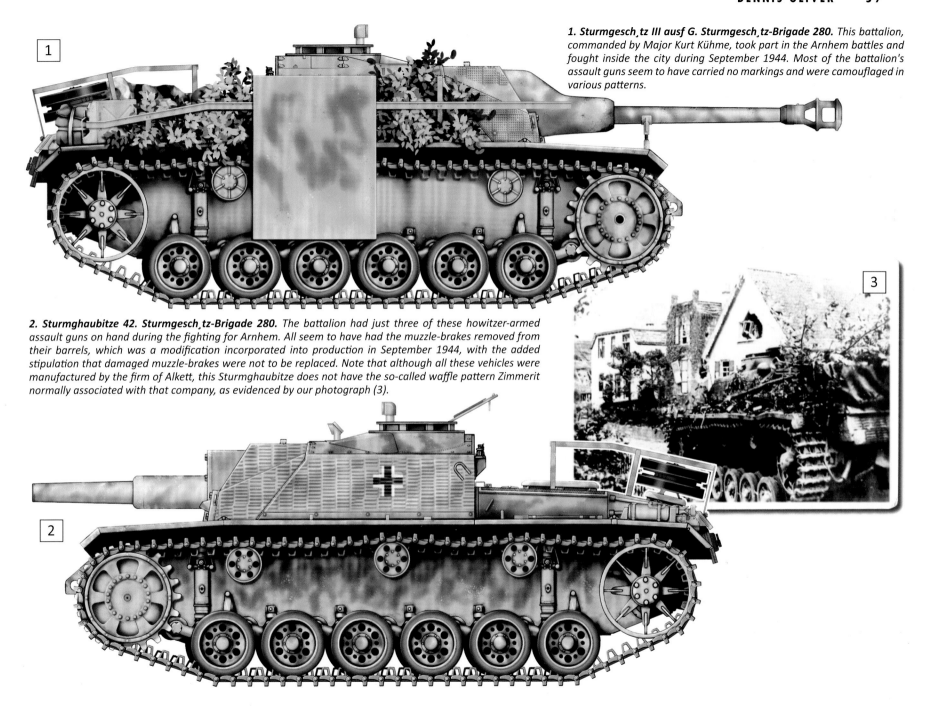

1. Sturmgeschütz III ausf G. Sturmgeschütz-Brigade 280. *This battalion, commanded by Major Kurt Kühme, took part in the Arnhem battles and fought inside the city during September 1944. Most of the battalion's assault guns seem to have carried no markings and were camouflaged in various patterns.*

2. Sturmghaubitze 42. Sturmgeschütz-Brigade 280. *The battalion had just three of these howitzer-armed assault guns on hand during the fighting for Arnhem. All seem to have had the muzzle-brakes removed from their barrels, which was a modification incorporated into production in September 1944, with the added stipulation that damaged muzzle-brakes were not to be replaced. Note that although all these vehicles were manufactured by the firm of Alkett, this Sturmghaubitze does not have the so-called waffle pattern Zimmerit normally associated with that company, as evidenced by our photograph (3).*

1. PzKpfw III ausf G. Panzer-Kompanie Mielke. *Detached from Panzer-Ersatz-Regiment Bielefeld for the defense of Arnhem in September 1944, this unit comprised two PzKpfw IV and six PzKpfw III tanks, two of the later being very early versions. All the PzKpfw III tanks carried a number, sometimes a single digit, which can also be seen in our photograph (2). The tank shown above had the number 213 painted on to the turret stowage box (3) while the other PzKpfw III ausf G (4) had the number on the turret side. Note that the Balkenkreuz has a thin black outline to the arms.*

5. PzKpfw IV ausf G. Panzer-Kompanie Mielke. *Unlike the company's PzKpfw III tanks, the PzKpfw IV vehicles seem to have been completely unmarked except for the Balkenkreuz carried on the turret Schürzen. Both PzKpfw IV tanks, one an ausf G and the other an ausf H, were lost during the fighting in the city.*

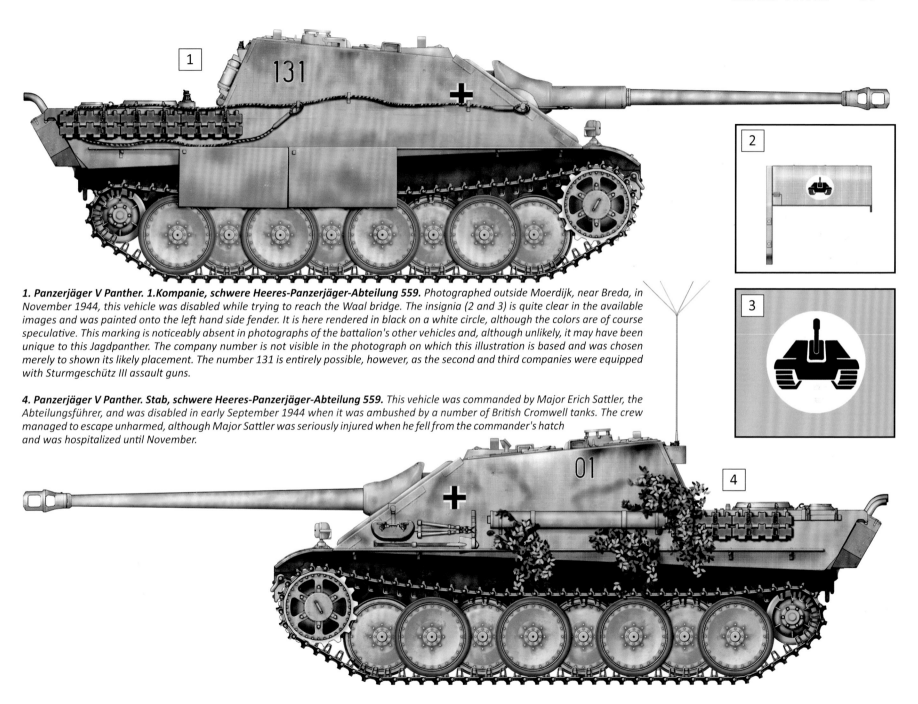

1. Panzerjäger V Panther. 1.Kompanie, schwere Heeres-Panzerjäger-Abteilung 559. *Photographed outside Moerdijk, near Breda, in November 1944, this vehicle was disabled while trying to reach the Waal bridge. The insignia (2 and 3) is quite clear in the available images and was painted onto the left hand side fender. It is here rendered in black on a white circle, although the colors are of course speculative. This marking is noticeably absent in photographs of the battalion's other vehicles and, although unlikely, it may have been unique to this Jagdpanther. The company number is not visible in the photograph on which this illustration is based and was chosen merely to shown its likely placement. The number 131 is entirely possible, however, as the second and third companies were equipped with Sturmgeschütz III assault guns.*

4. Panzerjäger V Panther. Stab, schwere Heeres-Panzerjäger-Abteilung 559. *This vehicle was commanded by Major Erich Sattler, the Abteilungsführer, and was disabled in early September 1944 when it was ambushed by a number of British Cromwell tanks. The crew managed to escape unharmed, although Major Sattler was seriously injured when he fell from the commander's hatch and was hospitalized until November.*

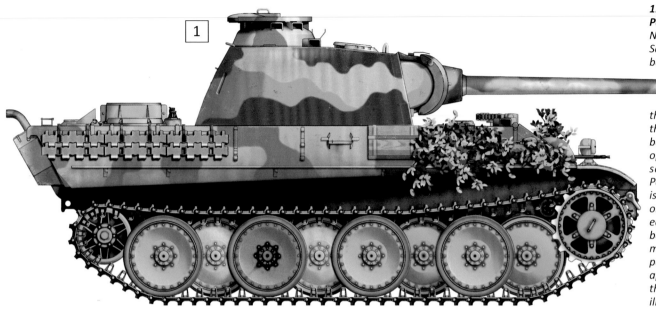

1. PzKpfw V Panther ausf G. II.Abteilung, Panzer-Lehr-Regiment 130. *Photographed in November 1944 near Schalbach, north-east of Sarrebourg, this tank was disabled when the battalion made an attack on positions held by* the US 114th Infantry Regiment. At this time, the Panzer-Lehr-Regiment consisted of a single battalion, with the sixth and eighth companies operating PzKpfw IV tanks while the fifth and seventh companies were equipped with Panthers. The hard-edged camouflage scheme is one of a number introduced as a result of an order issued on August 19, 1944, which stipulated that Panthers were henceforth to be painted before leaving the assembly plants in a pattern made up of patches of Olivgrün and Rotbraun painted onto a base coat of Dunkelgelb. The application varied between manufacturers and the differences are explained throughout these illustrations.

2. PzKpfw V Panther ausf G. Panzer-Regiment 15. *Photographed in Lorraine in November 1944, this tank is an ausf G model fitted with the cupola, and possibly the turret, from a Panther ausf D. Interestingly, a photograph taken on the Eastern Front at about this time shows an identical arrangement. The tanks in both cases were also coated with Zimmerit paste in a pattern of ridges normally associated* with vehicles manufactured by the firm of Demag, although that company never produced any late model Panthers. All this suggests that the addition of the early cupola, and perhaps turret, to the later hull was in the nature of a factory re-build, which may have been a series, and not a field modification. Of note are the hooks welded to the turret to hold lengths of spare track.

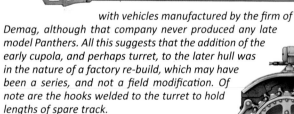

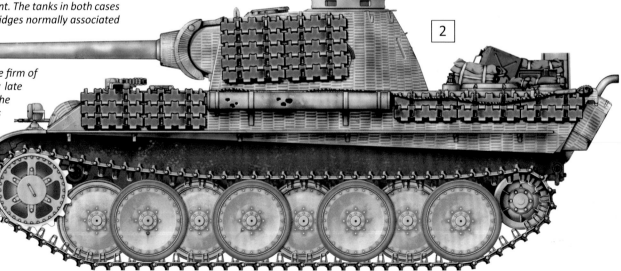

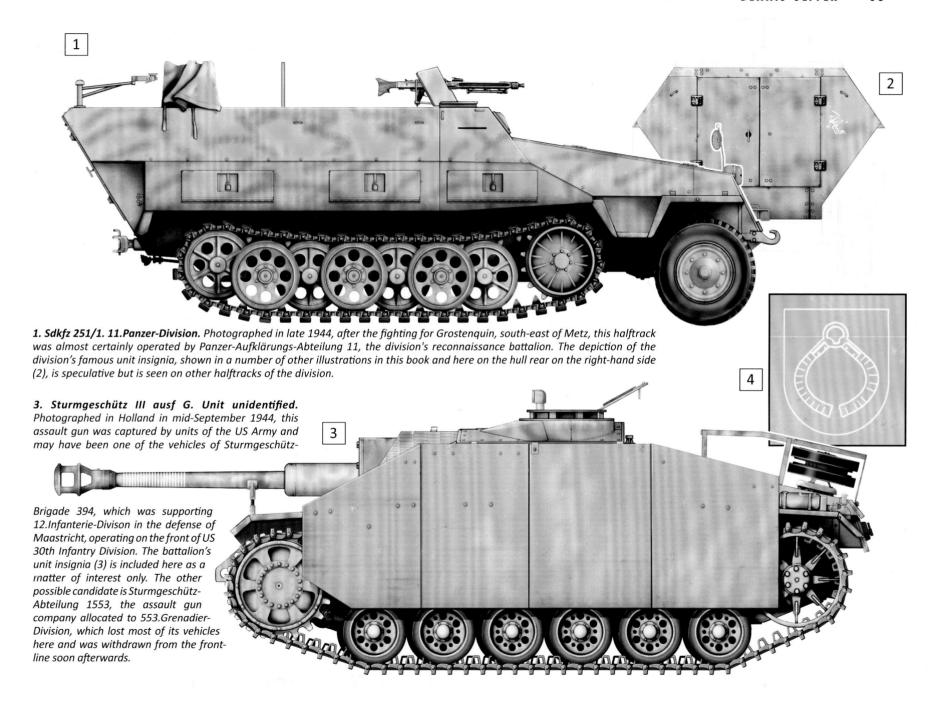

1. Sdkfz 251/1. 11.Panzer-Division. *Photographed in late 1944, after the fighting for Grostenquin, south-east of Metz, this halftrack was almost certainly operated by Panzer-Aufklärungs-Abteilung 11, the division's reconnaissance battalion. The depiction of the division's famous unit insignia, shown in a number of other illustrations in this book and here on the hull rear on the right-hand side (2), is speculative but is seen on other halftracks of the division.*

3. Sturmgeschütz III ausf G. Unit unidentified. *Photographed in Holland in mid-September 1944, this assault gun was captured by units of the US Army and may have been one of the vehicles of Sturmgeschütz-Brigade 394, which was supporting 12.Infanterie-Divison in the defense of Maastricht, operating on the front of US 30th Infantry Division. The battalion's unit insignia (3) is included here as a matter of interest only. The other possible candidate is Sturmgeschütz-Abteilung 1553, the assault gun company allocated to 553.Grenadier-Division, which lost most of its vehicles here and was withdrawn from the front-line soon afterwards.*

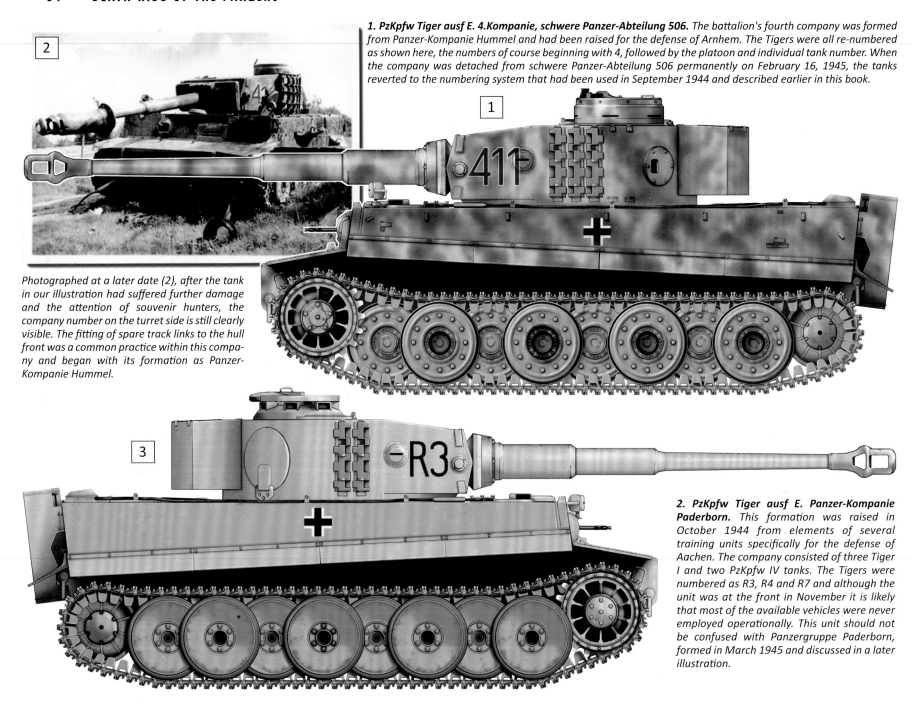

1. PzKpfw Tiger ausf E. 4.Kompanie, schwere Panzer-Abteilung 506. *The battalion's fourth company was formed from Panzer-Kompanie Hummel and had been raised for the defense of Arnhem. The Tigers were all re-numbered as shown here, the numbers of course beginning with 4, followed by the platoon and individual tank number. When the company was detached from schwere Panzer-Abteilung 506 permanently on February 16, 1945, the tanks reverted to the numbering system that had been used in September 1944 and described earlier in this book.*

Photographed at a later date (2), after the tank in our illustration had suffered further damage and the attention of souvenir hunters, the company number on the turret side is still clearly visible. The fitting of spare track links to the hull front was a common practice within this company and began with its formation as Panzer-Kompanie Hummel.

2. PzKpfw Tiger ausf E. Panzer-Kompanie Paderborn. *This formation was raised in October 1944 from elements of several training units specifically for the defense of Aachen. The company consisted of three Tiger I and two PzKpfw IV tanks. The Tigers were numbered as R3, R4 and R7 and although the unit was at the front in November it is likely that most of the available vehicles were never employed operationally. This unit should not be confused with Panzergruppe Paderborn, formed in March 1945 and discussed in a later illustration.*

2.01. Photographed between Rauray and Tilly-sur-Seulles in early July 1944, this Tiger I of 3.Kompanie, schwere SS Panzer Abteilung 101 was commanded by SS-Oberscharführer Rolf von Westernhagen, the younger brother of the battalion commander Heinz von Westernhagen. This Tiger was probably disabled during the fighting along the road between Caen and Villers-Bocage during the last days of June when tanks of the battalion's second and third companies, together with 7.Kompanie, SS-Panzer-Regiment 12 and a company from Panzer-Regiment 22, attempted to halt British units that were advancing towards Verson and Grainville. Accounts of these actions are extremely sketchy and our best source, Wolfgang Schneider, simply states that one tank was lost. The two available eyewitness accounts do not mention the tank commander or his crew and worryingly contain errors of fact. What is certain, however, is that Westernhagen survived and his tank was later recovered by the British and found to be in running order.

2.02. Captured near Cheux during the fighting for Carpiquet airfield, this Pzkpfw IV ausf H of 8.Kompanie, SS-Panzer-Regiment 12 is also depicted in the color illustration section. The unit insignia of 12.SS-Panzer-Division can be seen on the hull rear plate on the right hand side with the Balkenkreuz positioned above the muffler. The application of the turret number, black outlined with white, is unusually neat for this battalion. This particular tank was commanded by SS-Untersturmführer Jeran. This vehicle is also depicted in the colored illustration section on page 25.

2.03. A Pzkpfw IV ausf J of 8.Kompanie, Panzer-Regiment 3 photographed in the ruins of Pont-Farcy, south of Saint-Lô, in early August 1944. The unit insignia of 2.Panzer-Division is just visible on the front plate below the driver's hatch and the number 802, in the white outline style typical of this regiment, can be seen on the turret Schürzen. This tank is also shown in the illustration section. This vehicle is also depicted in the colored illustration section on page 34.

2.04. Photographed in early July on the road to Saint-Fromond, north of Saint-Lô, this Pzkpfw IV ausf J was operated by 6.Kompanie, SS-Panzer-Regiment 2. The unit insignia of 2.SS-Panzer-Division Das Reich is just visible on the left of the hull rear plate and the company number 622 can been seen on the turret Schürzen painted in a white outline. This vehicle is also depicted in the colored illustration section on page 27.

2.05. Photographed near Saint Denis-le-Gast on July 29, 1944, these Sdkfz 251 half-tracks are from 2.SS-Panzer-Division Das Reich and may be part of the column that included the Hummel self-propelled Howitzer named Clausewitz depicted in the following image. This division, with other units of 7.Armee, was attempting to withdraw when it was encircled at Roncey. The German units suffered severe losses in the ensuing fighting that including most of their heavy equipment.

2.06. Photographed near Notre-Dame-de-Cenilly, east of Coutances, this Sdkfz 251 half-track and Hummel self-propelled 15cm howitzer of 2.SS-Panzer-Division had been part of the column withdrawing after the fighting at Saint-Denis-le-Gast, which ran into elements of US 2nd Armored Division late in the evening of July 28, 1944. Of note is the name Clausewitz painted on the side of the Hummel towards the front in black outlined in white. On the rear of the half-track can be seen the tactical symbol identifying the first battery of a self-propelled artillery unit below the division's unit insignia.

2.06a. A Pzkpfw IV ausf J of 8.Kompanie, SS-Panzer-Regiment 2 knocked out during the fighting in Saint Denis-la-Gast on July 31, 1944. The use of white outline turret numbers was common to all the tanks of II Abteilung and examples are shown and discussed in the color illustration section on page 27.

2.07. A Sturmgeschütz IV assault gun of SS-Panzer-Abteilung 17 destroyed by US fighter-bombers while the battalion was moving along the Marigny-Montreuil road in late July during the Operation Cobra. Although the vehicle is badly damaged, much of the Zimmerit is still in place suggesting that these vehicles carried few, if any, markings. The production of the Sturmgeschütz IV was undertaken by Krupp and was intended to be an interim measure to fill the gap caused by the Allied bombing of the Alkett works in Berlin, which manufactured the Sturmgeschütz III. The new vehicle was essentially made up from the superstructure of an Alkett Sturmgeschütz III married to the chassis of a Krupp Pzkpfw IV with a large armored box at the hull front for the driver.

2.08. A Panther ausf A of I.Abteilung, Panzer-Regiment 6 attached to Panzer-Lehr-Division knocked out during the Operation Cobra battles in July 1944. The battalion had sixteen of its operational Panthers in its frontline positions when the preliminary bombardment for US Army's offensive commenced on the morning of July 25, 1944 and almost all were disabled. The method of application of the of Zimmerit anti-magnetic mine paste is typical of Daimler-Benz manufactured vehicles where an initial rough application was scored with horizontal and vertical lines. The monocular gun sight on the left-hand side of the gun mantlet was introduced into production from November 1943.

2.09. An Sdkfz 251/7 ausf D Pionierpanzerwagen of 11.Kompanie, Panzergrenadier-Lehr-Regiment 901 said to have been photographed only hours after the US breakthrough near Saint-Lô on July 25, 1944. The wooden planks that were normally carried on the hull side below the bridge section are missing and would have obscured the number. Although the Panther tank in the background would seem to carry no visible markings, it is almost certainly from Panzer-Regiment 6, at this time attached to the Panzer-Lehr-Division, and was in fact the subject of a further series of photographs after it had been cleared from the road.

2.10. A Pzkpfw IV ausf H of 8.Kompanie, Panzer-Lehr-Regiment 130 photographed in late July during the opening phase of Operation Cobra. Other photographs of this tank show that it also carried the unit marking of the regiment's second battalion based on the family crest of Major Prinz Schönburg-Waldenburg shown in the illustration section. Photographs of other 8.Kompanie tanks would suggest that most company numbers were painted in the rudimentary style seen here.

2.11. This Sdkfz 250/1 Neu halftrack of Panzer-Aufklärungs-Abteilung, the reconnaissance battalion of 2.Panzer-Division, was photographed shortly after August 6, 1944 near l'Abbaye Blanche, just north of Mortain. The division's unit insignia can be seen on the rear access door above the tactical symbol identifying the third company of an armored reconnaissance company.

2.12. Just visible on the driver's side fender of the disabled LKW Opel Blitz is the unit insignia of 10.SS-Panzer-Division Frundsberg. This photograph was taken looking north along what is today Route-de-la-Libération at the crossroads north of Foligny known as Le Repas and as with many towns in northern France, little has changed since 1944. Although the roads are now paved, all the buildings visible here are still standing.

2.13. Photographed after the Normandy battles, this Sturmgeschütz III assault gun displays several features that were indicative of the vehicles of 2.Batterie, Sturmgeschütz-Brigade 341 including the large rain guard over the gun mantlet and the bent upper edges of the hull Schürzen. The use of fencing wire, visible here on the barrel of the 7.5cm gun, was commonly employed in Normandy as a means of holding foliage camouflage.

2.14. A Pzkpfw IV ausf J of Panzer-Regiment 33 from 9 Panzer Division photographed outside the town of Sées, 20km south of Argentan, in late August 1944. At this time the regiment's I.Abteilung had eighty-two of these tanks on hand.

2.15. This photograph was taken on August 12, 1944 looking south-west towards the Neufbourg railway station which can be seen in the background on Route-de-la-Gare. The village of Neufbourg is situated about 1 kilometer north of Mortain near Abbey Blanche and, although the railway station is no longer in use, both buildings seen here and the road have changed little since 1944. Several German transport vehicles are visible here including a Type 166 Schwimmwagen, a Type 82 Kübelwagen and, in the background, an Sdkfz 251 halftrack.

2.16. The next three images show Panther ausf A tanks of I.Abteilung, SS-Panzer-Regiment 1 of 1.SS-Panzer-Division photographed on the road between Saint-Barthélemy and Juvigny-le-Tetre north-east of Mortain in August 1944 in the aftermath of Operation Lüttich. The practice of marking the tank's number on the side of the gun mantlet, seen on Panther number 328, was necessitated by the spare tracks which normally covered the turret sides and was an identifying feature of this battalion. The lengths of spare track were attached to the hull sides by sturdy metal hooks which had been welded to the turret roof and overhung the sides.

2.17. The method of attaching the lengths of track to the turret sides can be seen here. The Zimmerit is applied in a pattern indicative of Panthers produced by Maschinenfabrik Augsburg Nürnberg AG (MAN).

2.18. The application and style of the company number can be clearly seen in this view of a 3.Kompanie tank. The standard camouflage scheme of the period made up of Rotbraun RAL and Olivgrün sprayed over the base color of Dunkelgelb is often obscured by the effects dust and to some extent by the way in which light is reflected off the ridges of the Zimmerit coating. However, it is very obvious on the barrel of the main gun.

2.19. A Panther ausf A of II.Abteilung, Panzer-Regiment 33 from 9.Panzer-Division knocked out in the area between Argentan and Chambois in August 1944. Note that the Zimmerit, applied in the fashion indicative of MNH manufactured vehicles, is extended to the lower hull behind the wheels. The tracks appear to be the earlier type without the Stollen or cleats manufacturer prior to September 1943.

2.20. Pzkpfw V Panther ausf G of 1.Kompanie, SS-Panzer-Regiment 12 captured almost intact by Canadian troops at Bretteville-sur-Odon, about 15 kilometers south-east of Bayeux, on June 9, 1944. This Panther is a MAN-produced tank, built in March or April 1944 before the introduction of the welded armored exhaust covers. In his history of the Hitlerjugend division, Hubert Meyer mentions that this tank was commanded by the commander of the company's third platoon.

2.21. A Tiger II tank of 1.Kompanie, schwere Panzer-Abteilung 503 abandoned north-west of Vimoutiers in early August 1944, although this photograph was taken at a much later date. The battalion fought in Normandy with twelve Tiger II tanks, all with the Porsche turret seen here, all allocated to the first company. The second and third companies were equipped with Tiger I tanks. A tank of this battalion is shown and discussed in the illustration section.

22.22. Developed for the extreme conditions encountered on the Eastern Front, the Skoda Radschlepper Ost, also known as Porsche Typ 175, was found to be totally unsuitable. Although 200 were ordered, only half that number were built and all were sent to France where this example was photographed. Some of these vehicles survived the fighting in Normandy and can be seen in photographs taken during the Ardennes Offensive.

2.23. Disabled near Saint-Lô in July 1944, this vehicle is an Italian AB 41 armored car. A least four of the vehicles were on hand with 2.Fallschirmjäger-Division which took part in the defense of Brest during August and September and it is possible that others served with Fallschirm-Aufklärungs-Abteilung 12, an independent battalion attached directly to II. Fallschirm-Korps, which fought against 1st Polish Armored Division at Mont Ormel in August 1944.

2.24. Photographed in September 1944, possibly at the large equipment collection point outside Baupte west of Carentan, most of the tanks seen here are former French army vehicles. Nearest the camera, and minus its turret, is a Renault R35 next to a Hotchkiss H35 painted in Dunkelgelb with the company number 224 marked in black on the turret. Both these types were operated by II.Abteilung of Panzer-Regiment 22 and Panzer-Ausbildungs und Ersatz-Abteilung 100, a training and replacement unit which nevertheless fought at the front. Towards the end of the line, identified by its long barrel, is a Panzerjäger 38(t) Marder III. These self-propelled guns were on hand with the anti-tank battalions of most of the infantry divisions that served in Normandy and with the Panzergrenadier regiments of 166.Panzer-Division.

2.25. British troops inspect a Pzkpfw IV ausf H which, from this angle, seems to have suffered very little damage. The large number 5 visible on the open Schürzen access door behind the muzzle brake is very similar in style to that used by Panzer-Regiment 22, although unfortunately no definitive identification is possible. The white tape in the foreground indicates that the area has been cleared of mines. The date is probably late July or early August 1944.

2.26. A Panther ausf A of I.Abteilung, Panzer-Regiment 15 from 11.Panzer-Division photographed in the ruins Meximieux near Lyon. The battalion lost ten Panthers and almost twenty other assorted vehicles in the fighting for this town.

2.27. Photographed on the railway line at Braine between Soisson and Reims, well to the east of Paris, these four tanks of schwere-Panzer-Abteilung 503 were captured when the train was stopped on the morning of August 29 by elements of the US 32nd Armored Regiment. Several photographs of this incident are known to exist and although all seem to indicate that these tanks carried no markings, it is however probable that these vehicles are the survivors of 2.Kompanie, which took over all the third company Tiger I tanks at the end of July. The battalion's first company had been equipped with Tiger II vehicles in June.

2.28. Photographed in front of the Notre-Dame church in the town of Marle, south-east of Saint-Quentin, this tank is often identified with schwere SS-Panzer-Abteilung 101 which was in action to the north-east of the town, losing two of its last tanks, at the end of August 1944. In his two-volume account of the history of the Tiger battalions, Wolfgang Schneider mentions that a tank of schwere SS-Panzer-Abteilung 101 with the rubber-rimmed wheels was abandoned in Marle. However, this identification is not universally accepted, and another possible candidate is Panzer-Kompanie (Funklenk) 316, which had been allocated three Tiger I tanks in April 1944.

2.29. Photographed just outside Paris in August 1944, this Panther ausf G may be one of the twenty held in reserve by the garrison commander of Paris or possibly one of the tanks of Kampfgruppe Hennecke, an ad-hoc formation formed from elements of the Panzer-Lehr-Division and dispatched to the city on Friday, August 25. Lead by Hauptmann Heinrich Hennecke, a company commander of I.Abteilung, Panzergrenadier-Regiment 901, the Kampfgruppe consisted of an under strength company of Panthers and the men of Hennecke's battalion.

2.30. Abandoned in the grounds of the Palais du Luxembourg during the brief fighting for the city of Paris in August 1944, this Sdkfz 11/1 Flak 38 may have been one of the vehicles assigned to Panzer-Kompanie Paris, an ad-hoc unit formed from a company of 525.Sicherungs-Division.

2.31. Photographed in Paris in late August 1944 near the Jardin des Tuileries, this Renault R-35, or Panzerkampfwagen 35R 731(f), is one of the vehicles of Panzer-Kompanie Paris. Some accounts suggest that this company was formed from 325.Sicherungs-Division, a security formation directly under the command of the Militärbefehlshaber Frankreich, although it may have been raised from vehicles and personnel of 5.Kompanie, Panzer-Abteilung 100 and the turret number would seem to confirm at least some connection.

2.32. After the Normandy fighting, the Allies established several collection points for captured German vehicles such as that shown here outside Trevieres west of Bayeux. Photographed on September 4, 1944 are a turretless Renault R-35, or Panzerkampfwagen 35R 731(f), a Marder I 7.5cm PaK40/1 auf Geschützwagen Lorraine Schlepper (f) self-propelled anti-tank gun, and three Panther ausf A models.

2.33. Sturmgeschütz III ausf G assault guns of Panzerjäger-Abteilung 243 photographed here being recovered and repaired by US Army units. This battalion was attached to 243.Infanterie-Division, which had been stationed in the Contentin Peninsula when the invasion began. The division's Panzerjäger battalion, commanded by Oberleutnant Franz Stratmann, was made up of three companies with the first company being equipped with fourteen Marder III 7.5cm tank destroyers, the second company, referred to as Sturmgeschütz-Abteilung 1243, had ten Sturmgeschütz III assault guns, and the third company fielding a number of 2cm Flak guns—both self-propelled and towed.

CHAPTER THREE

TO THE BORDERS OF THE REICH

The Borders of the Reich

In the first few days of September 1944, the British and Canadians had captured the port cities of Antwerp and Dieppe and were closing on Le Havre and the fortress city of Boulogne. In the south, units of US 3rd Army reached the Meuse River on Tuesday, September 5th, and on the following day managed to advance to the Moselle, thrusting towards Nancy and the gap between 3.Panzergrenadier-Division at Pont-à-Mousson and a single regiment from 15.Panzergrenadier-Division situated almost 20 kilometers south of the city. Model's plan of withdrawing to defensive positions behind the Somme had been thrown into disarray and any German units fortunate enough to have escaped the Falaise Pocket and the crossing of the Seine now faced the prospect of a protracted withdrawal towards the Rhine and the relative safety of the prepared positions of the Westwall.

However, the Führer's Fireman, as Model liked to refer to himself, was not a man given to panic. The Feldmarschall had gained a reputation as a defensive specialist and had been able to avert seemingly inevitable disaster many times in the battles of annihilation on the Eastern front. Now he reported to Hitler that he proposed to hold the front in the west along a line running from Antwerp, following the Albert Canal to the Meuse and then the Siegfried Line as far as the Franco-Luxembourg border. Model reasoned, and Hitler agreed, that although the Allied armies had made huge gains in ground taken, their troops must be exhausted after the battles in Normandy and the subsequent advance and they were still forced to haul their supplies forward from north-western France, and would be for some time. A drawn-out and necessarily costly assault against prepared positions might undermine the Allies will to continue or at least prevent the fighting from moving onto German soil.[1]

The flaw in Model's plan was that the front would need to be held by at least twenty-five fresh infantry divisions with a mobile reserve of five or six Panzer or Panzergrenadier divisions waiting in the rear as mobile reserve. At this time, although recruits were being trained in Germany, the army did not possess a single fresh division on either front. Undeterred, Hitler promised Model that the next two hundred Panther tanks to leave the assembly lines would be earmarked for Heeresgruppe B. In addition, every Tiger tank, Jagdpanther tank destroyer, and 8.8cm

---

1 The Allied supply problems were indeed quite real and the British referred to this period as the 'Supply Famine.' Hitler's belief that the Anglo-American alliance would eventually fall apart was just one example of the wishful thinking that often characterized his conduct of the campaign in the West. It is interesting that both sides at various times underestimated the others will or capacity to fight on.

anti-aircraft and anti-tank gun available in Germany would be transferred immediately to the West. The manpower problem was solved to some extent by Reichsmarschall Hermann Göring, who announced, to the complete surprise of both Hitler and Model, that the Luftwaffe had raised and was at that moment training six Fallschirmjäger regiments and expected to raise two more from wounded personnel returning from convalescent leave. This represented a force of some twenty thousand men with a further ten thousand expected from surplus aircraft crews and ground staff. These men would form the nucleus of 1.Fallschirm-Armee, which was created on September 4, 1944 and placed under the command of Generaloberst Kurt Student, a veteran paratroop commander who had taken part in the airborne operations of 1940 and had led combat formations in Italy and Normandy. He was informed of his new role by a curt telephone call from Hitler's headquarters in East Prussia that evening. The forces promised to Model may have sounded impressive, but they reflected the wholly defensive posture of that the Germans had now adopted in the West. The powerful tanks and anti-tank guns would be of limited use in chasing a British or American breakthrough and the vehicles needed for highly mobile operations, such as the Panzer IV medium tanks and Sturmgeschütz III assault guns, were

allocate to the armies in the east where the situation was, if anything, worse.

As a further reinforcement the serviceable units of II.SS-Panzerkorps, made up of the Frundsberg and Hohenstaufen divisions, were sent to Model on September 5th. Commanded by Obergruppenführer Wilhelm Bittrich, the corps had been reduced to the strength of a reinforced brigade by the fighting in Normandy and the attempts to save the units trapped in the Falaise pocket. They were completely exhausted. Model stationed both divisions in what he considered safe areas around Eindhoven and Arnhem, a seemingly insignificant decision which was to have far reaching implications for the very near future.

Central to Model's plan was the continued occupation of Antwerp, or at least the denial of its port facilities to the Allies. He immediately ordered his only available unit, 719.Infanterie-Division under Generalmajor Karl Sievers, to move towards the front and assist in the defense of the city.

Sievers was an experienced soldier who had commanded 16.Lufwaffen-Feld-Division during the fighting in Normandy and realized that his slow moving infantry formation could not possibly arrive in time to intervene in the battle for the city. Largely on his own initiative, he positioned his division on the eastern outskirts of Antwerp along the Albert canal between Merksem

and Hasselt, a front of some sixty kilometers. Although stretched to their absolute limit, Sievers' men could at least deny the bridges across the canal to the enemy.[2]

Travelling between the canal crossings, Sievers personally organized retreating units and stragglers and incorporated them into his division. Fortuitously, the artillery and engineer battalions of 347.Infanterie-Division arrived in the area by train and, together with the first battalion of SS-Grenadier-Regiment Landstorm Nederland, made up of Dutch volunteers, Sievers was able to reinforce his front.[3]

On Sievers left, running south towards

2 Sievers was correct in his assumptions about Antwerp. On the day Model ordered him to move towards the front, British armored units had occupied the city. The port facilities would, however, remain in German hands for some time and were tenaciously defended by the remnants of 64.Infanterie-Division. Interestingly, the records of LXXXVIII.Armeekorps show that Panzerjäger-Abteilung 719 had ten 7.5cm PaK 40/1 Lorraine Schlepper self-propelled anti-tank guns on hand, although Sievers makes no mention of them in his detailed account of the battles along the Albert Canal.

3 The Dutch volunteers of the Waffen-SS were unusual in that they fought on their home soil, at one time against their countrymen. Almost all volunteer formations made up of western Europeans, and there were many, served exclusively in the east.

Maastricht, the line was held by the survivors of 85.Infanterie-Division, commanded by Generalleutnant Curt Chill, a veteran of the Russian front. The division had been severely depleted by the Normandy battles and the retreat across northern France and had been ordered to return to Germany. Realizing the gravity of the situation, Chill disregarded his orders, absorbed the survivors of 59.Infanterie-Division together with other stragglers, and moved his men towards the Albert Canal.[4]

On September 7, after heavy fighting, advance elements of the British Guards Armored Division forced a crossing of the Albert Canal at the junction of Sievers' and Chill's divisions, taking the town of Helchteren and advancing as far as the crossroads at Hechtel, some 15 kilometers from the

Dutch-Belgian frontier on the road to Eindhoven. Held by the battalion of Ersatz-und Ausbildungs-Regiment Hermann Göring from Chill's Kampgruppe, the garrison was quickly reinforced by two battalions of Fallschirmjäger under the command by Major Franz Grassmel, which had been positioned in the nearby village of Wijchmaal. Armed with nothing heavier than Panzerfaust anti-tank weapons, Major Grassmel's men held out against two full armored regiments, which were unable to dislodge the defenders but did manage to surround the town. Although several attempts were made to reinforce the Fallschirmjäger, including a determined assault conducted on September 8 by the Jagdpanthers of Major Erich Sattler's schwere Heeres-Panzerjäger-Abteilung 559, all met with failure.

On September 10, the British regiments attacking Hechtel succeeded in outflanking the German position, reaching the banks of the Meuse-Escaut Canal, almost 30 kilometers in the German rear. Within forty-eight hours, the Irish Guards had secured a crossing near the town of Neerpelt. The capture of Neerpelt presented the British with a direct route along Highway 69 to Eindhoven, Nijmegen, Arnhem, and the Rhine. Major Grassmel, realizing that his position at Hechtel had lost any strategic significance, withdrew the garrison and left behind over 200 wounded men who could not be evac-

uated. The town itself was almost completely destroyed.

Within twenty-four hours, the Germans had organized the first in a series of counterattacks against the bridgehead at Neerpelt. The initial attacks were made by Fallschirmjäger Regiment von Hoffmann and Fallschirmjäger Regiment von der Heydte, both elements of Kampfgruppe Chill, and reinforced by a mixed Waffen-SS unit led by Sturmbannführer Heinrich Heinke, who commanded the replacement battalion of 10.SS-Panzer-Division. Heinke's group was made up from infantrymen of his own battalion and SS-Panzergrenadier-Regiment 21 and supported by a number of Sturmgeschütz III assault guns, almost certainly from schwere Heeres-Panzerjäger-Abteilung 559.[5]

The British managed to hold out against the counterattack by continuously reinforcing the bridgehead. Student blamed Oberstleutnant von der Heydte, the overall commander of the counterattacking force, and replaced him on September 14 with Oberst Erich Walther, an experienced paratroop officer who had fought in Norway, Holland, Crete, Sicily, and at Monte Cassino. Kamp-

---

4   *What became known as Kampfgruppe Chill would remain in the frontline until November 1944, when it was eventually disbanded. In addition to the units of Chill's own division, the battle group controlled the first battalion of Fallschirmjäger- Regiment 2, four battalions of Fallschirmjäger- Regiment 6, elements of Ersatz-und Ausbildungs-Abteilung Hermann Göring and Bataillon Ohler, the staff and II.Abteilung of Artillerie-Regiment 185, three batteries of an artillery training unit of the Hermann Göring division, two batteries of a Waffen-SS replacement regiment, and a battery of 8.8cm guns of Flak-Abteilung 925.*

---

5   *The suggestion in many accounts that the assault guns were from SS-Panzerjäger-Abteilung 10 is certainly incorrect, as the battalion was stationed in the Aachen area until at least September 19, 1944.*

fgruppe Walther was reinforced with additional units including Luftwaffe-Bewährungs-Bataillon 6, a penal unit, which had been transferred from Italy in such haste that the men were still wearing their tropical uniforms. On September 15, in driving rain, Walther sent von der Heydte's men into the attack once more while a battalion of Hoffman's regiment and Heinke's SS grenadiers conducted a diversionary assault. Once again the Germans were unsuccessful, driven back by intense artillery fire and losing three of the Panzerjäger battalion's assault guns in the process. On the following day Student ordered Walther to continue with his attacks, but it was soon apparent that the British were far too strong. Walther convinced Student that it would be wiser to consolidate his defenses and the Germans limited themselves to minor probes.

Although very much on the defensive, the Germans had slowed the Allies progress in the north and in places pushed the British and Canadians back. Although Model's plan to hold a line on the Albert Canal had been thwarted, the rapid advances of August had degenerated into a series of bloody localized battles so fluid that the concept of a frontline was often meaningless in an area where the maze of water obstacles meant that the German always had another line to fall back on. No small part was played by the displays of leadership and initiative of commanders such as Generalleutnant Chill, whose actions alone would allow Student the time to deploy 1.Fallschirm-Armee. Other scratch units made up of Luftwaffe and Kriegsmarine personnel were also rushed to the front. The survivors of 15.Armee quickly followed, whom the British had allowed to escape through Antwerp.

Further to the south, Patton's US 3rd Army had been ordered to advance until his tanks ran out of fuel. By September 6, they were closing on Nancy on the Moselle River. During the evening of September 7, the tanks of Panzer-Brigade 106 Feldherrnhalle, commanded by Oberst Dr. Franz Bäke, attacked the exposed flank of US 90th Infantry Division around Thionville. Both Bäke and the commander of 1.Armee, drawing on their experiences of the Russian front, had assumed that the American infantry would panic and retreat in confusion when confronted with a night attack. The Germans were surprised, however, to find that it was not long before the defenders were mounting their own counterattacks. As the sun rose, the American infantrymen were joined by their tanks and Bäke's Panzers found themselves out of contact with their commander, scattered in a maze of small villages and hamlets, prey to American bazooka teams. By the end of the day, Panzer-Brigade 106 had lost half of its tanks and tank destroyers, over sixty armored halftracks, and almost three-quarters if its personnel killed, wounded or taken prisoner. This had been the first action in which these independent brigades, an initiative of Hitler's, had been sent into action. It had proven a dismal failure. In addition, Panzer-Brigade 106 had been slated to take part in a counterattack in the direction of Reims, planned by Hitler since August, which would now be seriously weakened. Within days, units of 3rd Army reached Trier and had occupied large sections of the Maginot Line, while 1st Army had reached the Siegfried Line east of Aachen. On September 15, after more than a week of fighting, US troops entered Nancy, which the Germans had evacuated on the previous day.

On September 18, in an attempt to reduce the bridgehead which 3rd Army had established on the eastern bank of the Moselle, General Hasso von Manteuffel's 5.Panzerarmee launched a counteroffensive towards Lunéville, approximately 15 kilometers south-east of Nancy. The attack began with Oberst Heinrich-Walter Bronsart von Schellendorf's Panzer-Brigade 111 attacking directly towards Lunéville. Although heavy fog kept the US fighter bombers away, the weather was so bad that the German attacks were completely uncoordinated from the start and soon devolved into a series of isolated skirmishes. The American units around Lunéville were soon reinforced by elements of two armored divisions and the German's were repulsed, leaving over twenty disabled tanks on the battlefield. Having failed to take Lunéville by direct assault on the first day, Manteuffel simply bypassed the town and moved towards the north.

On September 19, Oberst Freiherr von Seckendorf's Panzer-Brigade 113 attacked the salient which had formed around the town of Arracourt. Starting off at 8:00 am, the tanks of Panzer-Abteilung 2113 managed to overrun the eastern and southern flanks of the American position. They pushed as far as the headquarters, where they were driven back by a battalion of self-propelled howitzers firing over open sights. The heavy fog that had initially given the Germans the advantage of surprise now came to the aid of the defenders, with the Panzers advancing blindly to within visual contact of the enemy. At close range the heavier armor and superior range of the German tanks counted for little and the Americans were constantly being reinforced with fresh infantry and armored units. The defenders were further aided by the German commanders' persistence in pursuing the same avenues of attack.

On the following day, the remnants of Panzer-Brigade 111 and parts of Panzer-Regiment 15 of 11.Panzer-Division renewed the attack on the salient. Although they were able to threaten the American positions, they were beaten back by the end of the day by the tanks of US 4th Armored Division and, rather bizarrely, a bazooka-armed observation plane. On September 21, the skies at last began to clear and US fighter bombers ranged across the battlefield all day. Four days of intense and confused fighting had bought the Germans absolutely no advantage at great cost in both men and equipment. Hitler blamed Blaskowitz, the commander of Heeresgruppe G, and replaced him with General Hermann Balck, who immediately set about organizing an attack for the following day.

On September 22, Manteuffel sent his tanks against the northern edge of the Arracourt salient. They ran head-on into the screen of American light tanks and armored cars that shielded the main force of 4th Armored Division, which was dangerously close to driving a wedge between 5.Panzerarmee and General Otto von Knobelsdorff's 1.Armee. These units were no match for the tanks of Panzer-Brigade 111, but they held the Germans long enough for a force of tanks and tank destroyers to be rushed to the threatened area. As the morning fog lifted, the Panzers found themselves confronted by a wall of fire thrown at them by the collective force of tanks, artillery batteries, and the inevitable fighter bombers, which appeared as soon as the skies cleared. Panzer-Brigade 111 effectively ceased to exist as a fighting force, losing most of its tanks and personnel, including Oberst Bronsart von Schellendorff, who was killed as he led his brigade. Manteuffel felt that the American defense might break if any further pressure were applied and committed the remaining tanks of Panzer-Brigade 113. The brigade made repeated attacks throughout September 22 and the following day, when the brigade commander, Oberst von Seckendorff, was killed. Although 5.Panzerarmee had by now been reduced to just twenty-five serviceable tanks, Manteuffel continued to conduct offensive operations for three more days until the clearing weather brought the US fighter bombers out in large numbers and forced the Germans to abandon the offensive. Somewhat ironically, a determined attack made by the infantrymen of 559.Volksgrenadier-Division on September 24 almost overran the lead elements of 4th Armored Division near Château-Salins and the Grenadiers were only beaten back by sustained air attacks. What became known as the Battle of Arracourt was the largest armored engagement that US forces had taken part in up to that time and the performance of the American tank crews had surprised the German commanders. But while the battle was in progress, 3rd Army was informed that its fuel supplies would be restricted and the consequent pause in the American advance convinced the Germans that their offensive, though costly, had been ultimately successful.

Although the days between the capture of Nancy and the commencement of the fighting around Arracourt had been comparatively quiet along much of the front line in Belgium and Holland, by the evening of September 16, German units were reporting signs of continuous movement behind the enemy's lines that suggested a large assault was imminent. Throughout the following morning, the men of Kampfgruppe Walther watched in awe as wave after wave of Allied transport aircraft flew directly over their positions heading towards the north-east, only to return some hours later flying in the opposite direction. At exactly 2:00 pm, intense and accurate artillery fire began falling on the German positions, followed almost immediately by an aerial bombardment blasting the length of the Valkenswaard road. An hour later, tanks of the Irish Guards moved out of their bridgehead in the opening phase of Operation Garden, the ground offensive aimed at linking up with the Allied airborne forces dropped earlier that day between Eindhoven and Arnhem as part of Operation Market. The British expected that the airborne units would easily seize the Arnhem bridge over the Nederrijn, as the Rhine is known in Holland, while British armor would smash a path through Eindhoven, Nijmegen, and then on to Arnhem to relieve the paratroops with two to three days—that is by September 20 at the latest.

The British offensive ran into trouble from the very beginning, for although the initial bombardment had destroyed all nine anti-tank guns of a Panzerjäger company set up along the Valkenswaard road, a single infantry platoon armed with Panzerfaust anti-tank weapons accounted for nine tanks and a personnel carrier and was able to hold up the entire British column long enough to deny them Eindhoven and its bridge, which they had expected to take by late afternoon.[6]

When the Eindhoven Bridge was finally captured, a full forty-eight hours later, the British paratroopers in Arnhem had been completely surrounded. In a further setback, Eindhoven was attacked by the Luftwaffe during the night of September 19, while the town was packed with British tanks and supply vehicles.

The airborne phase of the operation had also met with much stiffer resistance than

---

6 This Panzerjäger company, attached to Fallschirmjäger Regiment von Hoffmann, was equipped with captured Russian 7.62cm anti-tank guns, which lacked any transport and having to be manhandled were all apparently in exposed positions. The company commander, Hauptmann Brockes, was mortally wounded. This sector of the front was held by the first battalion of Hoffmann's regiment, commanded by Major Helmut Kerrut, which was able to hold up the British tanks for the first day with only the weapons they carried.

was anticipated. It will be remembered that Model had moved the divisions of Obergruppenführer Bittrich's II.SS-Panzerkorps to the Arnhem area to rest and refit and these veterans of the Russian and Normandy fronts would now supply the core around which the German defense was built. Importantly, Bittrich's divisional commanders had taken it upon themselves to retain many of their armored vehicles, which should have been handed over to other units. On the western edge of the city, a Kampfgruppe commanded by Generalleutnant Hans von Tettau and composed of army, navy, and air force personnel was formed and thrown into combat within hours of the first landings. Kampfgruppe von Tettau could also call on the battle-hardened NCO candidates of the SS-Unterführerschule Arnheim and the tanks of Panzer-Kompanie 224. The latter were French vehicles captured in 1940 and, although obsolete, were more than a match for airborne infantry.

Most of the fighting at the Rhine Bridge was undertaken by the reconnaissance battalions of the Frundsberg and Hohenstaufen divisions from Bittrich's corps. They were supported by the first battalion of Panzergrenadier-Regiment 21 and the Tigers of schwere Panzer-Kompanie Hummel, an Alarmheit unit raised from Panzer-Ersatz-Abteilung 500. The other available units of the Hohenstaufen division, formed into three Kampfruppen, made up the bulk of the German force on the eastern side of Arnhem at Oosterbeek. They were later re-inforced by Sturmgeschütz-Brigade 280 and the Tiger tanks of 3.Kompanie, schwere Panzer-Abteilung 506. On the southern edge of the city, known as the Betuwe, the remainder of the Frundsberg division with Kampfgruppe Knaust were tasked with holding up the expected attempt to relieve the paratroopers in Arnhem. On September 19, they were perfectly positioned to intercept the landing of the Polish Parachute Brigade.

During the next week, while fighting raged in Arnhem and Oosterbeek, the units of Kampfgruppe Walther facing the armored advance along the Valkenswaard road managed to not only delay the British but to cut the highway at several points in their rear. Indeed, on September 23, the British commander had been forced to detach a task force from the Guards Armored Division and send it some 19 kilometers to the south to secure the road. On the following day the road was again cut, this time at Veghel, approximately 30 kilometers north of Eindhoven, by the tanks of Major Berndt-Joachim Freiherr von Maltzahn's Panzer-Brigade 107 which had arrived in the area from Aachen just days before. On the same day, the Allied command decided to abandon the operation's main objective, a crossing of the Rhine, and to establish a front at Nijmegen. Although the British managed to re-open the highway on the following day, they now found themselves defending a huge salient which Model lost little time in counterattacking.

On September 30, in an effort to widen what was now being called the Nijmegen Corridor, the Allies launched an attack towards the town of Overloon, which lies some 25 kilometers east of Eindhoven close to the western bank of the River Maas, this time with the US 7th Armored Division in the lead. The front line here was held by Fallschirmjäger-Regiment 21, a Luftwaffe Flak unit, and a Kampfgruppe under the command of Sturmbannführer Franz Roestel, which had been sent south after taking part in the defense of Arnhem and was primarily composed of SS-Panzerjäger-Abteilung 10 equipped with fifteen Jagdpanzer IV L/48 tank destroyers.

This battle, which was overshadowed at the time by the fighting taking place along the Moselle, was in fact one of the fiercest struggles of the campaign. The American tanks valiantly threw themselves at the German lines time and again but were stopped on each occasion by a combination of the extensive minefields and the skilful deployment of Panzer-Brigade 107 and Kampfgruppe Walther, both of which were used as a mobile reserve. Persisting with their attacks, the Americans reached Overloon on October 2, but were once again pushed back in savage fighting, which at one point descended into a hand-to-hand struggle. The Allies began to realize that, once again, they had underestimated their opposition. As if to drive home the lesson, the Germans managed to launch no less than seven counterattacks on Wednesday, October 4 alone. By the end of the week, 7th Armored Division was completely exhausted and was replaced by the British 11th Armored and 3rd Infantry divisions. The British formations took four days to prepare their assault on Overloon and, at around noon on October 12, advanced in two columns from the east and west, preceded by a massive artillery barrage. The British found themselves mired in the same swampy ground that had held up the Americans but managed to enter the town after two days of hard fighting. The last German defenders, barricaded in the church, refused the offer of surrender and fought on to the last man. The outlying village of Loobeek was taken on Monday, October 16 and Venray, further to the south, was taken on the following Thursday. The Battle of Overloon ended the general Allied advance in this area as the divisions would be needed for the operations to clear the Scheldt Estuary far to the north.

On October 1, while the fighting around Overloon was underway, the Germans launched a limited offensive to recapture the town of Elst, situated almost exactly halfway between Arnhem and Nijmegen.

The Panzergrenadiers of 9.Panzer-Division, supported by the Tiger tanks of schwere Panzer-Abteilung 506 and the survivors of Kampfgruppe Knaust, made the initial assault and met with some success. However, the units of 10.SS-Panzer-Division, which were to support the right wing of the attack, stalled at the very outset and at around noon the main thrust ran into a fresh British infantry division supported by tanks. During the night the tanks of 116.Panzer-Division, which were supposed to have taken part in the first assault, arrived and the following morning the attack was resumed. This time the British were prepared and the second battalion of Panzergrenadier-Regiment 11 was so badly battered in a firestorm of artillery fire and aerial bombing that it was withdrawn behind the Rhine. Although Generalleutnant Elverfeldt, the commander of 9.Panzer-Division, threw the assault guns of Panzerjäger-Abteilung 50 into the battle on October 3, they were unable to dislodge the British. On the following day, the British counterattacked with such force that Elverfeldt pulled his men back behind the Rhine. By October 7, his division was withdrawn to Germany and 116.Panzer-Division was sent to support the units fighting around Aachen.

The ancient city of Aachen had little military value and the Allies had hoped to capture it quickly and advance into the industrialized Ruhr Basin. However, as the burial place of Charlemagne, considered by Hitler to be the founder of the First Reich, the city's symbolic importance was tremendous. Additionally, the Germans were fighting on their own soil for the first time and any ideological considerations would be forgotten in defense of the Homeland. In addition, the city was part of the Westwall defensive network, the so-called Siegfried Line, and would not be such an easy nut to crack.

The fighting around Aachen had in fact begun in mid-September, when the city was defended by General Gerhard Graf von Schwerin's 116.Panzer-Division. While launching a counterattack against the US forces approaching the city from the southwest, Schwerin was secretly attempting to negotiate Aachen's surrender. A letter written by the general to the Allied commander instead found its way into the hands of Hitler and he was immediately replaced.[7]

---

7 *Schwerin had been previously removed from the command of his division during the Mortain offensive by Hausser after at least two instances of insubordination. He was charged with treason over the Aachen letter but suffered no more than a severe reprimand and was sent to a command in Italy after being promoted. Why a confirmed traitor, who was a general and a Prussian aristocrat into the bargain, should have been treated so leniently by Hitler remains a mystery. Almost certainly involved in the July Plot, Schwerin survived the war to die in 1980.*

The Allied assault on the city began on October 2. It was preceded by an aerial bombardment that had almost no effect on the network of concrete pill boxes, which would have to be taken and held one at a time. However, by the afternoon the main defensive line had been breached and the American units advancing from the north reached the towns of Übach-Palenberg and Rimburg, forming a line which straddled the defenses of the Westwall. That night the assault guns of Sturmgeschütz-Brigade 902 launched a counterattack but were beaten back by intense artillery fire. On the following day, the Americans were able to bring up their tanks and what German armor there was in the area could not hope to hold on in the face of such overwhelming numerical superiority, although the Tigers of schwere Panzer-Abteilung 506 did manage to retake the town of Alsdorf, just 6 kilometers from the center of Aachen. On October 8, a counterattack made by Oberstleutnant Friedrich-Heinrich Musculus' Panzer-Brigade 108, supported by an infantry regiment and almost forty armored vehicles scraped together from various sources, skirted Alsdorf and surprised the American armored force by suddenly appearing in their rear. On the same day the Americans launched an assault to the south of Aachen and by October 10 had captured the high ground outside the city, which came to be known as Crucifix Hill. Despite repeated German counterattacks, the Americans managed to hold the hill and also take the surrounding area. That evening the German commander, General Friedrich Köchling, received an ultimatum that unless the garrison surrendered immediately, the city would be bombed into submission. Köchling refused to capitulate and instead ordered his men to turn every cellar into a fortified pillbox. The following morning the American bombardment began and would not stop until October 21, when Aachen eventually fell. On October 11, in an attempt to relieve the pressure on Aachen, 3.Panzergrenadier-Division and 116.Panzer-Division, under the control of I.SS-Panzerkorps, began a series of counterattacks against the American units to the north and east of Aachen, which were attempting to link up and encircle the city. The heaviest fighting there took place on October 15 and 16 around the village of Würselen, where the Panzers were concealed in the houses to await the American advance units. However, by the evening of October 16 the Americans had infiltrated two infantry battalions through the German lines and the encirclement of Aachen was complete. Although the units of I.SS-Panzerkorps continued to attack from the east until October 19, and the garrison of Aachen fanatically fought to hold their positions, the American units literally blasted their way through the defenses using large caliber self-propelled guns.

On October 21, the last of the German garrison, barricaded behind the walls of the Hotel Quellenhof, surrendered.

While the Americans were occupied with the siege of Aachen and the Canadians were bogged down in the battles to clear the Scheldt Estuary, the fighting for the Nijmegen corridor in central Holland continued. On October 22, a combined British infantry and armored force advanced swiftly, capturing the outlying villages to the east and southeast of the town of 's-Hertogenbosch, an important road and rail junction and a stepping stone to the Moerdijk bridges over the River Maas. On the following day, a counterattack planned for the early morning to be made by the assault guns of Sturmgeschütz-Abteilung 1256 supported by infantry and artillery units was postponed at first due to a lack of fuel and then an enemy attack and did not begin until 4.30 pm. The attack immediately ran into trouble with two assault guns falling victim to their own artillery fire. As the grenadiers were riding on the vehicles in the open, infantry casualties were also high. Despite these losses, the Germans pressed on, advancing as far as Bruggen, where the attack was brought to a halt by intense artillery fire as night fell. This limited success was offset by a British advance at Hintham, on the eastern edge of 's-Hertogenbosch, which was co-incidentally the location of the German headquarters. A battalion of Grenadier-Regi-

ment 732, which had been ordered to restore the defensive line, was completely annihilated by the enemy's artillery fire and Hintham was abandoned during the night.

On October 24, the British attacked along the Nijmegen rail line, captured the command post of 712.Infanterie-Division, and pushed on to the iver Dieze, which runs through the center of 's-Hertogenbosch. By nightfall they had established a bridgehead along the Zuid-Willemsvaart on the river's south-western bank, where the assault guns of Sturmgeschütz-Abteilung 1256 succeeded in pushing the enemy back some way and taking a number of prisoners. To the south, the British were able to advance to the village of Vught, only 3 kilometers from the city center, but could go no further and Vught remained in the hands of 59.Infanterie-Division. The defenders were reinforced by a battalion of Artillerie-Regiment 256 with two batteries of heavy guns that evening and early the next day by a company of assault guns from schwere-Panzerjäger-Abteilung 559.

Early the next morning, the British assault was resumed. By the end of the day the Dommel canal had been reached, effectively bringing the center of the city under British control. During the night, the defenders experienced the heaviest artillery bombardment of the battle so far and all radio communications were lost; commanders were forced to rely on runners to carry their orders. On October 26, the British were able to secure the west side of the Dommel canal and the two pincers of the British attack were able to link up at the Vught bridge on the southern edge of 's-Hertogenbosch, all but ending the battle. The following day the Germans counterattacked with the meager forces at their disposal, including the assault guns of schwere-Panzerjäger-Abteilung 559, but could make no headway. During the evening the last defenders withdrew to the northern bank of the Maas across the bridge near Vlijmen, which they promptly destroyed.

In answer to the British attacks in the Nijmegen Corridor, Model directed 9.Panzer-Division to open an attack from Venlo, on the Maas River east of Eindhoven, towards Asten, which would then be exploited by 15.Panzergrendier-Division. On October 27 the attack began and went well enough, with the lead elements reaching the village of Meijel and the outskirts of Liessel, some 20 kilometers east of Eindhoven and just 5 kilometers short of their objective, despite the fact that Panzergrenadier-Regiment 11 could not be found and the Panther tanks of II.Abteilung, Panzer-Regiment 33 did not arrive until well into the afternoon. On the following morning, 15.Panzergrenadier-Division attacked to the north of 9.Panzer-Division and by the end of the day had advanced as far as the open fields to the east of Liessel.

Led by the division's reconnaissance battalion and elements of Panzergrenadier-Regiment 11, both under the command of Major Engelbert Bockhoff, 9.Panzer-Division reached the woods east of Asten but could go no further. The first of the Allied counterattacks was launched by US 7th Armored Division later that day. Although the American tanks were repulsed, it was clear that the Germans had lost the initiative and both division commanders suggested that the operation be called off. Model would not agree and another attack went forward on October 29, with 15.Panzergrenadier-Division capturing the town of Liessel. However, the resumption of the advance towards Asten by 9.Panzer-Division, the original objective of the assault, went badly and by noon Oberbefehlshaber West, overruling Model, called a halt to the operation. That evening Model asked that a final attempt be made the next day to capture Asten and Rundstedt relented. The attack went badly from the beginning, with an already-exhausted Panzergrenadier-Regiment 10 running head on into an American counterattack and suffering high losses. During the next day and into the night, the Germans went over to the defense and prepared for the counterattacks they knew would come, while 9.Panzer-Division was withdrawn from the front.

On October 29, the Polish Armored division took Breda, the last major town in southern Holland under German occupation, and as the winter approached the intensity of the fighting decreased. The weather became increasingly cold and wet through November and the fighting was restricted to a number of small engagements around the Venlo bridgehead, where the Allies resumed their attacks. In addition to the weather, the extensive flooding intentionally engineered by the retreating Wehrmacht also hampered operations. The fighting in Holland had been extremely costly for the Allies and in just over two months, with the exception of the clearing of the Scheldt Estuary, the British and Canadians had managed little more than an expansion of the corridor that had been taken as a result of the airborne assaults of September as part of Operation Market Garden. Although the Scheldt Estuary had been secured, the first ship would not enter the harbor facilities of Antwerp until November 28 and the port's use would be continually hampered by the stream of V2 rockets that fell on the city.

As winter approached, the Fortress of Metz finally capitulated to the Americans. The German defensive works were actually a collection of fortifications centered on Metz and Thionville made up of infantry strong points, concrete reinforced artillery positions, and interconnecting trenches. The trench works contained machine gun and rifle positions and were protected by an extensive barbed wire belt. An outer ring of the ten forts had been built by the French in the late 19th century and an inner ring had been completed by the German between 1899 and 1916. This inner ring contained the two most powerful forts, Feste Kaiserin and Feste Kronprinz, the latter known to the Americans as Fort Driant. Between these two forts lay a number of defensive works, which came to be known during the battle as the Seven Dwarves.

As early as mid-September units, of US 3rd Army had pushed aside the depleted 17.SS-Panzer-Division Götz von Berlichingen to advance towards the city, which was defended by General Otto von Knobelsdorff's 1.Armee. The bulk of the German defense was made up of infantry formations; however, Knobelsdorff could call on the remnants of the Götz von Berlichingen division and the tanks of 11.Panzer-Division. On September 27, two separate assaults were repelled by the Germans; however, in a separate operation, the Americans were able to establish a small bridgehead across the Moselle to the south of Metz. During October the attackers limited themselves to small scale assaults and offensive patrols and it was November 3 before a concerted attack was launched, which resulted in the capture of the outer defenses. On November 14, Generalleutnant Heinrich Kittel was appointed as the commander of the German

forces holding Metz and the system of forts while the mobile units of 1.Armee fell back to the Saar Heights, where Knobelsdorff hoped to slow the Allied advance long enough for his infantry formations to entrench themselves in front of the prepared positions of the Westwall. On the day Kittel took up his new command, the Americans managed to capture three of the Seven Dwarves. The attackers were making steady—if slow—progress and by November 17, most of the forts had been isolated and Metz itself was under attack. That evening the last civilians, who were mostly Nazi functionaries, were evacuated from the city and Kittel ordered the remaining bridges over the Moselle and Seille Rivers to be destroyed. On Saturday, November 18, US infantrymen entered the city from several different directions, struggling from street to street, and during the fighting on the following Tuesday, Generalleutnant Kittle was wounded and taken prisoner. Although the city of Metz was formally surrendered on the following day, a number of the outlying forts held out for weeks, mainly due to the Allied reluctance to expend the ammunition they would need for the advance to the Saar and the Siegfried Line.

On November 21, the day Generalleutnant Kittel was captured, units of US 10th Armored Division began the assault on the German positions between the Saar and Moselle Rivers at a point referred to as

the Siegfried Switch, more than 30 kilometers north of Metz. Despite the pounding the German defenders received from the preliminary artillery bombardment, the attackers were only able to advance to within 2 kilometers of the town of Orscholz, their major objective, at the center of the defensive belt. On either side of the main thrust, the Allied tanks made no progress all and the attempts to bridge the extensive ditches and destroy the Dragon's Teeth anti-tank obstacles were thwarted by intense machine gun fire. On the following day, the German defenses were further bolstered by the arrival of the tanks of Generalleutnant Heinz von Randow's 21.Panzer-Division.

The Americans now held back their armor, trusting their infantry to create a gap in the defenses which their tanks could exploit. In three days of close fighting, the attackers managed to occupy the fortified villages of Oberleuken and Butzdorf; however, they had been forced to bypass the town of Tettingen, which remained in German hands. During the night a force of infantry and tanks from 21.Panzer-Division attacked Butzdorf and, although the American defenders were relieved the next morning by an armored column, the Germans had infiltrated reinforcements into Tettingen and the Americans fell back behind a heavy artillery barrage.

Further to the south, on November 24, the tanks and armored infantry of US 3rd

Army's XII Corps ran into the positions occupied by 361.Volksgrenadier Division south of Sarre-Union. The Americans had little trouble in overrunning the German defenders and continued to advance towards the village of Barendorf, where that afternoon they came into contact with the Grenadiers of the Panzer-Lehr-Division. Unknown to the Americans, the Panzer-Lehr commander, Generalleutnant Bayerlein, had been ordered to prepare an attack towards the south against US XV Corps. Bayerlein was now forced to split his division to address the threat at Barendorf. In the early hours of November 25, Bayerlein's tanks attacked the American positions and although the Panzers were shielded by a heavy fog, the Germans were almost immediately forced to take up defensive positions. In the four days of skirmishing that followed, Panzer-Lehr-Division was so depleted that General Balck, the Heeresgruppe G commander, withdrew Bayerlein's men from the front line.

To the north of Barendorf, Allied units had crossed into German territory and were advancing towards the Saar Heights. Balck was determined to defend the strategically important high ground or at least force the Americans pay a high price for its possession. The struggle for the Saar Heights lasted for two days, with the fiercest fighting taking place on Wednesday, November 29, when a Kampfgruppe made up of units from 21.Panzer-Division with the remnant of Panzer-Lehr-Division launched no less than ten counterattacks against the Americans in an effort to keep them from clearing the heights and reaching the Saar River. On the following day, completely exhausted, the Germans finally gave up and withdrew to Saarlautern. To the north, other American units had encountered far less resistance, and as the Panzers pulled back from the Heights, closed up to the banks of the Saar. On the following day, despite the efforts of 25.Panzergrenadier Division, the Americans entered Saar-Union. On December 3, an attack by elements of 11.Panzer-Division was unable to force the American units from the town and Balck withdrew the divisions on his left to new positions in the Maginot Line bunkers at Rohrbach-les-Bitche. On the same day, US Army units were able to penetrate the Westwall defenses near Saarlautern and, although the fighting to secure the town would continue for some time, within forty-eight hours 3rd Army was advancing into Germany on a 50 kilometer front. By December 10, Hagenau and Saargemünd had fallen, as had the positions at Rohrbach-les-Bitche where Balck had hoped to hold the Americans. On December 13, the last of the fortifications around Metz, the Feste Kaiserin, finally surrendered. On the same day, the bloody battles in the Hürtgenwald, where a handful of German units including 3.Panzergrenadier-Division and 116. Panzer-Division had held up the Allied advance since late September, were drawing to a close. It seemed that the Germans were all but finished and the end of the war was in sight. But in less than thirty-six hours the Germans would launch a major offensive, employing units that were thought to have been destroyed (or at least decimated) in an area the Allied command considered almost impassable. The last great attack in the west would ensure, if nothing else, that the war would continue well into 1945.

SCHWERE PANZERJÄGER-ABTEILUNG 559, SEPTEMBER 1944

Typically, each German division had an organic Panzerjäger-Abteilung, or anti-tank battalion, in addition to the anti-tank platoons attached to the headquarters of the infantry and Panzergrenadier regiments. The success of the independent, fully-armored Panzerjäger units that were deployed during the French campaign of 1940 led to the creation of more heavily armed formations. By the end of the war, the army's schwere Panzerjäger-Abteilungen, or heavy anti-tank battalions, were equipped with the Nashorn self-propelled 8.8cm gun, the Panzerjäger V Jagdpanther, and the Panzerjäger Tiger ausf B, better known as the Jagdtiger. In addition, a number of independent battalions operated the 8.8cm PaK 43, a towed version of the gun fitted to the Tiger II and Nashorn. Most of the Jagdpanther units served in the east, although five battalions fought on the Western Front, and small numbers of these powerful anti-tank weapons were issued to Panzer units very late in the war. The formation shown here is schwere Panzerjäger-Abteilung 559 and is depicted at the time of the battles for Arnhem in central Holland in September 1944.

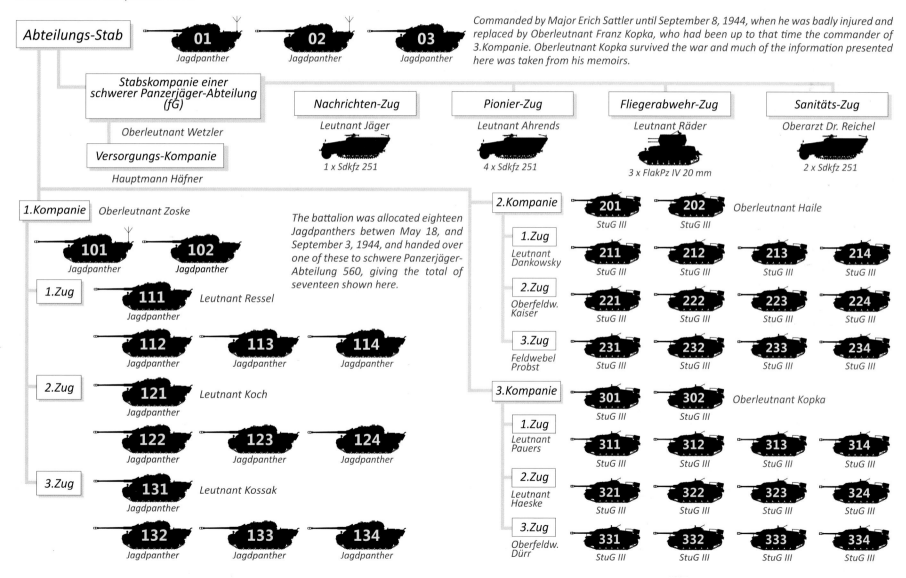

Commanded by Major Erich Sattler until September 8, 1944, when he was badly injured and replaced by Oberleutnant Franz Kopka, who had been up to that time the commander of 3.Kompanie. Oberleutnant Kopka survived the war and much of the information presented here was taken from his memoirs.

The battalion was allocated eighteen Jagdpanthers betwen May 18, and September 3, 1944, and handed over one of these to schwere Panzerjäger-Abteilung 560, giving the total of seventeen shown here.

SCHWERE PANZER-ABTEILUNG (TIGER-FUNKLENK) 301, OCTOBER 1944

From the earliest days of the war, the German Army recognized the need for a specialist vehicle that would be capable of clearing minefields and eliminating enemy pillboxes and bunkers. The first models, developed by the firm of Borgward, were fully tracked, radio-controlled vehicles that could be used to tow mine-detonating rollers. By May 1942, the rollers had been superseded by a completely new vehicle capable of carrying a 500kg demolition charge under fire and placing it near the target or within a minefield where the resulting explosion would detonate the mines. This vehicle was the schwerer Ladungsträger Borgward B IV Sdkfz 301 which, with slight variation, would remain in service until the end of the war, although production had ceased by late 1944. These vehicles were used with some success in late 1942 and at Kursk in June 1943, where, for the first time, they were controlled from specially adapted Sturmgeschütz III assault guns. Formed in late 1942, Panzer-Abteilung 301 had served in Russia and Italy before being transferred to Truppenübungsplatz Grafenwöhr in Germany in mid-1944 to begin training on Tiger I tanks specially adapted to control the Borgward demolition vehicles. The first Tigers were received on September 1, and the following day the battalion was renamed schwere Panzer-Abteilung (Tiger-Funklenk) 301. Further deliveries followed, including ten vehicles transferred from schwere SS-Panzer-Abteilung 503 on October 21, 1944. The battalion never received its full allocation of tanks, however, as can be seen from the diagram below. It seems that one tank was left at Grafenwöhr in November when the battalion moved to the front. In addition, the battalion's fourth company was permanently detached and was used in February 1945 to form Panzer-Abteilung (Funklenk) 303. The battalion fought on the Western front until April 16, 1945, when the last three serviceable tanks were destroyed by their crews.

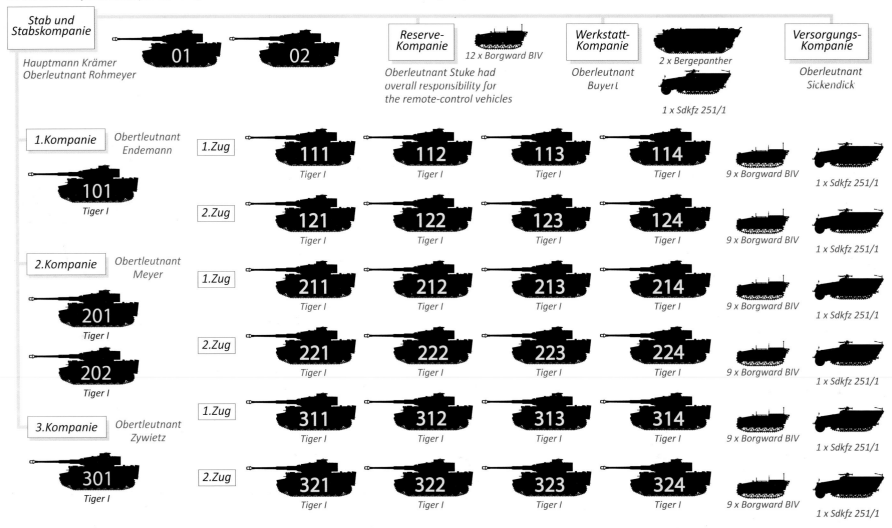

PANZERS IN THE WEST, SEPTEMBER-OCTOBER 1944

		SEPTEMBER													OCTOBER													
		Stug III	Stug IV	StuH 42	JagdPz IV	Jagdpanther	Wirbelwind	Möbelwagen	Tiger II	Tiger I	Panther	Pz IV/70(V)	Pz IV/70(A)	PzKfpw IV	Stug III	Stug IV	StuH 42	JagdPz IV	Jagdpanther	Wirbelwind	Möbelwagen	Tiger II	Tiger I	Panther	Pz IV/70(V)	Pz IV/70(A)	PzKfpw IV	
2.Panzer-Division	Panzer-Regiment 3																							8		10		
	Panzerjäger-Abteilung 38														11													
9.Panzer-Division	Panzer-Regiment 33										12																	
11.Panzer-Division	Panzer-Regiment 15				4						30		16															
21.Panzer-Division	Panzer-Regiment 22										40		10							3	3							
	Panzerjäger-Abteilung 200																	3										
116.Panzer-Division	Panzer-Regiment 16	10																										
	Panzerjäger-Abteilung 228							10																				
Panzer-Lehr-Division	II/Panzer-Lehr-Regiment 130																										28	
	I/Panzer-Regiment 6																				18							
3.Panzergrenadier-Division	Panzer-Abteilung 103																										2	
15.Panzergrenadier-Division	Panzer-Abteilung 115											33							2								8	1 PzKpfw III tank in October
	Panzerjäger-Abteilung 33			29																								
25.Panzergrenadier-Division	Panzer-Abteilung 25														31													
1.SS-Panzer-Division	SS-Panzer-Regiment 1										15									4	4			22		26		
	SS-Sturmgeschütz-Abteilung 1	1													21													
2.SS-Panzer-Division	SS-Panzer-Regiment 2																	3										
9. SS-Panzer-Division	SS-Panzer-Regiment 9										20															3		
10.SS-Panzer-Division	SS-Panzer-Regiment 10																				18							
12.SS-Panzer-Division	SS-Panzer-Regiment 12				4						12													20		27		
17.SS-Panzergrenadier-Division	SS-Panzerjäger-Abteilung 17			10																								
Panzer-Brigade 105					4						36*	11*																* Panzer-Abteilung 2105
Panzer-Brigade 106					4						36*	11*																* Panzer-Abteilung 2106
Panzer-Brigade 107					4						36*	11*																* Panzer-Abteilung 2107
Panzer-Brigade 108					4						36*	11*																* Panzer-Abteilung 2108
Panzer-Brigade 111		10			4	4					45*		45															* I/Panzer-Regiment 16
Panzer-Brigade 112		10			4	4					45*		45															* I/Panzer-Regiment 29
Panzer-Brigade 113		10			4	4					45*		45															* I/Panzer-Lehr-Regiment 130
Sturmgeschütz-Brigade 244		19													19		12											
Sturmgeschütz-Brigade 280		22		18											17													
Sturmgeschütz-Brigade 394		22															5											
Sturmgeschütz-Brigade 667				12											19													
Sturmgeschütz-Brigade 902		17															12											
Fallschirm-Sturmgeschütz-Brigade 12															19		12											
Schwere Panzerjäger-Abteilung 512																		28										
Schwere Panzerjäger-Abteilung 519																		17	4									
Schwere Panzerjäger-Abteilung 559					30	4												28										
Schwere Panzerjäger-Abteilung 560																			4									
Schwere Panzer-Abteilung 506					4				45																			
Panzer-Kompanie Hummel										14																		
Panzer-Kompanie Paderborn																								3		2		
Panzer-Kompanie 319 (Fkl)		10*																										* With 36 Borgward BIV
O.B. West with 34 units				34																								

Not included here are the armored vehicles allocated to the Panzerjäger battalions of Infanterie, Volksgrenadier of Lufwaffe Feld-Divisionen. At this time, the Jagdpanzer 38(t) Hetzer tank destroyer was making its appearance, with a total of seventy-two reported during September and October. All were with infantry formations and the independent Heeres-Panzerjäger-Abteilung 741. Also omitted are fully-tracked recovery vehicles such as the Bergepanther, Bergepanzer III, and Bergehetzer which were generally, but not always, allocated to Panther battalions, assault gun units, and Panzerjäger units respectively. Panzer-Kompanie Hummel was originally a temporary grouping but became the fourth company of schwere Panzer-Abteilung 506 on December 8, 1944, just before the commencement of the Ardennes Offensive.

1. PzKpfw V Panther ausf G. 8.Kompanie, Panzer-Regiment 33. *From August 19, 1944, vehicles were painted in standard camouflage patterns before leaving the assembly plants and the schemes adopted can often identify a particular manufacturer. That shown here was common to many Panthers produced by*

Maschinenfabrik Niedersachsen-Hannover (MNH) and the application of the Balkenkreuz on the turret side, or its complete absence, is often an identifying feature of these tanks. The small number 80 on the turret, in black with a white outline, probably identifies the 8.Kompanie commander. At this time, the regiment was attached to 9.Panzer-Division and the tank depict- was photographed at Humain, south-east of Belgium, in December 1944.

3. PzKpfw V Panther ausf G. 2.Kompanie, SS-Panzer-Regiment 1. *Commanded by Untersturmführer Hubert Kaufmann, this tank, as part of Kampfgruppe Peiper, was knocked out in the attack on Stoumont in December 1944. All the regiment's Panthers were painted in factory-applied schemes, the example shown here being indicative of vehicles manufactured by Maschinenfabrik Augsburg-Nürnberg (MAN) and Daimler-Benz. This is the most commonly seen pattern. Another scheme, the so-called disc pattern of MAN, is shown in our photograph (2) of a Panther ausf G of 1.Kompanie, SS-Panzer-Regiment 1.*

1. PzKpfw V Panther ausf G. 3.Kompanie, SS-Panzer-Regiment 12. *This tank was disabled in the attack on Krinkelt-Rocherath in December 1944, together with the battalion adjutant's vehicle. The camouflage scheme suggests that this vehicle was assembled by either MAN or Daimler-Benz. It is fitted with both the raised fan housing on the rear deck and the Flammvernichter exhaust mufflers, the latter shown in our photograph (2).*

2. PzKpfw V Panther ausf G. 2.Kompanie, SS-Panzer-Regiment 1. *This tank was commanded by Unterscharführer Krüger and was disabled at Stoumont, fifteen kilometers west of Malmedy. This vehicle, although damaged, was photographed from several angles, allowing for an accurate representation of the camouflage pattern. The small dots, painted onto the bands of color in a contrasting shade, are typical of the factory-applied scheme employed by Daimler-Benz and is today commonly referred to as Ambush camouflage.*

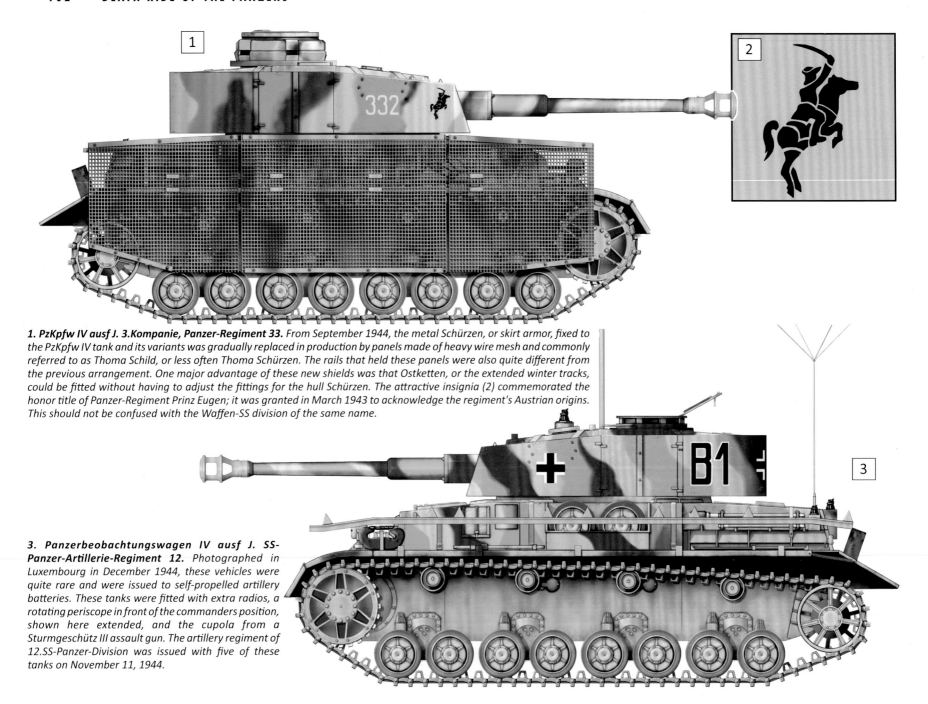

1. PzKpfw IV ausf J. 3.Kompanie, Panzer-Regiment 33. *From September 1944, the metal Schürzen, or skirt armor, fixed to the PzKpfw IV tank and its variants was gradually replaced in production by panels made of heavy wire mesh and commonly referred to as Thoma Schild, or less often Thoma Schürzen. The rails that held these panels were also quite different from the previous arrangement. One major advantage of these new shields was that Ostketten, or the extended winter tracks, could be fitted without having to adjust the fittings for the hull Schürzen. The attractive insignia (2) commemorated the honor title of Panzer-Regiment Prinz Eugen; it was granted in March 1943 to acknowledge the regiment's Austrian origins. This should not be confused with the Waffen-SS division of the same name.*

3. Panzerbeobachtungswagen IV ausf J. SS-Panzer-Artillerie-Regiment 12. *Photographed in Luxembourg in December 1944, these vehicles were quite rare and were issued to self-propelled artillery batteries. These tanks were fitted with extra radios, a rotating periscope in front of the commanders position, shown here extended, and the cupola from a Sturmgeschütz III assault gun. The artillery regiment of 12.SS-Panzer-Division was issued with five of these tanks on November 11, 1944.*

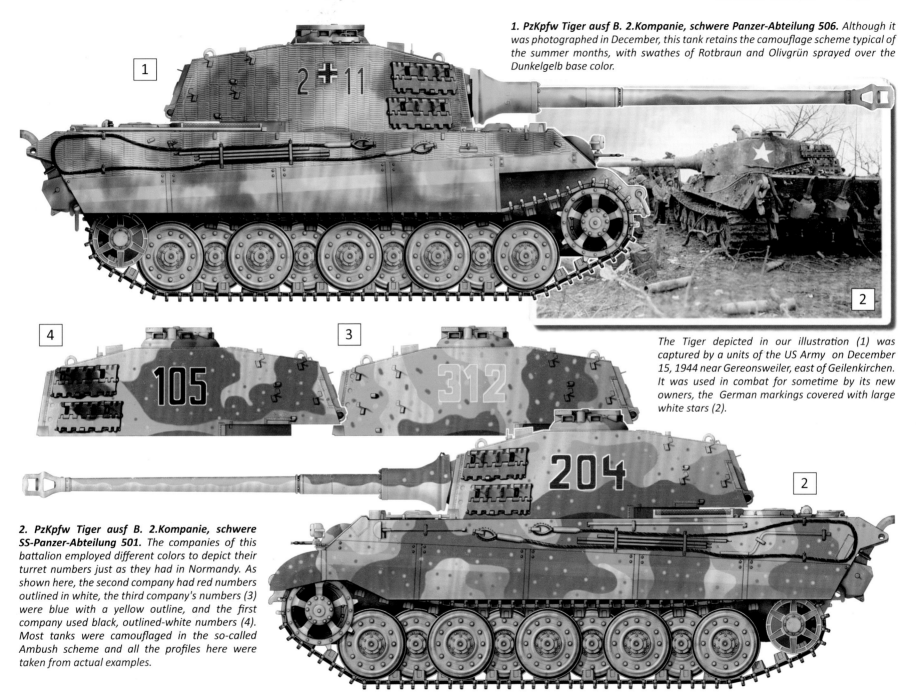

1. PzKpfw Tiger ausf B. 2.Kompanie, schwere Panzer-Abteilung 506. *Although it was photographed in December, this tank retains the camouflage scheme typical of the summer months, with swathes of Rotbraun and Olivgrün sprayed over the Dunkelgelb base color.*

The Tiger depicted in our illustration (1) was captured by a units of the US Army on December 15, 1944 near Gereonsweiler, east of Geilenkirchen. It was used in combat for sometime by its new owners, the German markings covered with large white stars (2).

2. PzKpfw Tiger ausf B. 2.Kompanie, schwere SS-Panzer-Abteilung 501. *The companies of this battalion employed different colors to depict their turret numbers just as they had in Normandy. As shown here, the second company had red numbers outlined in white, the third company's numbers (3) were blue with a yellow outline, and the first company used black, outlined-white numbers (4). Most tanks were camouflaged in the so-called Ambush scheme and all the profiles here were taken from actual examples.*

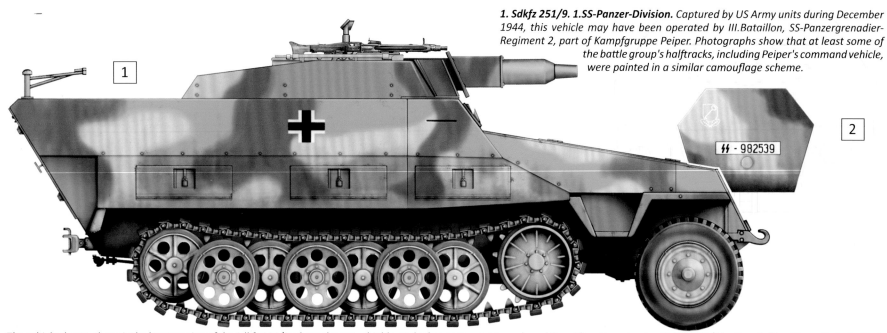

1. Sdkfz 251/9. 1.SS-Panzer-Division. Captured by US Army units during December 1944, this vehicle may have been operated by III.Bataillon, SS-Panzergrenadier-Regiment 2, part of Kampfgruppe Peiper. Photographs show that at least some of the battle group's halftracks, including Peiper's command vehicle, were painted in a similar camouflage scheme.

The vehicle shown above is the later version of the Sdkfz 251/9 where the gun, shields, and other parts were issued as a kit and fixed to a standard Sdkfz 251/1 halftrack. The silhouette is decidedly higher that that of the earlier, factory-produced version shown below. The placement of the unit insignia (2) is based on photographs of other halftracks of the division.

3. Sdkfz 251/9. 2.Panzer-Division. Although this halftrack was photographed in December 1944, the division's reconnaissance battalion, Panzer-Aufklärungs-Abteilung 2, also had a number of these vehicles on hand during the Normandy battles. They were finished in almost identical markings and camouflage schemes and this may be a survivor of those early battles. The markings on the front of the hull (4) show the division's unit Insignia and the tactical symbol identifying an armored infantry company.

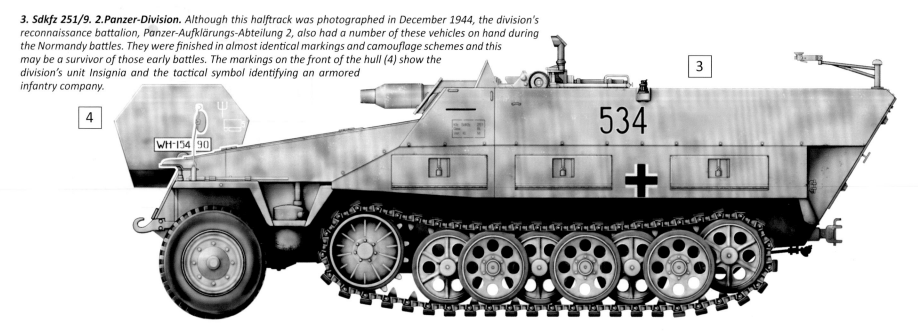

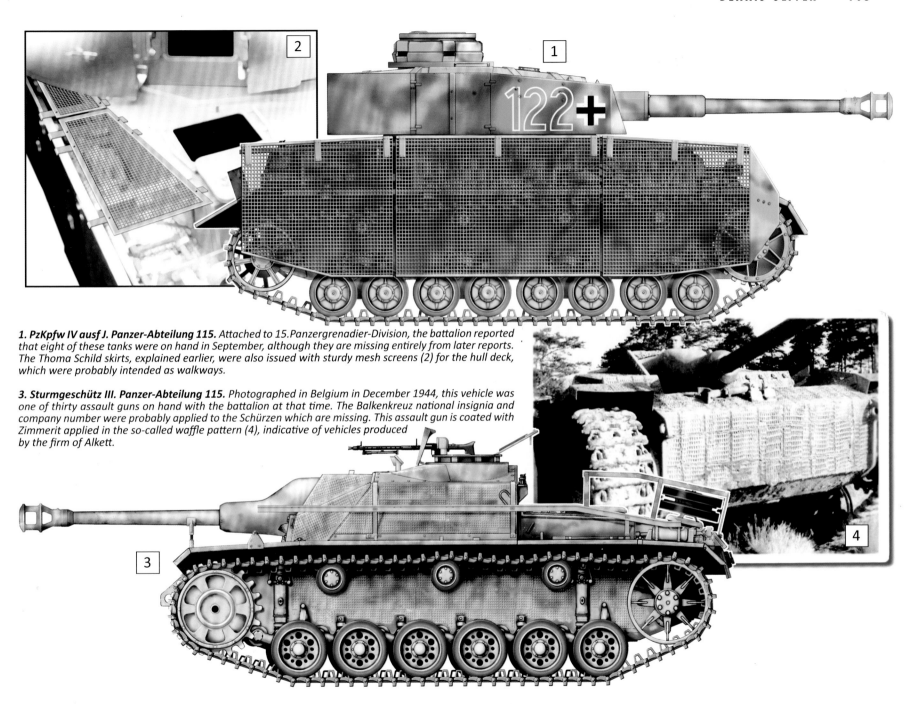

1. PzKpfw IV ausf J. Panzer-Abteilung 115. *Attached to 15.Panzergrenadier-Division, the battalion reported that eight of these tanks were on hand in September, although they are missing entirely from later reports. The Thoma Schild skirts, explained earlier, were also issued with sturdy mesh screens (2) for the hull deck, which were probably intended as walkways.*

3. Sturmgeschütz III. Panzer-Abteilung 115. *Photographed in Belgium in December 1944, this vehicle was one of thirty assault guns on hand with the battalion at that time. The Balkenkreuz national insignia and company number were probably applied to the Schürzen which are missing. This assault gun is coated with Zimmerit applied in the so-called waffle pattern (4), indicative of vehicles produced by the firm of Alkett.*

1. Sturmgeschütz III. Heeres-Sturmartillerie-Brigade 667. *This assault gun carries the battalion's colorful unit insignia, unusual at this stage of the war, at both the hull front (2) and rear (3). From late 1944, a thick layer of concrete was applied to the superstructure front (4) as extra protection, although it is rare to see an unpainted example as this appears to be. The Balkenkreuz and Fahrgestellnummer, or chassis number, were applied (5) on the hull front. The elaborate camouflage scheme was almost certainly applied at the factory.*

6. Sdkfz 234/2. Puma. Aufklärungs-Abteilung 2. *During the Ardennes Offensive, the battalion had ten of these vehicles on hand as part of Kampfgruppe von Böhm, the lead element of 2.Panzer-Division. Note the troop number painted in white on the mudguard between the first and second wheels. The division's unit insignia and the tactical sign identifying an armored car company can be seen behind the exhaust. This may be one of the vehicles that Hauptmann von Böhm's battle group were forced to abandon near Foy-Notre-Dame after the fighting on Christmas Day 1944.*

1. Jagdpanzer 38(t) Hetzer. Panzerjäger-Kompanie 1167. Attached to the Panzerjäger-Abteilung of 167, Volksgrenadier-Division, this company had fourteen of these vehicles on hand in December and supported 1.SS-Panzer-Division in the attack on Bastogne. The camouflage scheme is typical of vehicles manufactured by the Böhmisch-Mährische Maschinenfabrik at Prague.

As a means of compensating for the greatly reduced manpower of the infantry divisions raised or reorganized from late 1943, it was planned that each would contain a Panzerjäger-Abteilung made up of a company of towed anti-tank guns, a company of assault guns, and a light anti-aircraft gun company. The assault gun company was to contain ten vehicles, either Sturmgeschütz III or IV assault guns or Hetzer tank destroyers, and was generally referred to (somewhat confusingly) as a Sturmgeschütz-Abteilung. Usually, but not always, the assault gun company was numbered separately from its parent battalion, the number arrived at by adding 1000 to the division's number. For example, the assault gun company of Panzerjäger-Abteilung 31 was referred to as Sturmgeschütz-Abteilung 1031. From late November or early December 1944, the assault gun companies of infantry Panzerjäger battalions were referred to as Sturmgeschütz-Kompanien, although Panzerjäger-Sturmgeschütz-Kompanien is sometimes encountered. It was intended that all infantry divisions would eventually contain a Sturmgeschütz company, but the enormous numbers of vehicles needed to fully implement this change were never available and many units did not receive their authorized allocation.

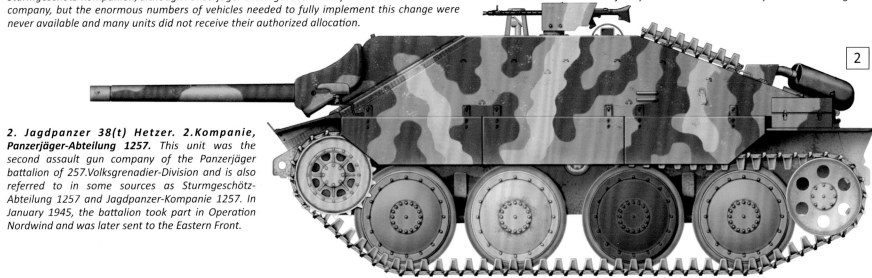

2. Jagdpanzer 38(t) Hetzer. 2.Kompanie, Panzerjäger-Abteilung 1257. This unit was the second assault gun company of the Panzerjäger battalion of 257.Volksgrenadier-Division and is also referred to in some sources as Sturmgeschütz-Abteilung 1257 and Jagdpanzer-Kompanie 1257. In January 1945, the battalion took part in Operation Nordwind and was later sent to the Eastern Front.

1. Beobachtungspanzerwagen IV ausf J. SS-Panzer-Artillerie-Regiment 1. *This vehicle was part of Kampfgruppe Peiper and may have been attached to the artillery regiment's II.Abteilung. The rail to which the steel-mesh Schürzen or Thoma Schild was attached can be more clearly seen in the photograph (2) and is of a much simpler construction than the earlier type. Just ninety-six of these specialist artillery observation tanks were issued between September 1944 and March 1945, when production ceased, and most were conversions based on older models.*

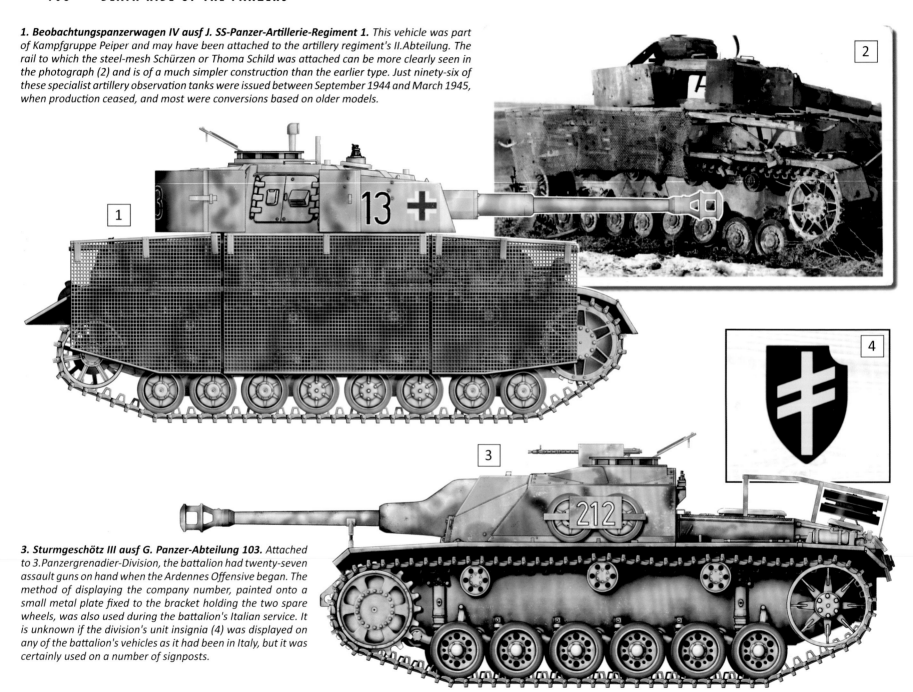

3. Sturmgeschötz III ausf G. Panzer-Abteilung 103. *Attached to 3.Panzergrenadier-Division, the battalion had twenty-seven assault guns on hand when the Ardennes Offensive began. The method of displaying the company number, painted onto a small metal plate fixed to the bracket holding the two spare wheels, was also used during the battalion's Italian service. It is unknown if the division's unit insignia (4) was displayed on any of the battalion's vehicles as it had been in Italy, but it was certainly used on a number of signposts.*

1. PzKpfw Tiger ausf E. Panzer-Kompanie Hummel. *When this company was detached from schwere Panzer-Abteilung 506 in February 1945, the tanks reverted to the practice of using numbers beginning with 1, although there is some debate about which colors were used. During the spring of 1945, the company was temporarily attached to Panzer-Brigade 106. It would seem that this unit retained its original title, although Hauptmann Hummel was killed in November 1944, in the fighting near Linden, and replaced by Leutnant Flör.*

2. PzKpfw Tiger ausf E. Schwere Panzer-Abteilung 301 (Funklenk). *Most tanks of this battalion had black company numbers painted onto the turret side toward the front. The lack of a number here may indicate that this is one of the tanks handed over from schwere SS-Panzer-Abteilung 103 in October 1944. Note the bracket welded to the turret stowage box, which was an identifying feature of this battalion's tanks and is also visible in our photograph (3).*

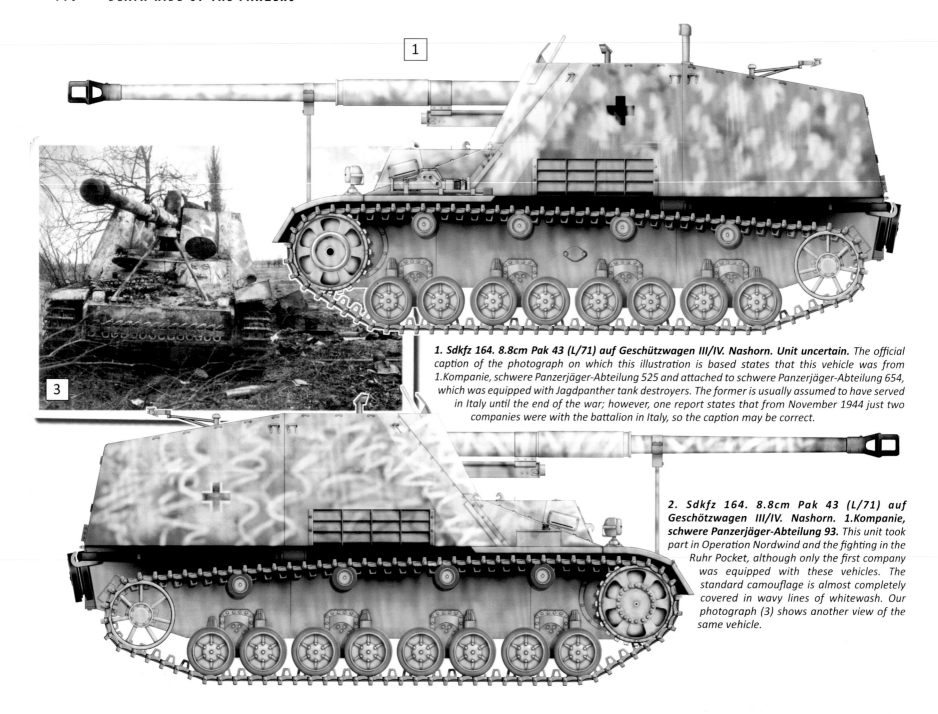

1. Sdkfz 164. 8.8cm Pak 43 (L/71) auf Geschützwagen III/IV. Nashorn. Unit uncertain. *The official caption of the photograph on which this illustration is based states that this vehicle was from 1.Kompanie, schwere Panzerjäger-Abteilung 525 and attached to schwere Panzerjäger-Abteilung 654, which was equipped with Jagdpanther tank destroyers. The former is usually assumed to have served in Italy until the end of the war; however, one report states that from November 1944 just two companies were with the battalion in Italy, so the caption may be correct.*

2. Sdkfz 164. 8.8cm Pak 43 (L/71) auf Geschötzwagen III/IV. Nashorn. 1.Kompanie, schwere Panzerjäger-Abteilung 93. *This unit took part in Operation Nordwind and the fighting in the Ruhr Pocket, although only the first company was equipped with these vehicles. The standard camouflage is almost completely covered in wavy lines of whitewash. Our photograph (3) shows another view of the same vehicle.*

1. PzKpfw V Panther ausf G. Führer-Grenadier-Brigade. *The first, second, and third companies of Panzer-Regiment Führer-Grenadier-Brigade were equipped with Panther tanks. It seems that the tanks had the company numbers painted on the turret sides, although any number would be obscured here by the lengths of spare track. The photograph (2) shows the same vehicle from the rear.*

2. PzKpfw V Panther ausf G. Unit uncertain. *Photographed in the Haguenau Forest near Strasbourg in early January 1945, this tank may be from either Panzer-Abteilung 5 of 25.Panzergrenadier-Division or Panzer-Regiment 22 of 21.Panzer-Division. A series of images was made at the time and all the tanks featured a variation of this unusual dazzle-style camouflage scheme. Some were completed in the style shown here and others with very wide diagonal bands.*

3.01. Knocked out near Périers, 25 kilometers west of Saint-Lo, in July 1944 during the early stages of Operation Cobra, this Sturmgeschütz IV assault gun is from 17.SS-Panzergrenadier-Division Götz von Berlichingen. The division's Panzer-Abteilung 17 was equipped with forty-two of these assault guns when it was committed to the fighting in Normandy, the last shipment arriving just a few weeks previously. Accounts suggesting that these vehicles were allocated to the division's Panzerjäger-Abteilung are incorrect, as is the claim that a number of Sturmgeschütz III were also on hand. Examples of the latter were received by the battalion but not before late August 1944, when most of the division had either been destroyed or withdrawn from front.

3.02. Photographed in Belgium, this Sturmgeschütz III ausf G assault gun has the bolted-on supplementary armor referred to as Zusatzpanzer. Officially dropped from production in May 1943, these plates were in fact fitted to some vehicles until the following November when they were replaced by a single 80mm thick plate. Note that this assault gun also has an extra piece of armor plate welded to the lower hull front. The left hand side of the superstructure is covered with a thick coat of concrete above the driver's position and extending back to the commander's cupola, giving it a very rounded appearance when compared to the right.

3.03. Photographed outside Hyères, near Toulon on the French Mediterranean coast in late September 1944, this well camouflaged concrete emplacement was used as a plotting and range finding station and its commanding view of the surrounding area is obvious.

3.04. Photographed near Xertigny, south of Épinal, on September 21, 1944 this Flakpanzer IV Möbelwagen was disabled by its crew. Armed with the 3.7cm FlaK 43 L/89 gun just 240 of these vehicles were built and most served with the anti-aircraft platoons of the Panzer divisions and independent Panzer brigades on the Western Front.

3.06. This Flakpanzer IV Wirbelwind was disabled in the fighting around Metz in late 1944 and may have been allocated to Panzer-Regiment 15 of 11.Panzer-Division or the Panzer battalion of 17.SS-Panzergrenadier-Division, both of which fought in this area at the time and had a number of these vehicles on hand.

3.06a. Another view of the Flakpanzer IV Wirbelwind shown in the previous photograph. The Zimmerit paste applied to the upper surfaces of the hull is clearly visible here on the opened radio operator's hatch. Commonly referred to as Keksdose, or biscuit tin, by the troops very few of these vehicles were produced, perhaps less than 100 although the exact number is unknown. Almost all were issued to units fighting on the Western front between August 1944 and February 1945 when they disappear from official strength returns.

3.05. Photographed near Malry, west of Metz, in early September this Panther ausf G of Panzer-Brigade 106 Feldherrnhalle was disabled during the German counterattack, which began during the late evening of 7 September 1944. This tank is also shown in the illustration section. This vehicle is also depicted in the colored illustration section on page 53.

3.07. Photographed near Antwerp in September 1944, this 4.7cm Pak auf R35 self-propelled anti-tank gun is almost certainly one of the vehicles operated by the Panzerjäger battalion of 346.Infantrerie-Division, which reported that twelve of these vehicles were on hand in September. Although quite rare, a number also appeared later during the fighting around Veghel attached to 59.Infanterie-Division.

3.08. The badly damaged assault gun in this photograph, taken near the village of Erp, approximately 5 kilometers east of Veghel in late September, may be from one of the companies of Sturmgeschütz-Brigade 280 which was operating in this area in support of Panzer-Brigade 107. The production features of this vehicle that can be discerned, including the Alkett pattern of Zimmerit application and the gun travel lock, were both commonly seen on the vehicles of the battalion.

3.08a. A heavily camouflaged Sturmgeschütz III ausf G, probably of schwere Panzerjäger-Abteilung 559, photographed in the town of 's Hertgenbosch, approximately thirty kilometers north of Eindhoven. At this time, only the battalion's first company had been issued with Jagdpanther tank destroyers while the second and third companies were both equipped with Sturmgeschütz III assault guns. On Monday, October 23, 1944, the battalion's 3.Kompanie, which was at the time stationed at Utrecht and commanded by Oberleutnant Franz Kopka, was ordered to proceed towards s'Hertgenbosch to support the grenadiers of 712.Infanterie-Division in an attempt to secure the town.

3.09. Disabled and abandoned in the town of Oosterbeek, at some time after the battles for Arnhem, this Tiger II of 3.Kompanie, schwere Panzer-Abteilung 506 was attached to Kampfgruppe von Allworden. Despite the extensive fire damage traces of the tank's camouflage scheme can still be seen. It appears that the gun's muzzle brake is still in place, although curiously it is missing in most of the other photographs of this vehicle. Although Allied reports would suggest otherwise, this was the only Tiger lost in Oosterbeek.

3.10. This Befehlspanzerwagen V Panther ausf G of Panzer-Brigade 107 was disabled near Erp, north-east of Eindhoven, on September 23, 1944 by a British Sherman tank. The brigade operated three of these command vehicles, identified by the Sternantenna D at the right rear of the hull, and this tank was commanded by Major Hans-Albrect von Plüskow, the Abteilungsführer of Panzer-Abteilung 2107. The other command tanks were probably allocated to Major Berndt-Joachim Freiherr von Maltzahn, the brigade commander, and Leutnant Graf Von Brockdorff-Ahlefeld, one of Plüskow's company commanders. As part of Kampfgruppe Walther, the battalion's Panthers were advancing towards the road between Veghel and Uden when, at around noon, a 75mm anti-tank round fired from the rear slammed into the left side track. It was quickly followed by two more, which hit the turret killing Major Plüskow.

3.11. The Jagdpanther of schwere Heeres-Panzerjäger-Abteilung 559 shown here was captured by the Allies after it was disabled on September 8, 1944 near Hechtel in Belgium. The single piece barrel of the 8.8cm Pak 43/2 was installed in the early production models and the mantlet of the main gun is also the early, internally bolted version. This vehicle was in fact the Panzerbefehlswagen version of the Jagdpanther and the provision for the Sternantenna D radio aerial and its armored cover was fitted on the rear of the fighting compartment behind and below the commander's hatch. This vehicle is also depicted in the colored illustration section on page 61.

3.12. In this view of the Jagdpanther shown in the previous photograph, the vehicle's number 01 is clearly visible and can be seen to have been applied with a stencil. The two hatches for the commander and loader in the superstructure roof were apparently removed before the vehicle was recovered and their absence is obvious in several existing photographs of this vehicle taken shortly after the action at Hechtel. The large ventilator to the left of the commander's hatch and the smaller ventilator behind the loader's position are undamaged. The four u-shaped metal brackets are armored covers which each housed a periscope, although these are also missing. Note that those at the front and rear are able to rotate while the two at the sides are fixed. The curved metal plate at the left front of the roof is a swiveling cover with an aperture for the Sfl Zf5 gun sight. Behind that is the Nahverteidigungswaffe, or close defense weapon, which could fire a variety of projectiles, including a smoke grenade or high explosive charge. This vehicle is also depicted in the colored illustration section on page 61.

3.13. Photographed in Holland, this Panther ausf G has the earlier rounded gun mantlet fitted to these tanks until September 1944. Traces of the camouflage scheme generally referred to today as the Disc Pattern can be discerned on the glacis below the hull machine gun aperture. This pattern and the placement of the Balkenkreuz on the turret side would suggest that this vehicle was produced by the firm of Maschinenfabrik Augsburg-Nürnberg AG. This factory applied camouflage scheme was short lived and may have only been applied to the vehicles manufactured between August 19 and the middle of September 1944.

3.14. This Panther ausf G of 2.Kompanie, Panzer-Abteilung 2107 attached to Panzer-Brigade 107 was disabled during the fighting around the town of Overloon on the Meuse river south of Nijmegen in late September 1944. Today this tank is on exhibit at the Nationaal Oorlogs-en Verzetsmuseum, just a short distance from where it was recovered.

3.15. Said to have been photographed near Bruyéres, east of Épinal, in late October 1944, this halftrack is a Schützenpanzerwagen U 304 (f), a modification based the French Unic P107 vehicle. Several hundred of these halftracks were captured by the Germans and converted into various configurations including command, anti-aircraft, and mortar-carriers. The version shown here was used as an armored personnel transport by the Panzergrenadier battalions of 21.Panzer-Division.

3.16. This Panther ausf G of Panzer-Brigade 113 was disabled in late September near Rechicourt, north-east of Metz, when the brigade supported elements of 11.Panzer-Division as part of Kampfgruppe Hammon. This battle group was made up of the surviving infantry of the first and second battalions of Panzergrenadier-Regiment 2113 and as many as twenty-five tanks from the brigade's tank battalion and I.Abteilung, Panzer-Regiment 130, which was attached to the brigade at the time. The reconnaissance battalion of 11.Panzer-Division also supported Oberstleutnant Erich Hammon's Kampfgruppe. The pattern of Zimmerit is typical of vehicles manufactured by the firm of Maschinenfabrik Niedersachsen-Hannover.

3.17. Photographed near Woensdrecht on October 27, 1944, this Sturmhaubitze 42 of Sturmgeschütz-Brigade 280 was destroyed during the fighting around the Scheldt Estuary in Holland. Although heavily damaged, it is possible to see the Zimmerit applied to the hull front and other surfaces in the so-called waffle pattern indicative of assault guns assembled by the Alkett company, which was in fact the sole manufacturer of these howitzer-armed vehicles. The hole in the welded gun mantlet for the coaxial machine gun was incorporated into production in June 1944, while the muzzle brake was also discontinued from production in September 1944, although some units had simple removed them prior to that time.

3.18. Photographed in the town of Kinzweiler, about 10 kilometers north-east of Aachen in late 1944, this Sturmgeschütz III ausf G is coated with Zimmerit anti-magnetic mine paste that has been scored to give a very neat grid pattern indicative of vehicles produced by Mühlenbau und Industrie AG (MIAG) of Braunschweig. The first Sturmgeschütz III rolled of the company's production line in February 1943, with the last vehicle being produced in March 1945. This vehicle may have been one of the assault guns reported as on hand during November 1944 with Panzerjäger-Abteilung 103 of 3.Panzergrenadier-Division. The OKW situation maps show the division in this exact location at that time and strength returns suggest this to be the only unit in the area equipped with the Sturmgeschütz III.

3.19. Photographed on October 20, 1944 in Kohlscheid, north of the city of Aachen, this Sdkfz 251 half track is one of several vehicles of Kampfgruppe Rink that were captured by a US Army tank unit as they attempted to evacuate their wounded from the besieged city. This battle group was commanded by Obersturmführer Herbert Rink and made up principally of men from the second battalion of SS-Panzergrenadier-Regiment 1. The account of a former member of the regiment's 7.Kompanie, which describes the distinctive badge of a stylized mailed fist holding a sword over a flame, suggests that this half track may have been one of the vehicles that the company received in Normandy. Interestingly, other photographs from this series show that a number of the battle group's half tracks had Wehrmacht number plates and the formation insignia of 1.SS-Panzer-Division. The cap badge and rank insignia of the man standing in the half track identify him as a Revier-Oberwachtmeister of the Schutzpolizei, the national uniformed police service.

3.20. Photographed just outside what is almost certainly the village of Halloville, 20 kilometers east of Lunéville, this Jagdpanzer 38(t) Hetzer tank destroyer is one of fourteen vehicles on hand at the time with Sturmgeschütz-Abteilung 1708 of 708. Volks-Grenadier-Division, most of which were destroyed during the early morning hours of November 14, 1944. This division was formed from the remnants of 708.Infanterie-Division as part of the German Army's 32nd recruitment conducted between September and October 1944. All such divisions contained a Panzerjäger-Abteilung made up of a company of towed anti-tank guns, another of towed anti-aircraft guns and a Sturmgeschütz company equipped with self-propelled tank destroyers or assault guns, which was somewhat confusingly referred to as an Abteilung .

3.21. Photographed at Moerdijk, about 10 kilometers north of Breda, in November 1944 this Panzerjäger V Jagdpanther of schwere Heeres-Panzerjäger-Abteilung 559 was disabled while attempting to reach the bridge over the river Waal. This vehicle is also shown and discussed in the illustration section and the marking on the near side fender is depicted in detail.

3.22. Photographed at Sierck-les-Bains, north-east of Thionvillle, in late November 1944, this Raupenschlepper Ost (RSO) tractor was captured from 19.Volksgrenadier-Division, identified by the unit insignia of a stylized mailed fist holding a sword which can be seen on the cab front just to the right of the Notek headlight. Above that and slightly to the right is the tactical sign denoting a towed artillery unit. The cloth covering on the cab roof is a US Army aerial recognition device. The RSO/01 model seen here is easily identified by its rounded cab while the RSO/02 and RSO/03 both featured a more angular version.

3.23. Disabled during the fighting near the Hürtgenwald between Aachen and Düren in late 1944 this Sturmgeschütz III ausf G was manufactured between March 1944, when the later style muzzle brake seen here was adopted, and early September after which Zimmerit paste was no longer applied. Although there is no possibility of identifying the unit to which this vehicle belongs Sturmgeschütz-Brigade 341, Sturmgeschütz-Brigade 394 and Sturmgeschütz-Brigade 902 all operated in the area at this time as part of LXXXI.Armeekorps reserve.

3.24. Photographed in La Bourgance, south-east of Lunéville, this Sdkfz 251/21 Drilling was destroyed by artillery fire in mid-November 1944. These vehicles utilized the large quantity of 1.5cm MG 151/15 or the 2cm 151/20 guns which were no longer required by the Luftwaffe. The three guns were fixed to a pedestal bolted to the floor of the crew compartment and the gunner's protective shield, the sight, and the breech of the right hand gun can be seen here behind the additional armor on the hull side. Another gun would be directly below the site and it would appear that the left hand gun is missing. This half-track shows several features indicative of late production models, including the late style road wheels with a metal ring over the hub and the distinctive Bosch headlight.

3.25. This Panther ausf G is one of a number of tanks lost by II.Abteilung, Panzer-Regiment 33 of 9.Panzer-Division in November 1944 in the fighting around Geilenkirchen. Just visible in another photograph of this tank behind the turret rear access door is a white-outlined number which appears to be either 611 or 811, both being possible. A common practice within this regiment was to repeat the number on the turret's side, however any marking that may be have been there is unfortunately covered by the thick foliage camouflage.

CHAPTER FOUR

WINTER

By mid-December 1944, the British and Canadians had advanced into northern Holland as far as the Waal River after finally clearing the Scheldt estuary. In the center of the front the Americans had taken Aachen, the first German city to fall to the Allies, and advanced as far as Jülich, just 30 kilometers from Cologne. Further to the south, they had occupied Strasbourg and crossed the Saar and, although 19.Armee held a pocket around Colmar on the western bank of the Rhine, the only sector of the front where the Allies were not pressing forward was the heavily wooded area on the German-Belgian frontier known as the Ardennes. Despite increased armored vehicle production, Heeresgruppe B, the largest formation facing the Allies, could only muster 239 tanks, compared to a combined British and American total of over two thousand. Although the US Army's intelligence services knew that a number of German armored formations were in the process of being rebuilt, in particular Dietrich's 6.Panzerarmee, the Americans had faced one of the refitted divisions, Bayerlein's Panzer-Lehr, and had found it to be both under-equipped and under-trained.[1] In addition, it was felt that OB West was unlikely to risk any strategic reserve that could be built up with crossing of the Rhine and the advance into Germany just weeks away at most.

Both sides had for some time used the Ardennes as something of a rest area. It was here that Hitler had decided that a decisive breakthrough, aimed at recapturing Antwerp, would force the western Allies into a negotiated peace, allowing the Wehrmacht to shift the bulk of its force to the Eastern front. Codenamed Wacht am Rhein, the planned offensive was Hitler's creation in its entirety and an outline was first presented to a conference of generals as early as September 16, 1944.[2] Preceded by a whirlwind artillery barrage, units of Model's Heeresgruppe B were expected to break through the American lines in the weakly-held Ardennes sector by the end of the first day. By nightfall on the second day, the Panzers were to have exploited the success of the initial assault and then pushed on to reach the Meuse between Liège and Dinant by the end of the third day. By the end of the fourth and final day of the operation, Antwerp and the western side of the Scheldt estuary would be in German hands.

To pad out the depleted divisions on the Western front and to raise new formations, the 16- and 17-year-old age classes were

---

1 Often referred to incorrectly as 6.SS-Panzerarmee, this formation was not incorporated into the Waffen-SS until April 1945. The Panzer-Lehr division had been rushed to the front in late November in an effort to deny Strasbourg to the Allies. After heavy loss it was returned to OB West reserve at the insistence of Rundstedt.

2 The codename translates into English as Watch on the Rhine and was taken from the name of a patriotic song. It was deliberately chosen for its defensive connotations. Bayerlein, who attended the September meeting, later remarked on the sense of unease felt by all those present except, apparently, Hitler.

called up and many workers who had previously been considered essential to the war effort now found themselves in uniform. Replacements were also drafted from army units and paramilitary organizations, such as the RAD, which were on garrison duty in those eastern European countries still under German control.[3]

In this way the Oberkommando der Wehrmacht was able to raise the number of available personnel on the Western front from around 400,000 to over one million. Although many would receive only rudimentary training before going into battle, they were highly motivated and, contrary to some accounts, reasonably well equipped. In addition, many German boys had received a form of military training in the Hitler Youth, membership of which had been compulsory since March 1939, and were at least proficient in field craft and the use of small arms. To outfit these new formations, German industry had actually increased production despite the intense Allied bombing campaign, and the initial attack would involve over 1,200 tanks and assault guns and more than 4,000 artillery pieces. This was

at a time when Allied intelligence estimated that the Germans could field just 200 tanks to defend the whole front. No amount of effort, however, could alleviate the critical shortages of fuel and ammunition; these would have a telling effect in the coming weeks and months.

Four armies would take part in the offensive and Hitler had personally chosen 6.Panzerarmee and its commander, Oberstgruppenführer Josep 'Sepp' Dietrich, to assault the crucial northern sector. From Monschau to just south of Losheim, 6.Panzerarmee was to advance across the Belgian border towards Malmedy and Stavelot along the Amblève River. This formation was given the task of breaking through the American lines, crossing the Meuse and, if all went well, swinging north to retake Antwerp. This was of course the most important aspect of the plan and Dietrich was given the most powerful armored formations, including four Waffen-SS Panzer divisions and an army Panzergrenadier division. In addition, 6.Panzerarmee contained four newly raised Volksgrenadier divisions and, although their manpower allocation was less than a normal infantry division, they were organized with an increased number of automatic weapons. Importantly, each division's Panzerjäger battalion had been issued with a company of assault guns. A Kampfgruppe, under the command of Obersturm-

bannführer Joachim Peiper and composed of tanks from SS-Panzer-Regiment 1 and the Tigers of schwere SS-Panzer-Abteilung 501, would act as a spearhead. Another Kampfgruppe under Sturmbannführer Ernst Krag was made up of units from II.SS-Panzerkorps. Privately, both Dietrich and Peiper were less than optimistic, particularly in light of the condition that Peiper's men would need to capture stocks of fuel if they were to have any chance of reaching the bridges over the Meuse.

Protecting Dietrich's left flank was General von Manteuffel's 5.Armee, whose front stretched south as far as the area between Prum and Vianden, east of Bitburg. Manteuffel had at his disposal four Volksgrenadier divisions supported by the tanks of 116.Panzer-Division, 2.Panzer-Division, Panzer-Lehr-Division, and the Führer-Begleit-Brigade. The latter had been raised around a cadre made up from Hitler's personal bodyguard and was commanded by Oberst Otto Ernst Remer, who had played a pivotal role in foiling the July assassination plot and had been given command of the brigade as a reward for his loyalty. As well as its own tanks, the Führer-Begleit-Brigade was temporarily reinforced by the assault guns of Sturmgeschütz-Brigade 200. Further to the south were the division's of 7.Armee under General Erich Brandenberger. As 7.Armee was expected to guard

---

3 *The RAD or Reichsarbeitdienst was a national labor service whose members were armed and had received some basic military training. In 1945, the RAD would supply the recruits for four infantry divisions and two mountain brigades.*

Manteuffels' southern flank and absorb the impact of the anticipated American counterattack from Luxembourg, it had been allocated little armor apart from the tanks of the Führer-Grenadier-Brigade, although three of Brandenberger's four Volksgrenadier divisions had each been equipped with a company of Hetzer tank destroyers.[4]

The infantry formations were, however, all near full strength and, in the paratroopers of 5.Fallschirmjäger-Division, Brandenberger had what were probably the best trained ground troops available to the Wehrmacht. In the north, immediately behind Dietrich's army, was 15.Armee under General Gustav-Adolf von Zangen, which was to be used in the event of an American counterattack in the 6.Panzerarmee sector. Recently reinforced, many of Zangen's men were veterans of the battles in Normandy and the defense of the Netherlands.

In addition to these conventional formations, the offensive employed an airborne unit to be dropped behind the American lines and a Panzer brigade made up of personnel wearing US Army uniforms and riding in captured American vehicles or disguised German tanks and assault guns. Nei-

ther had any real impact on the operation.[5]

Although the line-up of the attacking force may appear impressive, it made up just 70 percent of the total number which Hitler had calculated would be needed to drive the Allied armies back and take Antwerp. Bayerlein, the Panzer-Lehr-Division commander, later stated that not a single general officer believed the offensive had any chance of success, if for no other reason than that there was insufficient fuel available. To add to the supply difficulties, the German columns would have to advance under skies

that were controlled by over 14,000 Allied combat aircraft, against which the Luftwaffe hoped to deploy 800 fighters and bombers. Model thought the plan overly ambitious and Rundstedt, who had returned as OB West in September, confided to his diary that only with the aid of the Almighty could the Panzers hope to reach the Meuse, let alone Antwerp.

At precisely 5:30 am on the morning of December 16, 1944, an artillery barrage delivered by two thousand guns pounded the American positions between Monschau and Echternach, a narrow front of just over 100 kilometers in length. Before the artillery had lifted, German infantrymen were infiltrating the American lines with the Panzers following close behind.

At the head of 6.Panzerarmee, Peiper's Kampfgruppe moved towards Losheim but was held up by two collapsed overpasses along the Losheim to Losheimergraben road, which was also protected by an extensive minefield, and had to be diverted to Lanzerath. In an effort to preserve Peiper's armor, a battalion of Fallschirmjäger-Regiment 3 was ordered to take the town but could not move the small American garrison until around 4:00 pm, by which time a large traffic jam had built up behind Peiper's tanks. Ironically, the poor weather, which the Germans had hoped would keep the Allied fighter bombers grounded, had actually

---

4 *Like Remer's brigade, the Führer-Grenadier-Brigade had been formed from one of Hitler's escort units. Both were upgraded to divisions in early 1945.*

5 *As part of Operation Greif, German soldiers dressed in American uniforms were to infiltrate the Allied lines and generally cause confusion by spreading rumors, misdirecting traffic, and altering or removing signposts. Their primary mission was, however, to seize a number of bridges across the Meuse River. Commanded by the legendary Obersturmbannführer Otto Skorzeny, the brigade was supposed to have been made up from men who could pass for native English speakers outfitted in US Army uniforms and equipped with American vehicles and equipment. In actuality, Skorzeny was forced to accept soldiers who spoke little or no English and sometimes dressed in outdated or incorrect uniforms. There were also not enough captured US Army vehicles and ten Panthers and Sturmgeschütz III assault guns were disguised, rather unconvincingly in the case of the latter, to give the appearance of an Allied armored vehicles.*

hampered their advance and, coupled with the difficult terrain and unexpected resistance, ensured that none of the first day objectives had been taken.

Early the following morning, as Kampfgruppe Peiper reached the village of Buchholz, the infantry of 12.Volksgrenadier-Division completed the occupation of Lanzerath. At the same time just to the south, elements of 18.Volksgrenadier-Division reached Schönberg, 10 kilometers from St. Vith. By 12:30 pm Peiper's men had reached the village of Baugnez, between Malmedy and Ligneuville, and after a brief skirmish with an artillery unit of US 7th Armored Division, advanced to Honsfeld. At Hosfield, they were able to destroy a number of Allied tanks and armored vehicles and take prisoner a large part of an American infantry battalion. Importantly, Peiper was able to secure over 50,000 gallons of fuel here, allowing him to push on towards the west, reaching the area around Hünningen.[6]

Behind Peiper, elements of 12.SS-Panzer-Division finally secured Losheimergraben and began their assault on the villages of Rocherath and Krinkelt. That evening, Peiper's tanks were just outside Stavelot, 5 kilometers south-west of Malmedy, and although the Germans managed to capture the town on the following day, the American defenders had been able to evacuate much of the large fuel dump and destroy what could not be saved. Desperate to maintain the momentum of his attack, Peiper sent an advance guard to secure the bridge at Trois-Ponts. They reached by 11:30 am only to find that it had been destroyed. Swinging north, Peiper's men headed towards La Gleize but outside Cheneux, less than a kilometer south of Stoumont, they were hit by the US fighter bombers now making their presence felt as the weather cleared. Within minutes the burning wrecks of two tanks and five halftracks blocked the narrow road. It was 4:00 pm before the Germans were able to get moving again and a further two hours before they could return to their original route heading towards the village of Lienne, where the Americans managed to destroy one of the two remaining bridges as the Germans approached. Undeterred, Peiper pushed his Kampfgruppe further north and halted to rest in the forested area between La Gleize and Stoumont. That night he learnt that Stoumont, and the last bridge before the Meuse, was strongly held and that the Amer-

icans were steadily bringing up reinforcements. To the east, the tanks and Grenadiers of 12.SS-Panzer-Division had given up their attempts to take Rocherath and Krinkelt and decided to bypass the town. Another battle group from 1.SS-Panzer-Division under Sturmbannführer Gustav Knittel had been directed to move towards Peiper and, after fighting their way through Stavelot, which was now under attack, they reached La Gleize. However, after a determined assault, the Americans had retaken Stavelot and both Knittel and Peiper faced the prospect of being cut off. Ominously, as December 18 drew to a close just 36 hours after the commencement of the offensive, the commands of both 6.Armee and 5.Armee reported shortages of fuel.

Although Manteuffel's 5.Armee lacked the armored strength of 6.Panzerarmee, they still enjoyed a marked numerical superiority over the Allied divisions that they faced. In the first days of the offensive, they were able to surround two infantry regiments and force their surrender. The German's success here was largely attributable to Manteuffel's tactic of infiltrating the Allied lines before the preliminary artillery barrage had lifted. Manning their positions as the bombardment ended, American infantrymen were surprised to find that they were being attacked from all sides. Perhaps significantly, Dietrich declined to adopt this

---

6 *At least eighty-four of the men captured at Baugnez were later murdered by a follow-up unit of 1.SS-Panzer-Division. Although the exact circumstances remain unclear, Peiper, Dietrich, and other Waffen-SS officers were later tried for the crime and convicted. Another similar massacre, which has only recently come to light, took place on the same day at Wereth, about 10 kilometers north-east of St. Vith.*

method, preferring to rely on the artillery to smash a way through the Allied defenses. By December 20, the major road junction of Bastogne had been cut off and surrounded by units of XLVII.Panzerkorps. Their commander, General von Lüttwitz, left 26.Volksgrenadier-Division and a single Panzergrenadier regiment of Panzer-Lehr-Division to deal with the defenders and the mobile units of his corps raced westward. Led by a Kampfgruppe from 2.Panzer-Division and elements of Panzer-Lehr-Division, the Germans were able to very quickly advance to St.Vith, a major communications center, where they ran into elements of an American armored division that managed at least to slow their advance.[7]

The town was evacuated on December

---

7 *The battle group from Panzer-Lehr-Division was commanded by Oberstleutnant Joachim Ritter von Poschinger and consisted of Panzergrenadier-Lehr-Regiment 902 supported by two companies of tanks from Panzer-Lehr-Regiment 130. The lead units of 2.Panzer-Division were organized into two Kampfgruppen. The first, under Hauptmann von Böhm, was formed around the division's reconnaissance battalion; the second, stronger battle group under Major Ernst von Cochenhausen contained a full Panzergrenadier regiment and the Panthers of I.Abteilung, Panzer-Regiment 3. Both battle groups from 2.Panzer-Division were completely destroyed in the fighting after Christmas Eve.*

21 and, although the American troops were able to fall back to prepared defensive positions, within two days the Germans had forced them to withdraw as far as the Salm River, some 15 kilometers to the west. Despite these successes, the original plan had called for the town of St. Vith to be taken by 6:00 pm on December 17 at the latest; within the framework of the strict timetable that Hitler had imposed, the German units were far behind schedule. In addition, the Germans had advanced along a very narrow corridor and this now caused problems of supply and reinforcement. By the evening of December 22, the 2.Panzer-Division Kampfgruppe had pushed forward to Foy-Nôtre-Dame, within sight of the Meuse crossing at Dinant. However, they were constantly harassed by flanking attacks all through the next day and although their goal was within reach, the threat of encirclement was ever-present. On December 24, the tanks of Panzer-Lehr-Division captured the town of Celles but could go no further, faced by a determined American defense which by now had been reinforced with British armored units. Late on the same day Manteuffel called off the attacks in this sector.

On the extreme southern flank of the German advance, the divisions of General Brandenberger's 15.Armee had been halted after an initial advance of just 6 kilometers by a strong American defense, which in-

cluded units of US 10th Armored Division. Brandenberger's northern wing joined Manteuffel's army near Vianden and fared much better, with the paratroops of 5.Fallschirmjäger-Division pushing forward almost 20 kilometers to the area between Martalange and Bastogne.

Meanwhile, on December 19 in the northern sector, infantry units of Kampfgruppe Peiper had infiltrated the American defenses around Stoumont in an early morning surprise attack. As the tanks of SS-Panzer-Regiment 1 broke through the eastern edge of the perimeter, an American tank battalion arrived and by 10:30 am, after a two-hour tank battle, the Germans were in possession of the town. Very soon after this Knittel and his Kampfgruppe arrived, but any relief that Peiper may have felt at being reinforced was soon dispelled. Knittel informed him that Stavelot was now in enemy hands and that they were effectively surrounded, although another battle group under Sturmbannführer Max Hansen was on its way. Unsure of what help, if any, Hansen could bring, Peiper immediately ordered Knittel to return to Stavelot and retake the town. He realized that his tanks did not have sufficient fuel to advance beyond Stoumont and at first ordered his men to take up defensive positions west of the town and later that night to withdraw into the streets and houses at the edge of the town. Beating off several attacks made by US 30th Infantry Division, Peiper abandoned Stoumont during the night of December 21 and withdrew his men towards La Gleize where, he had been told, he would meet reinforcements. Although Dietrich urged Gruppenführer Hermann Priess, the commander of I.SS-Panzerkorps, to increase his efforts to relieve Peiper and his men, Hansen's Kampfgruppe was caught up by the American resistance along the southern route to La Gleize. The remainder of Priess' corps, including Knittel, were trying to recapture Stavelot. On December 23, with little ammunition and no food or fuel, Peiper realized that he would not be relieved and ordered his men to abandon their vehicles and heavy equipment and break out towards the east and the German lines.

On the same day that Peiper and the last 800 men of his command set out for the relative safety of their own frontline, the weather began to clear and allowed the Allied air forces to take part in the counteroffensive. As fighter bombers attacked the German forward positions and rear elements, transport planes were able to drop much needed supplies into Bastogne, which was still under siege.

By December 24, it was obvious that the heavily defended Meuse bridges would not fall to the Germans. The units which had made the furthest penetrations were without supplies and it was unlikely that they would

receive any. In the south, US 3rd Army was now pushing forward steadily towards Bastogne, threatening to cut off all the German formations to the west of the town. In the center of what became known as "The Bulge," the forward elements of 2.Panzer-Division were destroyed while the tanks of 9.Panzer-Division were pinned down by an American attack towards Marche. By December 27, further Allied advances, notably the relief of Bastogne, convinced OB West that no further offensive action towards the Meuse was possible and Rundstedt and Model both suggested that the army be pulled back to the fortifications of the Westwall to preserve what was left of the mobile reserve. Hitler, however, would not listen to any talk of retreat. On January 1, 1945 the divisions of Heeresgruppe G and Oberkommando Oberrhein launched a major offensive against Allied positions in the Saar valley along a thinly held front of just over 100 kilometers in an attempt to retake Strasbourg.

Codenamed Nordwind, the main assault was led by 17.SS-Panzergrenadier-Division and 36.Volksgrenadier-Division. Although the initial attacks met with some success becauase the American units in this area had been weakened by sending troops north to deal with the Ardennes offensive, it became increasingly clear that any progress would be limited. On January 4, the town of Wingen-sur-Moder, over 30 kilometers

north-east of the operation's main objective, was captured by elements of 6.SS-Gebirgsjäger-Division and this would prove to be the high-water mark of the offensive. On the following day a supplementary operation, codenamed Sonnenwende, commenced with an attack made by a Kampfgruppe commanded by Major Hannibal Graf von Lüttichau, which quickly led to the establishment of a bridgehead on the Rhine at Gambsheim between Strasbourg and Hagenau.[8]

On January 6, the tanks of Generalmajor Heinrich-Hermann von Hülsen's 21.Panzer-Division drove into the American lines from the area around Wissembourg on the northern edge of the German front. Over the next few days, Hülsen's tanks and the remnants of 25.Panzergrenadier-Division, combined as Kampfgruppe Feuchtinger, were able to push towards Lüttichau's bridgehead as far as Hatten, a distance of approximate-

8 *Major von Lüttichau's command consisted of a company of Panzer IV tanks from Panzer Regiment 2, two companies of tank destroyers, three companies of Jagdpanzer 38(t) Hetzers, most of Grenadier-Regiment 1119, and several ad hoc units under the orders of Oberkommando Oberrhein. The codename Sonnewende or Solstice was, rather confusingly, used for several operations during the war, including the commando raid on Tito's headquarters in Yugoslavia and a major counterattack conducted in Pomerania in 1945.*

ly 15 kilometers. By January 16, with the offensive stalling, 10.SS-Panzer-Division led an attack south from Lauterbourg on the extreme left wing of the German northern sector in an attempt fight their way to the Gambsheim bridgehead. Reaching Herrlisheim on the following day, the division was able to intervene in an attack made by US 12th Armored Division on the bridgehead, effectively destroying two Allied battalions, but failing to link up with the German units in Gambsheim. After repeated attempts to break through to the bridgehead, 10.SS-Panzer-Division was moved to new positions in the Hagenau forest, where the Americans were defending a line along the Moder River as the Allies began an attack aimed at Colmar, approximately 60 kilometers south of Strasbourg.

On January 22, the formations of Heeresgruppe G and Oberkommando Oberrhein were able to link up south of Hagenau but could not force a crossing of the Moder River. On the same day the Allies intensified their attacks around Colmar, where a pocket had formed on the western bank of the Rhine between the village of Rhinau in the north and Mulhouse in the south. Defended by a handful of infantry formations, the pocket held out until February 8, when Hitler authorized the withdrawal of all German troops. On the same day, British and Canadian troops launched a major offensive into the Reichswald, the heavily forested area between the Maas and Rhine Rivers, in an effort to break through the Siegfried line defenses in preparation for an assault on the Ruhr industrial region. In the American sector, the last of the seven Ruhr dams was captured on February 10. Extensive flooding, caused by the demolition work of German engineers, ensured that any Allied offensive operations would be slow and painful. It was February 23 before the Americans could resume their advance. It would be early March before any real advance was made into the Ruhr, with the capture of Köln coming in the first week of the month.

The German offensives of December and January had caused surprise and shock in the Allied camp and, for at time, a great deal of consternation. The advance into Germany, and with it the end of the war, had been stalled while reinforcements were rushed from other areas of the front to reduce the Bulge in the Ardennes. Allied leaders, who had hoped that the conflict would end by Christmas, were now forced to admit that the war would drag on into 1945, possibly until as late as August. Although the Germans had been beaten back to their starting positions, one of Hitler's main objectives had been to drive a wedge, both militarily and politically, between the Anglo-American armies and he had come closer than was evident at the time to achieving his aim. However, the last reserves of both manpower and armor had been used up in ultimately fruitless attacks, ensuring that any future German offensive operations would be localized counterattacks. The Luftwaffe was completely spent as a military force and would take almost no further part in the war in the west, consumed as it was with the defense of Germany's cities. The real winner of the winter battles in the west was Stalin, whose Red Army had advanced to the eastern bank of the Oder River, just 60 kilometers from Berlin, by the end of January 1945.

THE GERMAN ARMY IN THE WEST, DECEMBER 1944

By November 1944, in the defensive fighting in Normandy and the subsequent withdrawal across France and the Low Countries, the German armed forces in the west had suffered almost three-quarters of a million casualties. In an extraordinary logistical and administrative effort, the army had been able to rebuild many of its shattered divisions by absorbing personnel from the Kriegsmarine and the Luftwaffe, by extending the call-up to all males between 16 and 60 years of age, and by conscripting men who had previously been exempt as essential to the war effort. By these measures, the Wehrmacht was able to increase its manpower strength on the Western Front from just over 400,000 to over one million. By December 1944, the German Army in the West was organized into three separate Heeresgruppen or army groups and a single higher command. The three army groups, referred to as Heeresgruppen B, G, and H, were under the control of Generalfeldmarshall von Rundstedt as Oberbefehlshaber West. The strongest was Generalfeldmarschall Model's Heeresgruppe B, which would provide the main strike force for the coming Ardennes Offensive. Oberkommando Oberrhein, often incorrectly referred to as an army group, came under the command of Reichsführer-SS Heinrich Himmler in his position as commander of the Ersatzheer. Note that only armored units are shown in detail.

PANZERS IN THE WEST, DECEMBER 1944

		Panzer III	PzBeoWag III	Bergepanzer III	Panzer IV	PzBeoWag IV	Bergepanzer IV	Pz IV/70 A	Pz IV/70 V	Jagdpanzer IV	Möbelwagen	Wirbelwind	Flakpanzer 38	Panther	Bergepanther	Tiger I	Tiger II	Hetzer	Marder II	Marder III	StuG III	StuG IV	StuH 42	
2.Panzer-Division	Panzer-Regiment 3				28				3*		4	4	3	64							24			*Received during December
Reported December 14, 1944	Panzerjäger-Abteilung 38																				21*			*Received at the end of November
9.Panzer-Division	Panzer-Regiment 33				28						4	4		57										3 Panther and 14 StuG in transit December 14, 1944
Reported December 14, 1944	Panzer-Artillerie Regiment 102		2			2																		
	Panzerjäger-Abteilung 50							14	9															
11.Panzer-Division	Panzer-Regiment 15				31						7	8		47	4									30 Panzer IV and 37 Panthers in transit December 14, 1944
Reported December 14, 1944	Panzerjäger-Abteilung 61									14														
21.Panzer-Division	Panzer-Regiment 22				34						3	5		38										
Reported December 29, 1944	Panzerjäger-Abteilung 200			1						1														
116.Panzer-Division	Panzer-Regiment 16				21									41							19			5 Panzer IV, 23 Panther and 14 StuG in transit December 16, 1944
Reported December 16, 1944	I.Abteilung, Panzer-Regiment 24													9										Handed over to Panzer-Regiment 16 in late November
	Panzerjäger-Abteilung 228			1					11															
Panzer-Lehr-Division	Panzer-Lehr-Regiment 130				27						4	3		30	2									10 Panzer IV and 10 Panther in transit December 8, 1944
Reported December 8, 1944	Panzerjäger-Lehr-Abteilung								21															Reported on hand at the end of November 1944
3.Panzergrenadier-Division	Panzer-Abteilung 103	1*			2*																41			*Both Befehlspanzer
Reported December 10, 1944	Panzerjäger-Abteilung 3								17											7				
15.Panzergrenadier-Division	Panzer-Abteilung 115	1*			14						2										30			*Befehlspanzer
Reported December 9, 1944	Panzerjäger-Abteilung 33																				2			
25.Panzergrenadier-Division	Panzer-Abteilung 15													11										30 Panthers in transit December 14, 1944
Reported December 14, 1944	Panzerjäger-Abteilung 25			1				11	5												32			
Panzer-Brigade 103	II.Abteilung, Panzer Regiment 2				6			11																
Reported December 16, 1944																								
Panzer-Brigade 106	Panzer-Abteilung 2106				2						4	4		10							5*			*Not included in some sources
Reported December 14, 1944																								
Panzer-Brigade 150	9.Kompanie, Kampfabteilung 2150													5										Usually referred to as Kampfgruppe X
Reported December 16, 1944	1.Kompanie, Kampfabteilung 2150																				5			Usually referred to as Kampfgruppe Y
Führer-Begleit-Brigade	Panzer-Regiment FBB		2		17				5		4	4												
Reported December 16, 1944	II.Abteilung, Panzer-Regiment GD				7				38															
	Panzerjäger-Abteilung 673																				5	5		
	Panzer-Artillerie-Regiment 120		5																					
Führer-Grenadier-Brigade	III.Abteilung, FGB				8				12		4			37	2						13	1		
Reported December 16, 1944	Sturmgeschütz-Abteilung 911			2																	34			Temporarily attached to Führer-Grenadier-Brigade
1.SS-Panzer-Division	SS-Panzer-Regiment 1				37						4	4		42	2									
Reported December 3, 1944	Schwere-SS-Panzer-Abteilung 501														2		45							Temporarily attached to SS-Panzer-Regiment 1
2.SS-Panzer-Division	SS-Panzer-Regiment 2				28						4	4		58							28			
Reported December 10, 1944	SS-Panzerjäger-Abteilung 2								3											20				
9.SS-Panzer-Division	SS-Panzer-Regiment 9				32						8			33							28			25 Panthers in transit on December 8, 1944
Reported December 8, 1944																								
10.SS-Panzer-Division	SS-Panzer-Regiment 10				2						8			10	1									34 Panzer IV and 25 Panthers in transit December 8, 1944
Reported December 10, 1944	SS-Panzerjäger-Abteilung 10							10	3															
12.SS-Panzer-Division	SS-Panzer-Regiment 12				37									41	1									
Reported December 8, 1944																								
17.SS-Panzergrenadier-Division	SS-Panzer-Abteilung 17			1																		19		17 Stug and 4 Wirbelwind in transit December 29, 1944
Reported December 29, 1944	SS-Panzerjäger-Abteilung 17																				23			
Panzer-Abteilung (Fkl) 301															2	27								
Reported December 15, 1944																								
Panzer-Kompanie (Fkl) 319																					5			
Reported December 15, 1944																								
Schwere-Panzer-Abteilung 506															1		42							6 Tigers in transit December 10, 1944
Reported December 10, 1944																								

1. PzKpfw Tiger ausf E. Panzergruppe Paderborn. *Not to be confused with the Panzer-Kompanie Paderborn mentioned earlier in this book, this unit was formed at the end of March 1945 from the operational tanks of Panzer-Lehr und Ausbildungs-Abteilung Tiger.*

The group contained eleven Tiger I and six Tiger II tanks and a number of other vehicles. It fought in the area of Paderborn, south-west of Hanover, until April 12, 1945, when the last tank was destroyed. The Tiger I depicted here may have been the group's last operational vehicle.

The tank shown in the photograph at left and below is often associated with Panzer-Kompanie Hummel; however, other photographs of the same vehicle clearly show the turret number 201 and the field modification of a rack fitted to the turret stowage bin. The turret number would seem to eliminate Panzer-Kompanie Hummel as that unit's numbers began with a 1, when the company operated independently, or a 4, when it was attached to schwere Panzer-Abteilung 506. The configuration of the rack is almost identical to others seen of the tanks of schwere Panzer-Abteilung 301.

2. PzKpfw Tiger ausf E. Schwere Panzer-Abteilung 301 (Funklenk). *Photographed in February 1945 at Elsdorf, west of Cologne, this tank must have been one of the last serviceable vehicles available to the battalion. A rack has been fitted to the turret stowage bin and this vehicle has a debris guard covering the mantlet of the main gun. This can also be seen in the photograph (3), although it is quite damaged. The turret number almost certainly indentifies one of the second company's command tanks.*

1. Sturmgeschütz III ausf G. Unit unidentified. *Photographed near Ostenholtz in northern Germany in April 1945, this assault gun is often associated with Kampfgruppe Schulze, an ad-hoc formation raised from elements of the Panzerschule Bergen. However, if the location and date are correct, it is more likely that this is one of the two assault*

guns of Kampfgruppe Grosan. The Kampfgruppe was under the command of Oberst Erhard Grosan and was disbanded on April 21, 1945, although a single Tiger fought on until May 1, when it was destroyed by British tanks.

2. Sturmgeschütz III ausf G. Unit unidentified. *Photographed in western Czechoslovakia or possibly southern Germany in the spring of 1945, this vehicle is one of the assault guns converted from obsolete PzKpfw III tanks late in the war. Approximately 170 of these conversions were completed and the vehicles were fitted with a simple outward opening hatch (3) in place of the commander's cupola, concrete armor on the superstructure front, and a Bosch headlight on the left front fender (missing here). As an economy measure, the shield for the loader's machine gun was replaced by a simple bracket that held the gun.*

1. Sdkfz 251.21 Drilling. 4.Kompanie, Panzergrenadier-Regiment 60. *Attached to 116.Panzer-Division, this unit was in combat around Kirchhellen, north of Essen, in March 1945, when this vehicle was photographed. Note that this halftrack does not have the armor panels normally fitted around the top of the hull to protect the gun shield. These vehicles were armed with a triple mount (2) of either the 1.5cm MG 151/15 or 2cm MG 151/20 gun, which had become surplus to the requirements of the Luftwaffe.*

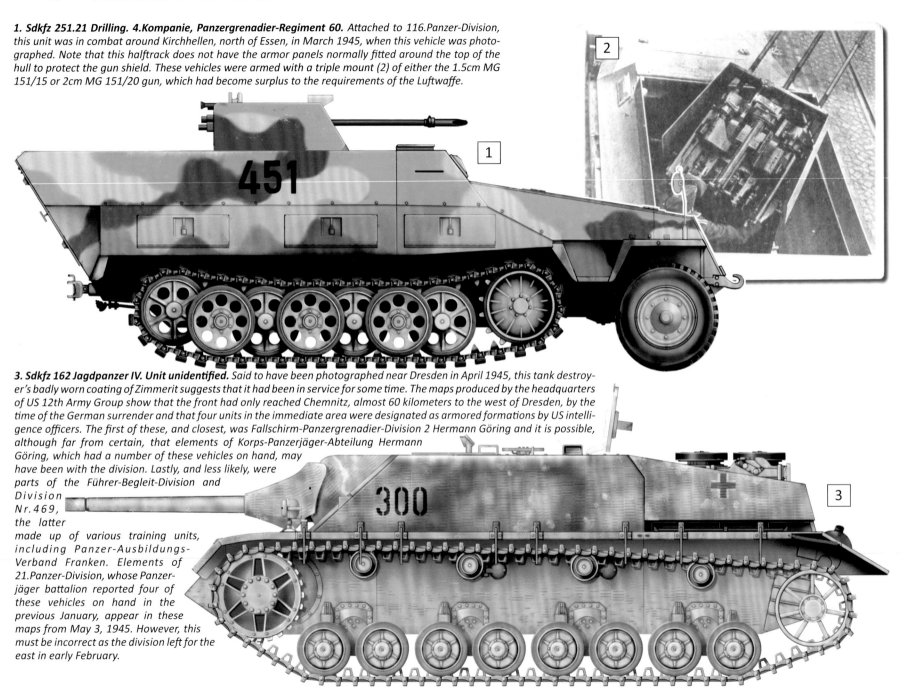

3. Sdkfz 162 Jagdpanzer IV. Unit unidentified. *Said to have been photographed near Dresden in April 1945, this tank destroyer's badly worn coating of Zimmerit suggests that it had been in service for some time. The maps produced by the headquarters of US 12th Army Group show that the front had only reached Chemnitz, almost 60 kilometers to the west of Dresden, by the time of the German surrender and that four units in the immediate area were designated as armored formations by US intelligence officers. The first of these, and closest, was Fallschirm-Panzergrenadier-Division 2 Hermann Göring and it is possible, although far from certain, that elements of Korps-Panzerjäger-Abteilung Hermann Göring, which had a number of these vehicles on hand, may have been with the division. Lastly, and less likely, were parts of the Führer-Begleit-Division and Division Nr.469, the latter made up of various training units, including Panzer-Ausbildungs-Verband Franken. Elements of 21.Panzer-Division, whose Panzerjäger battalion reported four of these vehicles on hand in the previous January, appear in these maps from May 3, 1945. However, this must be incorrect as the division left for the east in early February.*

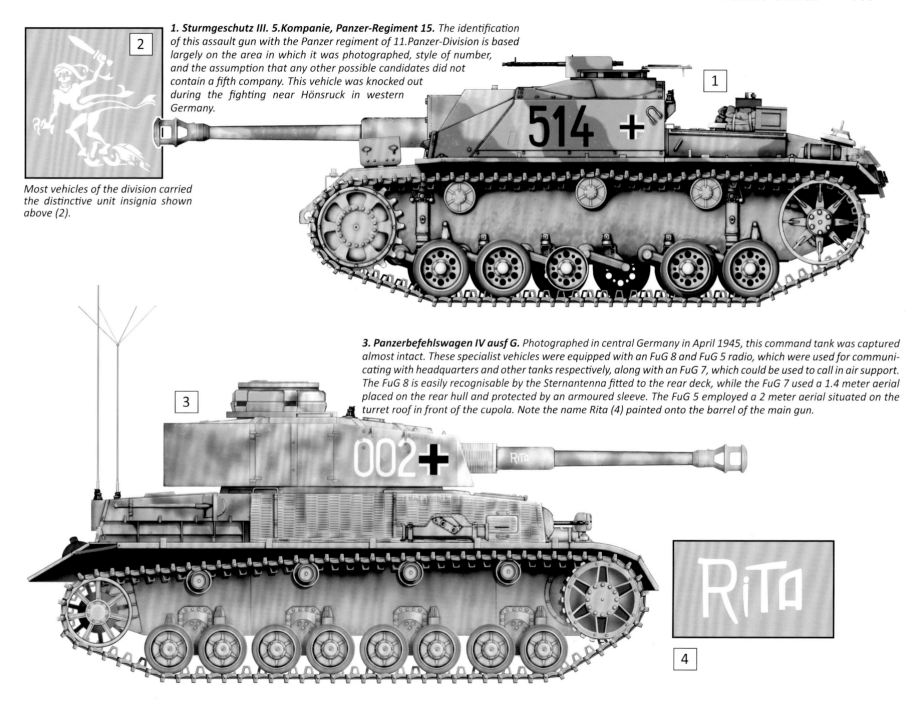

1. Sturmgeschutz III. 5.Kompanie, Panzer-Regiment 15. *The identification of this assault gun with the Panzer regiment of 11.Panzer-Division is based largely on the area in which it was photographed, style of number, and the assumption that any other possible candidates did not contain a fifth company. This vehicle was knocked out during the fighting near Hönsruck in western Germany.*

Most vehicles of the division carried the distinctive unit insignia shown above (2).

3. Panzerbefehlswagen IV ausf G. *Photographed in central Germany in April 1945, this command tank was captured almost intact. These specialist vehicles were equipped with an FuG 8 and FuG 5 radio, which were used for communicating with headquarters and other tanks respectively, along with an FuG 7, which could be used to call in air support. The FuG 8 is easily recognisable by the Sternantenna fitted to the rear deck, while the FuG 7 used a 1.4 meter aerial placed on the rear hull and protected by an armoured sleeve. The FuG 5 employed a 2 meter aerial situated on the turret roof in front of the cupola. Note the name Rita (4) painted onto the barrel of the main gun.*

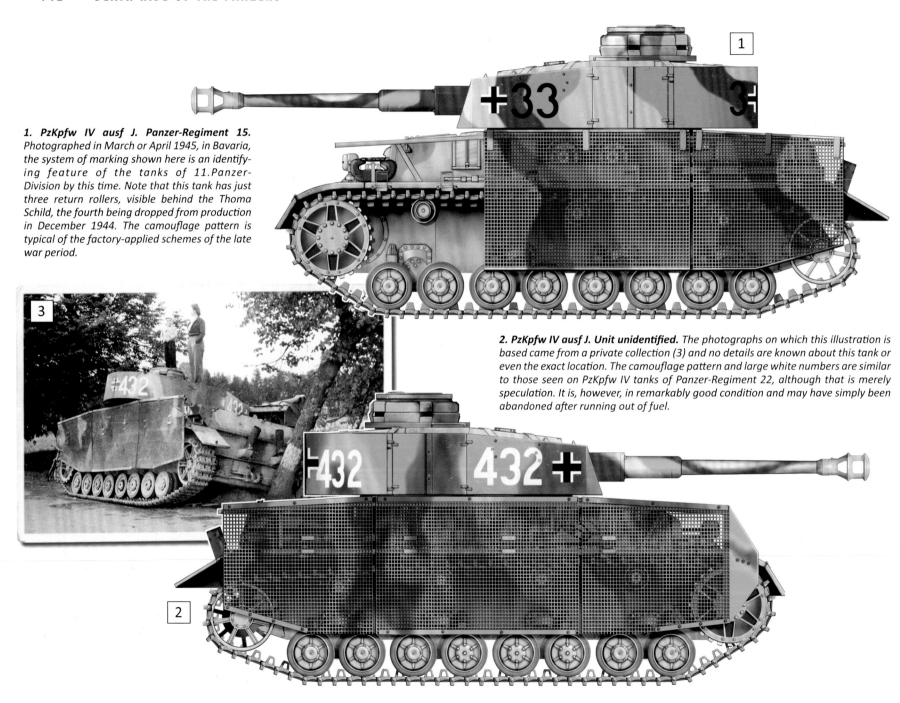

1. PzKpfw IV ausf J. Panzer-Regiment 15. Photographed in March or April 1945, in Bavaria, the system of marking shown here is an identifying feature of the tanks of 11.Panzer-Division by this time. Note that this tank has just three return rollers, visible behind the Thoma Schild, the fourth being dropped from production in December 1944. The camouflage pattern is typical of the factory-applied schemes of the late war period.

2. PzKpfw IV ausf J. Unit unidentified. The photographs on which this illustration is based came from a private collection (3) and no details are known about this tank or even the exact location. The camouflage pattern and large white numbers are similar to those seen on PzKpfw IV tanks of Panzer-Regiment 22, although that is merely speculation. It is, however, in remarkably good condition and may have simply been abandoned after running out of fuel.

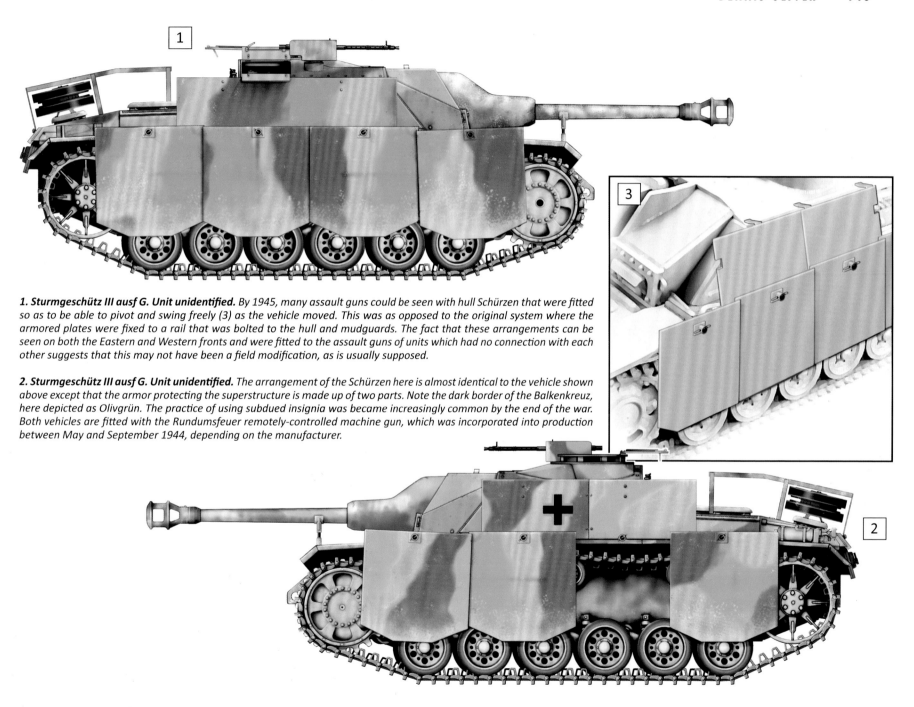

1. Sturmgeschütz III ausf G. Unit unidentified. By 1945, many assault guns could be seen with hull Schürzen that were fitted so as to be able to pivot and swing freely (3) as the vehicle moved. This was as opposed to the original system where the armored plates were fixed to a rail that was bolted to the hull and mudguards. The fact that these arrangements can be seen on both the Eastern and Western fronts and were fitted to the assault guns of units which had no connection with each other suggests that this may not have been a field modification, as is usually supposed.

2. Sturmgeschütz III ausf G. Unit unidentified. The arrangement of the Schürzen here is almost identical to the vehicle shown above except that the armor protecting the superstructure is made up of two parts. Note the dark border of the Balkenkreuz, here depicted as Olivgrün. The practice of using subdued insignia was became increasingly common by the end of the war. Both vehicles are fitted with the Rundumsfeuer remotely-controlled machine gun, which was incorporated into production between May and September 1944, depending on the manufacturer.

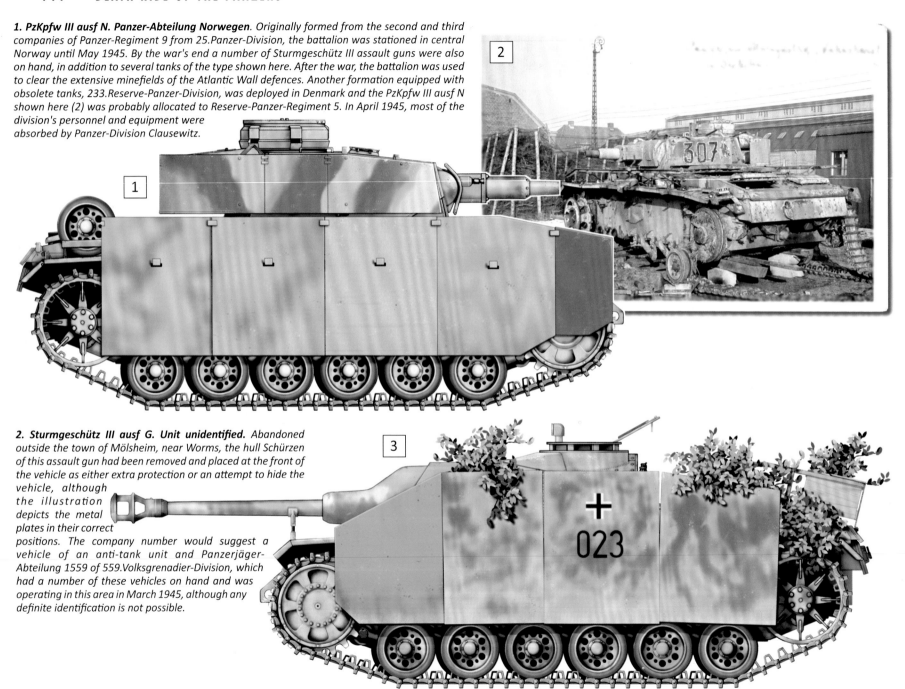

1. PzKpfw III ausf N. Panzer-Abteilung Norwegen. *Originally formed from the second and third companies of Panzer-Regiment 9 from 25.Panzer-Division, the battalion was stationed in central Norway until May 1945. By the war's end a number of Sturmgeschütz III assault guns were also on hand, in addition to several tanks of the type shown here. After the war, the battalion was used to clear the extensive minefields of the Atlantic Wall defences. Another formation equipped with obsolete tanks, 233.Reserve-Panzer-Division, was deployed in Denmark and the PzKpfw III ausf N shown here (2) was probably allocated to Reserve-Panzer-Regiment 5. In April 1945, most of the division's personnel and equipment were absorbed by Panzer-Division Clausewitz.*

2. Sturmgeschütz III ausf G. Unit unidentified. *Abandoned outside the town of Mölsheim, near Worms, the hull Schürzen of this assault gun had been removed and placed at the front of the vehicle as either extra protection or an attempt to hide the vehicle, although the illustration depicts the metal plates in their correct positions. The company number would suggest a vehicle of an anti-tank unit and Panzerjäger-Abteilung 1559 of 559.Volksgrenadier-Division, which had a number of these vehicles on hand and was operating in this area in March 1945, although any definite identification is not possible.*

1. PzKpfw Tiger ausf E. Tiger-Gruppe Fehrmann. This unit was hastily formed at the end of the war, with maintenance depots using whatever vehicles and parts could be scraped together. Consequently, the Tigers featured a mixture of early and late production features and even pre-1943 camouflage. All were, however, marked with a large letter F, for the commander Oberleutnant Fehrmann, followed by a two-digit number. Many numbers were quite roughly applied, as shown in the photograph at right (2). Several photographs have recently come to light showing the right-hand side of Tiger F01, as it is depicted here.

3. PzKpfw Tiger ausf E. Tiger-Gruppe Fehrmann. This Tiger has an early production turret, complete with drum-style cupola, large pistol port, and Schwartzgrau camouflage. The single headlight on the left-hand side at the front indicates that the hull was manufactured prior to October 1943, although the steel road wheels were introduced into production from February 1944.

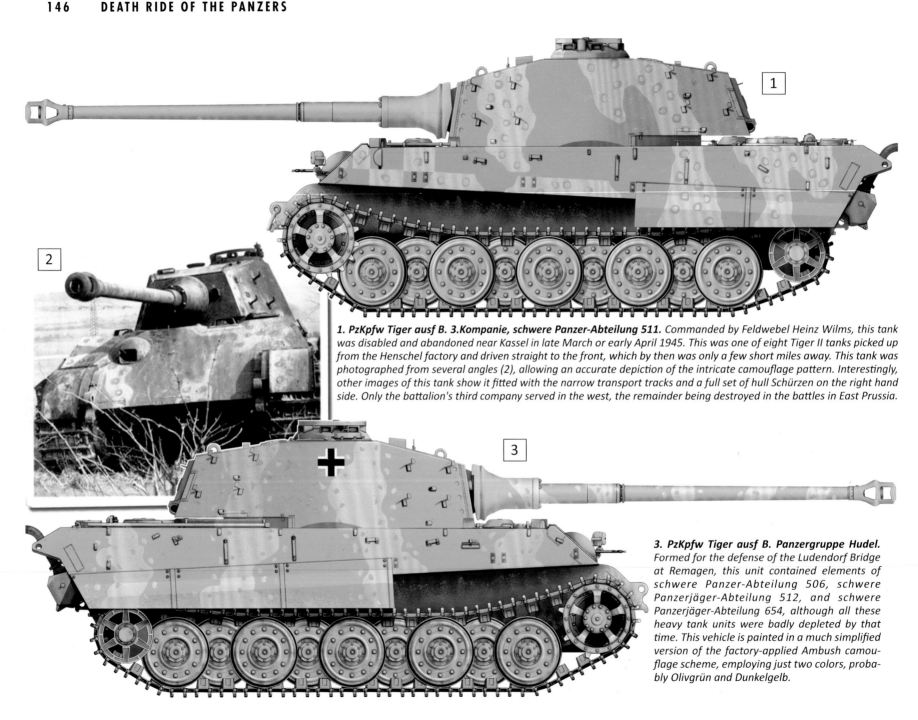

1. PzKpfw Tiger ausf B. 3.Kompanie, schwere Panzer-Abteilung 511. Commanded by Feldwebel Heinz Wilms, this tank was disabled and abandoned near Kassel in late March or early April 1945. This was one of eight Tiger II tanks picked up from the Henschel factory and driven straight to the front, which by then was only a few short miles away. This tank was photographed from several angles (2), allowing an accurate depiction of the intricate camouflage pattern. Interestingly, other images of this tank show it fitted with the narrow transport tracks and a full set of hull Schürzen on the right hand side. Only the battalion's third company served in the west, the remainder being destroyed in the battles in East Prussia.

3. PzKpfw Tiger ausf B. Panzergruppe Hudel. Formed for the defense of the Ludendorf Bridge at Remagen, this unit contained elements of schwere Panzer-Abteilung 506, schwere Panzerjäger-Abteilung 512, and schwere Panzerjäger-Abteilung 654, although all these heavy tank units were badly depleted by that time. This vehicle is painted in a much simplified version of the factory-applied Ambush camouflage scheme, employing just two colors, probably Olivgrün and Dunkelgelb.

1. PzKpfw V Panther ausf G. Unit unidentified.
Although any definitive identification of this vehicle is not possible, it may be one of the Panthers of Panzer-Abteilung 2106 handed over to Panzer-Division Clausewitz in April 1945. It has been suggested that the tanks from Panzer-Brigade 106 were allocated to Panzerkampfgruppe Wallenberg, part of the division's armored component, and although this is entirely possible I have not been able to find any confirmation. The formation of this division, the last German armored unit raised during the war, is discussed in detail in the main text of this book.

2. PzKpfw V Panther ausf G. Panzer-Abteilung Putlos. Photographed near Fallersleben, near Brunswick in western Germany, this tank is painted in the factory-applied camouflage scheme employed by the firms of MAN and Daimler-Benz and introduced from August 1944. The Flammvernichter, or flame-dampener, exhaust mufflers and the raised fan housing on the rear deck were both incorporated into production from October 1944. The photograph at left (3) shows the vehicle on which the illustration is based. The battalion was formed from elements of the Schiess-Schule Putlos and attached to Panzer-Division Clausewitz and has the fittings for the BIWA infrared sighting equipment, as many of the battalion's tanks did. The history of the US 407th Infantry Regiment describes a battle fought in this area on April 21, 1945, against ten Panther tanks. This may be one of those vehicles.

1. PzKpfw V Panther ausf G. Panzer-Abteilung Putlos. *Photographed near Fallersleben, north-east of Brunswick, in April 1945, this tank is one of several Panthers seconded from the tank gunnery school at Putlos and attached to Kampfgruppe von Benningsen, part of Panzer-Division Clausewitz. Many of this unit's Panthers were fitted with the attachments and brackets for the BIWA infrared sighting equipment, although it is almost certain that none were equipped with the actual sights. A number of tanks (2) were also handed over from Panzer-Abteiling 2106 and retained their original markings.*

3. PzKpfw V panther ausf D. Unit unidentified. *Photographed in the town of Bamberg in northern Bavaria in April 1945, this early model tank was almost certainly drafted from one of the training establishments as an emergency measure. The early road wheels, with their sixteen reinforcing bolts, were phased out of production from September 1943, and assembly of this model of the Panther ceased in the same month. Replacement barrels were delivered in the dark gray heat resistant primer depicted here. This example seems to have been roughly camouflaged with Olivgrün.*

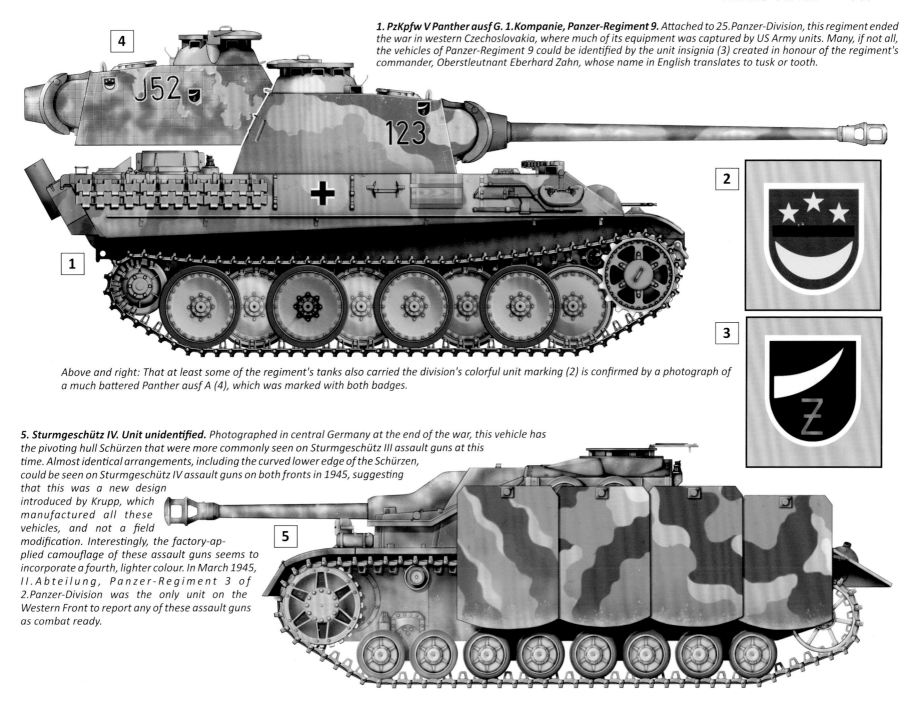

1. PzKpfw V Panther ausf G. 1.Kompanie, Panzer-Regiment 9. *Attached to 25.Panzer-Division, this regiment ended the war in western Czechoslovakia, where much of its equipment was captured by US Army units. Many, if not all, the vehicles of Panzer-Regiment 9 could be identified by the unit insignia (3) created in honour of the regiment's commander, Oberstleutnant Eberhard Zahn, whose name in English translates to tusk or tooth.*

Above and right: That at least some of the regiment's tanks also carried the division's colorful unit marking (2) is confirmed by a photograph of a much battered Panther ausf A (4), which was marked with both badges.

5. Sturmgeschütz IV. Unit unidentified. *Photographed in central Germany at the end of the war, this vehicle has the pivoting hull Schürzen that were more commonly seen on Sturmgeschütz III assault guns at this time. Almost identical arrangements, including the curved lower edge of the Schürzen, could be seen on Sturmgeschütz IV assault guns on both fronts in 1945, suggesting that this was a new design introduced by Krupp, which manufactured all these vehicles, and not a field modification. Interestingly, the factory-applied camouflage of these assault guns seems to incorporate a fourth, lighter colour. In March 1945, II.Abteilung, Panzer-Regiment 3 of 2.Panzer-Division was the only unit on the Western Front to report any of these assault guns as combat ready.*

4.01. Supporting the infantry of 560.Volksgrenadier-Division during the initial phase of the Ardennes offensive, the assault guns of 244.Sturmgeschütz-Brigade forced a crossing under fire of the Our River near Welchenhausen on the Belgian-German border where this vehicle was photographed. Completely destroyed in the battles on the Eastern front in July 1944, the brigade was rebuilt in Holland in October despite just seven of these vehicles being on hand in December and even the loss of one would have been sorely felt. Several features identify this as a late production vehicle, including the side opening loader's hatch to accommodate the Rundumsfeuer remotely controlled machine gun, the travel lock for the main gun introduced in June 1944 and the complete lack of Zimmerit, which was dropped from production in the following September.

4.02. Photographed in Clervaux, in the north-east corner of Luxembourg, this badly damaged Sturmgeschütz III is one of the six assault guns of II.Abteilung, Panzer-Regiment 3 of 2.Panzer-Division which attacked the town from the south on the morning of December 17, 1944. Supported by infantry from one of the division's Panzergrenadier battalions, the assault guns ran head on into five Sherman tanks of the US 707th Tank Battalion. In the ensuing battle, two German vehicles were knocked out and the Americans lost three Shermans. The burning hulks blocked the road, effectively halting any further German advance from this direction.

4.03. Just twenty of these vehicles were built as conversions based on the Jagdpanzer 38(t) Hetzer with the main gun replaced with a flamethrower and all served with Panzer-Kompanie (Flamm) 352 and Panzer-Kompanie (Flamm) 353 during the Ardennes Offensive in December 1944. The vehicle shown here is probably from the former. Both companies took part in Operation Nordwind in January 1945 after which the surviving vehicles were formed into a single company.

4.04. Captured near Gros-Réderching during the battles for Metz, this Flammpanzer 38(t) is one of the vehicles of Panzer-Kompanie (Flamm) 353 that supported the units of 17.SS-Panzergrenadier-Division. Both this company and Panzer-Kompanie (Flamm) 352 were attached to 1.Armee during this time.

4.05. A Pzkpfw V Panther ausf G of Panzer-Regiment 33, 9.Panzer-Division photographed in Humain on December 28, 1944 following the successful attempt by US 2nd Armored Division to retake the town. The division had taken over this section of the line just two days previously and suffered badly in the intense artillery barrage which preceded the attack and the ten hour battle that followed. A small number 80 is just visible on the turret side forward of the Balkenkreuz and this may indicate the commander of 8.Kompanie Oberleutnant Hugo Crisandt. This company was formed exclusively from members of 1.Kompanie, Panzer-Abteilung 2105 when that battalion was disbanded in October 1944. This vehicle is also depicted in the colored illustration section on page 100.

4.06. Panzer-Brigade 150 was formed specifically for the Ardennes Offensive and equipped with either captured US Army vehicles or German tanks and assault guns which were modified and painted to resemble Allied vehicles. The Sturmgeschütz III shown here was abandoned after the brigade's unsuccessful attack on Malmedy on December 21, 1944. All were painted in an olive green shade, probably RAL 6003 Olivgrün, and marked with large white stars and US vehicle codes, although the latter included the letters XY which would identify them to German military police units.

4.07. Photographed in the town of Hotton, 20 kilometers northwest of Houffalize in Belgium on December 26, 1944, this Panther ausf G of I Abteilung, Panzer Regiment 16 of 116.Panzer-Division and a Pzkpfw IV ausf J from 6.Kompanie of the division's II Abteilung were part of Kampfgruppe Bayer, which attempted to capture the town on the previous Thursday. The extended mantlet of the main gun on the Panther, often referred to as a chin, was introduced into production from September 1944. The small contrasting dots of color incorporated into the camouflage scheme are just visible on the turret and quite clear on the hull Schürzen.

4.08. Although this Bergepanzer III recovery vehicle was photographed in company with tanks of 9.Panzer-Division, there is no record of that formation having any of these vehicles on hand. These vehicles were usually allocated to companies or battalions equipped with the Sturmgeschütz III assault gun and one possible candidate is Panzerjäger-Abteilung 228 of 116.Panzer-Division, which was operating in the same area at the end of December 1944 and had a single Bergepanzer III on hand.

4.09. This Panther ausf G of 4.Kompanie, SS-Panzer-Regiment 2 is almost certainly one of the tanks disabled on the morning of December 24, 1944, when Hauptscharführer Franz Fraussher led four Panthers of his platoon in an attack towards Manhay from Grandmènil, approximately 12 kilometers north of Houffalize, in Belgium. The tank pictured here was overturned by a US Army Bulldozer in an effort to clear the road. This tank has the self-cleaning rear idler and raised housing for the crew compartment heater, indicating that it was assembled some time after October 1944.

4.10. On Christmas Day 1944, a Kampfgruppe made up from elements of the Führer-Grenadier-Brigade attacked US Army positions in front of the village of Heiderscheid, north-west of Diekirch in central Luxembourg, and were caught in the open field shown here. The Sturmgeschütz III is from the brigade's III. Abteilung, which had thirteen of these vehicles on hand and the half track is an SdKfz 251/17 equipped with a 20mm cannon, not visible here, fitted into the small turret above the driver's position. Very few of these vehicles were produced and just over 130 were delivered between October 1944 and February 1945. The number 21 is visible on the open rear access door of the halftrack and what may be a O is just discernible on the hull side above the center stowage locker.

4.11. This Sturmgeschütz III is another of the vehicles of III.Abteilung, Führer-Grenadier-Brigade, which attacked Heiderscheid on December 25, 1944. This is a late production vehicle as evidenced by the hole in the upper left corner of the gun mantlet for a coaxial machine gun that was fitted from October 1944. Although the well known Topfblende cast gun mantlet, often referred to today as the Saukopf, was incorporated into production from November 1943, there is some evidence that the firm of MIAG continued to install the welded version shown here until the end of the war.

4.12. Knocked out during the defense of Heiderscheid in central Luxembourg, this Panther ausf G was one of the thirty-seven tanks on hand with III.Abteilung, Führer-Grenadier-Brigade at the start of the Ardennes Offensive. The Panthers of the brigade supported 79.Volksgrenadier-Division here from December 22, 1944 and suffered heavily. The only markings visible are the Balkenkreuz on the hull side at the front and the vehicle's chassis number, or Fahrgestellnummer, on the glacis.

4.13. The caption of the US Signal Corps photograph provides little information about this Sturmgeschütz III, other than that it was photographed in the Ardennes. The tactical marking on the hull front, however, may provide a clue as to which unit this vehicle belonged. The rhomboid denotes a Panzer unit while the small number 12 identifies the company. Of all the armored units under the command of Oberbefehlshaber West in December 1944, only III.Abteilung of the Führer-Grenadier-Brigade contained a twelfth company and the battalion was in fact reinforced with a number of Sturmgeschütz III assault guns in late November or early December, eighteen of which were combat ready when the offensive began.

4.14. Photographed just 3 kilometers from St Vith, as the sign in the background clearly indicates, this Sturmgeschütz III ausf G may be from Panzerjäger-Abteilung 673 of the Führer-Begleit-Brigade. During the Ardennes offensive this unit was operating near the village Hünnigen, a village to the north of St Vith and incorrectly identified as of Hummange in the official caption, and had five combat ready assault guns on hand.

4.15. A Tiger II of 2.Kompanie, schwere SS-Panzer-Abteilung 501 photographed outside the town of La Gleize, just 8 kilometers to the west of Malmedy on the road to Stoumont, on December 24, 1944. Commanded by Unterscharführer Eduard Stadler, this tank was one of over 100 vehicles abandoned in this area by Kampfgruppe Peiper when the Germans were forced to retreat on foot. Another 2.Kompanie Tiger, numbered 213 and commanded during the battle by Obersturmführer Helmut Dollinger, is today on permanent display at the December 44 Historical Museum in La Gleize. This vehicle is also depicted in the colored illustration section on page 103.

4.16. A Pzkpfw IV ausf H, identified by the small muffler on the left hand side of the hull rear plate, photographed in Belgium in late 1944. Other images which seem to depict tanks disabled along this same stretch of road suggest that this vehicle may be from 6.Kompanie, SS-Panzer-Regiment 1 and the location may be somewhere near Wirtzfeld, 10 kilometers from Malmedy in Belgium. Commanded by Obersturmführer Werner Sternebeck, this company had been detached from the regiment's II.Abteilung and formed the armored spearhead of Kampfgruppe Peiper in the opening stages of the Ardennes Offensive.

4.17. This Tiger II of 3.Kompanie, schwere SS-Panzer-Abteilung 501 was disabled outside the village of Garonne near Engelsdorf on Christmas Day 1944. This photograph was taken almost two weeks later when it was apparently safe for civilians to return to the area. As they had been in Normandy, the tanks of this battalion were marked in different styles and colors for the headquarters and three companies and examples are shown in the illustration section. This vehicle is also depicted in the colored illustration section on page 103.

4.18. An Sdkfz 251/7 engineer halftrack destroyed at Amblève in December 1944. This vehicle was probably allocated to SS-Panzerpionier-Bataillon 1 under the command of Obersturmführer Franz Sievers and attached to Kampfgruppe Peiper. The American soldier is examining the bellows used to inflate the one of the rubber dinghies carried by these specialist halftracks.

4.19. The vehicle closest to the camera is a Panther ausf G of 3.Kompanie, SS-Panzer-Regiment 12 photographed in the streets of Krinkelt on December 18, 1944. When the Ardennes offensive began these tanks were part of Kampfgruppe Kuhlmann, which consisted of the Panthers of I.Abteilung, SS-Panzer-Regiment 12, the armored infantry of III.Abteilung, SS-Panzergrenadier-Regiment 26 supported by the Jagdpanzer IV/70, and Jagdpanther tank destroyers of schwere Panzerjäger-Abteilung 560. The Panthers were, however, detached to aid Kampfgruppe Muller in the capture of the twin villages of Krinkelt-Rocherath. Many of the tanks destroyed in the close confines of the town were victims of bazooka teams.

4.20. Photographed on the road south of Krinkelt, towards Kanlenberg, this Panther ausf G of 1.Kompanie, SS-Panzer-Regiment 12 may be one of the company's tanks that survived the savage fighting in the town as evidenced by the considerable amount of rubble on the rear deck. The company number 126 is clearly visible on the turret side.

4.21. Abandoned at La Gleize, east of Stoumont , this Panther ausf G of 2.Kompanie, SS-Panzer-Regiment 1 was commanded Hauptscharführer Heinz Knappich. The tank's company number of 221 is visible in at least one other photograph of this vehicle. Incredibly this tank was hit at least eight times, at close range, by a US 90mm anti-aircraft gun as it entered the town, but was only disabled and Hauptscharführer Knappich and the entire crew managing to escape. Just twenty-four of these Panthers, all built by MAN during September 1944, were fitted with steel road wheels seen here.

4.22. Two panther ausf G tanks of SS-Panzer-Regiment 1 attached to Kampfgruppe Peiper abandoned after the fighting in the Ardennes. The tank in the foreground is painted in the so-called ambush camouflage scheme sometimes referred to as the Dot Pattern, where large fields of color were covered with small dots of a contrasting shade. Examples are shown in the illustration section. This factory-applied scheme was indicative of vehicles manufactured by Daimler-Benz, as was the placement of the Balkenkreuz on the hull side. Just visible behind the gun mantlet is what appears to be a small number 301 painted in black although the battalion's 3.Kompanie was not present at the time.

4.23. This Panther ausf G was knocked out on December 18, 1944 as it left Cheneux, south of Stoumont, and approached the railway bridge across the Amblève river less than 500 meters to the south of the village. Although badly damaged, the remains of the so-called disc camouflage is clearly visible on the turret as is the tank's company number depicted in black with a white outline. In the original image it is possible to see that the number 131 has also been painted behind the gun mantlet. At least one other tank of this company, number 124, was painted in the same style of camouflage.

4.24. Although the identification of this Tiger II as a tank of 1.Kompanie, schwere Panzer-Abteilung 506 is beyond question, the location has been the subject of some debate, variously described as Villers-la-Bonne-Eau, Lutramange or Moinet. I believe that this may be one of two Tigers the battalion lost on January 13, 1945 in a fight with tanks of the US 6th Armored Division as described by Schneider. This is not the town of Moinet, which is much further to the north and closer to Oberwampach in Luxembourg, but rather the Moinet farm just off the road from Villers-la-Bonne-Eau to Lutramange. In the original print, a number 1 is visible to the left of the Balkenkreuz on the turret side and this is in keeping with the system used by this battalion.

4.25. This late production Pzkpfw V Panther ausf G of I Abteilung, Panzer Regiment 33 of 9.Panzer-Division was photographed between Clervaux and Hosingen in northern Luxembourg near the German border, probably in January 1945. Photographs of other tanks of this regiment's third company taken at the same time confirm that it was common practice to repeat the tank's number on the turret rear. This tank has the later style gun mantlet with the extension along the lower edge introduced into production from September 1944.

4.26. This Pzkpfw IV ausf J of I.Abteilung, Panzer-Regiment 33 from 9.Panzer-Divison may have been another of the regiment's tanks that were lost in near Langlire, north-east of Houffalize, in early January 1945. This tank is also depicted in the illustration section, where the distinctive unit insignia adopted by this battalion is shown in detail. This vehicle is also depicted in the colored illustration section on page 102.

4.27. Said to have been knocked out during the fighting for the village of Langlire, north-east of Houffalize, on January 13, 1945, this Panther ausf G is most often associated with Panzer-Regiment 33 of 9.Panzer-Division. However, that regiment's Panthers were all allocated to II.Abteilung, making the turret number highly unlikely. I believe that this tank is almost certainly from 116.Panzer-Division, whose I.Abteilung, Panzer-Regiment 24 took part in the battles conducted in this area while 9.Panzer-Division was operating much further to the north. The camouflage scheme is an example of the factory-applied patterns that came into use from August 1944. The example shown here is indicative of vehicles manufactured by either MAN or Daimler-Benz.

4.28. Photographed near the village of Marcourt, north-west of Houffalize, in early January 1945, this Sdkfz 251/1 halftrack has been fitted with a captured .50 caliber machine gun. This vehicle may have been operated by one of the Panzergrenadier battalions of 116.Panzer-Division.

4.29. Photographed in the area north of Houffalize in Belgium on January 13, 1945, this Pzkpfw IV is one of the tanks of Panzer-Abteilung 115 from 15.Panzergrenadier-Division. This division had been stationed in Italy as late as June 1944 and after being transferred to the Western front had spent much of November fighting around the city of Aachen. For the Ardennes Offensive, the Panzer battalion was reinforced with thirty Sturmgeschütz III assault guns. A somewhat reconstructed version of this vehicle, as it may have appeared before it was badly damaged and covered by snow, is included in the illustration section. This vehicle is also depicted in the colored illustration section on page 105.

4.30. A Flakpanzer IV Möbelwagen photographed near the town of Hosingen in northern Luxembourg in early 1945. Both 2.Panzer-Division and Panzer-Lehr-Division were involved in the fighting in this area and both had four of these vehicles on hand on when the Ardennes Offensive began on December 16, 1944. Although these vehicles were rushed into production as a stop gap, they served in the anti-aircraft platoons of all the Panzer divisions on the Western Front with 240 built on the chassis of damaged Pzkpfw IV tanks.

4.31. This Panther ausf G of I.Abteilung, Panzer-Regiment 130 of Panzer-Lehr-Division was disabled near the village of Buissonville, north of Rochefort, in the fighting which took place there in late December 1944. These tanks supported Kampfgruppe von Fallois, made up principally of the division's reconnaissance battalion commanded by Major Gerd von Fallois, and were stalled just short of the village by tanks of US 2nd Armored Division. Although the battalion's tanks were usually marked with a company number on the turret sides, this vehicle is devoid of any markings other than the Balkenkreuz on the rear stowage box and hull side behind the tool rack, the latter a possible identifying feature of Panthers manufactured by Daimler-Benz.

4.32. Disabled during the fighting for the outer suburbs of Strasbourg in January 1945, this Jagdpanzer38(t) Hetzer is almost certainly one of the five such vehicles on hand with Panzerjäger-Abteilung 1553 of 553.Volksgrenadier-Division at the beginning of the year. This unit also reported two Marder III and a single Marder II on hand at the same time.

4.33. Destroyed in the fighting in northern Luxembourg in late 1944 or early 1945, this Pzkpfw IV ausf J is fitted with the mesh Schürzen commonly referred to as Thoma Schild. More correctly termed Drahtgeflechtschürzen, these screens were adopted in September 1944 beginning with Pzkpfw IV ausf J Fahrgestellnummer 92301 and were found to be as effective as the steel plates in use at the time. The Thoma Schild screens were also incorporated into the assembly of the tank destroyers based on the Pzkpfw IV chassis and would probably have been extended to other vehicles had the war continued.

4.34. Photographed near Inden, east of Aachen, on December 17, 1944, this captured Sturmgeschütz III ausf G features the cast mantlet of the main gun which was a standard feature of these vehicles from November 1943. The gun travel lock, situated on the hull front directly below the main gun, was fitted from July 1944. The presence of Zimmerit anti-magnetic mine paste applied in the so-called waffle pattern identifies this as vehicle assembled by the firm of Alkett prior to September 1944. The wire brackets welded to the hull front and driver's side mudguard are non-standard and are almost certainly a filed modification. The addition of concrete to the front of the crew compartment was commonly seen on assault guns at this time on both the Western and Eastern Fronts and began to appear sometime in late 1944.

CHAPTER FIVE

THE END

By the spring of 1945, the strategic reserve that the Wehrmacht had built up in the last months of the previous year had been exhausted. The Anglo-American armies had been fighting on German soil since the struggle for control of Aachen in October 1944 and in the first weeks of the new year had pushed the Germans back to the starting points of the Ardennes Offensive. The campaign in the Rhineland against the Americans had further weakened the German Army, leaving only badly depleted units to defend the east bank of the Rhine.

An Allied offensive to crush the German divisions on the western bank of the river began on March 1 with an attack on a broad front towards Köln in the north and Trier in the south. Fighting with the few tanks and Grenadiers left to them, 9.Panzer-Division, 11.Panzer-Division, 3.Panzergrenadier-Division, and the remaining infantry formations of 15.Armee attempted to hold up the American armored divisions while engineers destroyed the twenty-two road bridges and twenty-five railway bridges across the Rhine. In five days of savage fighting the German divisions were largely destroyed. On March 6, US Army units entered Köln just as the explosive charges on the Hohenzollern Bridge were detonated. This bridge had been one of just four remaining Rhine bridges left standing by that date.[1] However, by an incredible stroke of luck, the Ludendorf Bridge at Remagen, over 40 kilometers to the south, was captured intact on the next day when some of the demolition charges fixed to the structure failed to explode. With-

---

1 *Although the city may be better know to readers as Cologne, I have chosen to use its German name here and throughout this book. The Hohenzollern Bridge was rebuilt after the war and is today the most heavily used railway bridge in Germany, which should give some idea of its importance in 1945. Of the remaining crossings, the Bonn Bridge was destroyed during the night of March 8, as was the Kronprinz Wilhelm Bridge at Urmitz on the following morning. The Ludendorf Bridge at Remagen was, of course, captured intact.*

in two days the Americans had a complete infantry division across the bridge and this was very quickly followed by two more infantry formations supported by tanks.

Over the next weeks the Germans threw every imaginable weapon at the bridge, including super-heavy artillery, floating mines, Kriegsmarine underwater demolition teams, and finally the Luftwaffe's new Arado Ar 234 jet bombers, escorted by ME 262 fighters. Hitler was incensed at the loss of the bridge and several officers were court-martialed and shot. The Führer also used the crisis at the front as an excuse to sack Rundstedt. He was replaced as OB West by Generalfeldmarschall Albert Kesselring, who arrived at Model's headquarters three days later to be briefed on the situation. An armored counterattack on the growing bridgehead was mounted on the same day by the remaining tanks of 9.Panzer-Division and 11.Panzer-Division, which attacked the American perimeter near Bad Honnef, about 7 kilometers downstream from Remagen. By this time, both German formations were divisions in name only—they could muster just thirty serviceable tanks for the attack, which did little more than consume the available stocks of fuel. Generalleutnant Fritz Bayerlein, the commander of the Panzer-Lehr-Division, was given the task of reducing the bridgehead. In addition to the infantry of five Volksgrenadier divisions, Bayerlein had under his control the tanks of his own division, Panzer-Brigade 106 Feldherrnhalle, and the staff of LIII.Armeekorps. The remnants of the two divisions that had made the attack on Bad Honnef remained in the area for some time and reinforcements were being assembled in the shape of Panzergruppe Hudel, an ad-hoc formation consisting of the Tiger II tanks of schwere Panzer-Abteilung 506, the equivalent of two full companies of Jagdpanthers from schwere Panzerjäger-Abteilung 654, and schwere Panzerjäger-Abteilung 512 equipped with Jagdtiger tank destroyers. Commanded by Major Helmut Hudel, a veteran of the Russian, North African, and Italian campaigns, this powerful armored group was continuously hampered by supply and mechanical problems, with three Jagdtigers lost to breakdowns and the Jagdpanther battalion never able to field more than eight or nine of its full complement at any one time. It was March 23 before Hudel's Kampfgruppe was fully assembled and able to take part in the fighting, by which time the Americans were breaking out of their bridgehead.

The inability of Bayerlein and Model to agree on a coordinated plan of attack, partly due to their mutual animosity, meant that the attempts to destroy the American bridgehead were limited to small unit actions where Allied penetrations were hampered more by the terrain and weather. On March 11, the day Kesselring arrived at Model's headquarters, the Americans were able to complete the first pontoon bridge over the Rhine and were pouring men and equipment into the Remagen bridgehead. Up to this point, the German resistance on the Western front had been conducted with aggressiveness and efficiency, meeting each new emergency by scraping together just enough tanks and troops to at least slow the Allied advance. Now mobile units could not find enough fuel to even reach the front line, if they were lucky enough to have any vehicles to move. Although German industry had been able to sustain—and in some cases increase—production through 1944, the Allied bombing campaign was at last having an effect and all classes of weapons and ammunition were in short supply. In addition, the bulk of the Wehrmacht's armored force was deployed against the Red Army, which had already overrun East Prussia and most of Pomerania. Until the end of the war, the defense in the west would be left for the most part to battle groups formed from depleted formations and training school personnel backed by the boys and old men of the Volkssturm.

On March 13, US 3rd Army commenced a large scale assault into the Saar-Palatinate region, crossing the Moselle on the following day and breaking through the Siegfried Line within three days. On March 21, US Army units advanced from the Remagen bridgehead as far as Siegburg, a distance of over 10 kilometers; that night, elements of 3rd Army crossed the Rhine at Nierstein-Oppenheim, 15 kilometers south of Mainz, almost unopposed. By March 23, Major Hudel's Kampfgruppe was at last committed to the battle. Supported by the Panzergrenadiers of 11.Panzer-Division in a counterattack near Eitorf on the northern flank of the Remagen bridgehead, the heavy tanks and tank destroyers could not hope to hold the strong American armored units. The next day Kesselring ordered Model to send what remained of 11.Panzer-Division to the south to support Oberkommando Oberrhein.

As Hudel's tanks were pushed back from the Remagen bridgehead, the British and Canadian armies in the northern sector of the front launched the largest offensive of the campaign since the D-Day landings, codenamed Operation Plunder. During the first weeks of February 1945, the area between the Maas and the Rhine east of the

Dutch-German border had been cleared and British tanks had fought their way through the thick forests of the Reichswald. They pushed the Germans back to Wesel, where General Alfred Schlemm's 1.Fallschirm-Armee was able to hold a sizeable bridge-head until March 10, when the last units withdrew across the Rhine and destroyed the bridges behind them. The Germans had been allowed to withdraw in good order and 1.Fallschirm-Armee, which was now defending the east bank of the river, had been able to save most its artillery and supply elements. In addition, Schlemm could call on the tanks of 116.Panzer-Division and 15.Panzergrenadier-Division, although these two formations combined were able to field the equivalent of two Panzer companies.

On March 23 the main assault on the Rhine began, preceded by an intense artillery barrage that seriously wounded General Schlemm. General Günther Blumentritt, the commander of LVII.Panzerkorps, would command briefly in his stead. As the British and Canadians were crossing the river, Hitler demanded that a counterattack be launched at the American bridgehead at Oppenheim, south of Mainz, only to be told that not a single reserve formation was available on the Western front. Indeed, the British crossing and the expansion of the resulting bridgehead had met with such surprisingly light resistance that Prime Minis-ter Churchill crossed the river on the second day, venturing as far forward as the Wesel railway bridge, just 200 meters from the town center. By March 25 the town of Wesel, which had been almost completely destroyed by the Allied artillery, was securely in British hands. On the southern front, both Mainz and Darmstadt were captured by American troops on March 26; it is telling that the OKW situation map for that day records no German units in the area except the headquarters of 7.Armee. However, at Aschaffenburg, just 20 kilometers to the east, the Germans hung on tenaciously until April 3, defending the town with little more than a battalion of engineers and an increasing number of stragglers.

As the Allies advanced deeper into German territory, the many training and replacement establishments were ordered to form defensive battle groups from whatever personnel and vehicles might be available. Many of these formations were organized with very little notice and some enjoyed a measure of success, such as Panzer-Lehr und Ausbildungs-Abteilung Tiger, formed from the staff of Truppenübungsplatz Paderborn, east of Dortmund. Fighting as infantry, the 160 men of the battalion were able to hold, and then push back, an American assault on the small town of Wewer. Two days later an armored group, made up of eighteen Tiger I and nine Tiger II tanks and referred to as Panzergruppe Paderborn, attacked US Army units at Borchen, 2 kilometers to the south.[2]

As courageous as the German defensive efforts were, they could not accomplish any more than small local successes. On April 1, 1945, the two US Armies, which had been heading east and north, linked up at Lippstadt on the Dortmund-Paderborn road and cut off over 300,000 German troops in the Ruhr area. On the following day British armored units, opposed by the last tanks of 15.Panzergrenadier-Division, reached the Dortmund-Ems canal but found that all the bridges had been destroyed. The far bank was held by a number of Hitler Youth boys, led by officers of the Waffen-SS who preferred to be killed rather than allow the enemy to pass. Making the best use of the terrain and harassing the British tank crews with accurate sniper fire, the Germans held on against concerted attacks and intense artillery bombardments. After two days of fighting the British armored divisions gave up and simply bypassed the German position. It was not until April 6 that the best part of two British infantry divisions were

---

2 *In addition to a number of the school's instructors, the Tiger tanks were operated by crews drafted from schwere Panzer-Abteilung 424 and schwere Panzer-Abteilung 508. By April 12, all the tanks had either been lost or were inoperable.*

able to dislodge the defenders.[3]

As the British armored units were pushing towards the east, a small Kampfgruppe was moving in the opposite direction, almost straight towards them. Consisting of just five Panther tanks from the Fallingbostel training area and under the command of Major Paul Schulze, the group was ordered to make contact with Panzer-Lehr-Division, which was fighting in the Ruhr Pocket. Joined by a platoon of six Tiger tanks led by Oberleutnant Rudolf Fehrmann, Schulze's tanks were able to push over 30 kilometers into the enemy's rear before they were forced into battle on April 9 at Wietersheim, about 40 kilometers east of Hanover. In the brief fight that followed, four of the Panthers were lost and one of the Tigers was damaged. The Germans were, however, able to break through the Allied defenses into the outskirts of Frille, north-east of Minden, and take prisoner thirty British paratroopers who were holding the town. The damaged Tiger, commanded by Unteroffizier Franzen,

returned to Fallingbostel on its own tracks and was repaired. By April 11, Schulze's remaining tanks had fought their way to Bückeburg, a few kilometers to the south of Wietersheim, where two of his Tigers become bogged down as they were negotiating the muddy tracks of a heavily wooded area. The surviving Panther attempted to recover the heavy tanks but also became bogged. Realizing that they could not be moved, Schulze ordered the crews to destroy all three tanks. Shortly after this, Oberleutnant Fehrmann and the crews of the abandoned tanks, unable to keep up with Schulze, were captured by a unit of the US Army advancing from the south. The remaining tanks moved on to Achum, where they were engaged by an American armored unit that was able to knock out the Tiger of Feldwebel Bellof, killing the crew. However, the last Tiger, with Major Schulze on board, accounted for three Sherman tanks and an armored car before capturing a fuel truck complete with its cargo and maps. During the night the Tiger, with the captured fuel truck, reached Lauenau and early the next morning passed through Nienstadt, directed by an American MP who failed to realize that they were Germans. On the western side of the town, the Tiger ran into a column of Allied vehicles. After destroying a tank and an armored car, it was also able to free about 200 German soldiers who had been held captive in a nearby barn. Now with a second American truck in

tow, Major Schulze decided to head back towards the German lines. At dawn on April 12, Schulze discovered a large Allied command post at Barsinghausen and made plans to attack it. However, the Tiger finally ran out of fuel at Hohenbostel, less than 2 kilometers short of their objective, where Major Schulze ordered the crew to destroy the tank and disbanded his Kampfgruppe. In the meantime, the Tiger of Unteroffizier Franzen, which had returned to Fallingbostel to be repaired, was ordered to move to Ostenholz and report to Kampfgruppe Grosan.

This battle group was commanded by Oberst Erhard Grosan and was made up of two Tigers, a single Panther, and two assault guns from the Panzertruppenschule Bergen with supporting infantry including sailors from the 2.Marine-Division. Oberst Grosan had been seriously wounded earlier in the war, losing a leg, and had been appointed acting commander of the Bergen tank school when he returned to duty. On April 11, Grosan's Kampfgruppe attacked British positions at Engehausen near Buchholz, managing to halt an enemy advance. On the following day, Franzen's Tiger arrived and was immediately used in an attack on the Aller bridgehead near Essel. Grosan's men were able to destroy two of the new British Comet tanks and several other vehicles before withdrawing to the cover of a nearby forest. On April 14, as the Kampfgruppe was mov-

---

3   *The Hitler Youth contingent is described in British accounts as the pupils of a 'Cadet School' located at Hanover, led by their instructors. However, most German language sources are clear that the officers were SS personnel. The 'Cadets' may have been the pupils of the Nationalpolitische Erziehungsanstalten located at Haselünne, to the north of the British frontline, which was the National Political Teaching Institute for the state of Hanover.*

ing south from Ostenholz, an armor-piercing round from a Comet slammed into the side of Franzen's Tiger as it drove along a creek bed from a range of just 60 meters. Although the tank was completely destroyed, Franzen and the crew managed to escape.

The remainder of Grosan's Kampfgruppe moved on to Ahlften, where they attacked British positions on the Halburger Strasse north of Soltau, between Bremen and Lüneburg. Withdrawing to the south through Bassel, one of the remaining Tigers ran out of fuel and Grosan ordered the crew to remain at the approach to the town to form a static defense position. Three days later, on April 17, British attempts to outflank Soltau were repulsed by this lone Tiger. On the following day, the remaining serviceable Tiger of Kampfgruppe Grosan managed to halt the forward elements of the British 7th Armored Division at Bispingen, 15 kilometers further to the north. At the same time, the tanks of Kampfgruppe Benningsen from Panzer-Division Clausewitz were able to drive the British from their positions around Wittingen, in the area east of Hanover, although they could not keep the enemy out of Ülzen and Lüneburg further to the north. On April 19, the British renewed their attacks around Wittingen but were forced to withdraw when a single Tiger of Kampfgruppe Benningsen from Panzer-Division Clausewitz was able to halt the advance of a complete tank regiment. Major von Ben-

ningsen's tanks fought throughout the day but lost contact with the other units of the division once darkness fell. They moved towards the forest near Ehra-Lessien, north of Wolfsburg, and managed to inadvertently outflank and almost annihilate an American blocking force. The next day was spent preparing an attack on the last remaining bridge across the Weser-Elbe canal near Fallersleben, and in the early hours of April 21 the road between Gifhorn and Brome was secured. In the morning gloom, the German tanks were able to mingle with an American transport column undetected until they reached the canal, where an anti-tank gun position suddenly opened fire and destroyed the lead tank. Benningsen's tanks returned fire and raced forward. They captured the bridge and moved forward to Ehmen, in the process passing a full company of American tanks that were too busy refueling to attempt to stop the Panzers[4] Reaching the safety of the Elm Mountains, without any fuel and little ammunition, Benningsen decided

---

4 *The suggestion that the Panthers which led the assault on the canal bridge were equipped with infra-red sighting equipment is almost certainly incorrect. Although a number of tanks were fitted with the devices, there is no record that any were used in combat and very good evidence that they were removed to prevent their capture. The Germans also believed that British and American tanks were fitted with sights that could detect and fire on the infrared signal.*

to disband the Kampfgruppe and ordered the men try to destroy their tanks and make their escape as best they could. The last tank of Panzer-Division Clausewitz, the Tiger that had stayed at Wittingen, continued to defend its position, holding up the British advance again on May 1 until it was simply overwhelmed.

Impressive as these local victories were, they could not alter the strategic situation. While Grosan and Benningsen's battle groups were fighting until they no longer had the means to do so, Schweinfurt and Nuremberg had fallen to the allies. In the north Bremen was taken and in the south the Danube had been crossed. On April 25, American soldiers were able to meet Soviet units on the Elbe River at Torgau, southwest of Berlin. On the day the last tank of Panzer-Division Clausewitz was battling a British armored regiment outside Wittingen, the remnants of General Walter Wenck's 12.Armee, which Hitler had earlier ordered to relieve Berlin, was surrendering to the Americans. In less than a week, units of US 3rd Army were fighting in Czechoslovakia. On Monday, May 7, Generaloberst Alfred Jodl, the Oberkommando der Wehrmacht chief of staff, signed Germany's unconditional surrender. All units of the Wehrmacht were to cease operations at 1 minute after midnight on the next day.

Although the war in Europe was over, one final duty remained for the Panzertruppen. On May 11, 1945, British authorities in the port city of Kiel formed a security unit composed of German prisoners of war, referred to as I.Abteiling, Feldjäger-Regiment 1. The battalion's personnel were drawn almost exclusively from Panzer-Regiment 35 and were armed with German army rifles and pistols. The officers and men were permitted to wear their insignia and decorations provided that any Swastikas or National Socialist references were removed. Overseen by the Feldjägerkommando, these men did not formally surrender their weapons until June 23, 1946 and must have been some of the last members of the Wehrmacht under arms.

PANZER-REGIMENT, APRIL 1945

On March 25, 1945, Oberkommando des Heeres, the high command of the army, ordered that all Panzer and Panzergrenadier divisions were to be re-organized in accordance with an instruction titled "Gliederung der Panzer-Division 45." Each division was to contain a single Panzer battalion made up of two companies of PzKpfw V Panther and two companies of PzKpfw IV tanks. Each company contained three platoons of three tanks, with a single tank allocated to the company headquarters. This new order called for the Panzer-Abteilung to be combined with a Panzergrenadier-Bataillon under a regimental headquarters to form a Gemischte, or mixed, Panzer-Regiment. In addition to the twenty Panthers on hand with the companies of the Panzer-Abteilung, the battalion staff and regimental headquarters were both allocated two PzKpfw V Panther tanks. The single exception to this order was 232.Panzer-Division, which was to retain its unique establishment. These mixed units should not be confused with the Panzer-Sturmgeschütz battalions, which were formed from mid-1943 and sometimes referred to as Gemischte Panzer-Abteilungen. Those divisions unable to comply with the March 1945 order, due to a lack of personnel or equipment, were to be reorganized as Kampfgruppe Panzer-Division 45, the structure of which was similar to the full division with a much reduced infantry and artillery component. Detailed instructions in the form of Kriegstärkenachweisung were issued on April 1, 1945, and all formations were to report their progress by the beginning of May. Detailed records from this period are fragmentary at best; however, it is known that of the divisions serving in the west, 116.Panzer-Division formed a Kampfgruppe from the remaining elements of the division, comprising a Panzer-Kompanie with fourteen Panthers and a platoon of four Sturmtiger 38cm self-propelled guns. The remaining tanks and personnel of 2.Panzer-Division were reorganized as a Kampfgruppe Panzer-Division after absorbing Panzer-Division Thüringen, which was actually a brigade-sized formation made up of training and replacement units. The reorganization of 9.Panzer-Division was somewhat unique in that the first battalion of the Panzer regiment was made up of two companies of PzKpfw V Panthers with a single PzKpfw IV company, while the second battalion was equipped with a mixture of Sturmgeschütz III, Jagdpanzer 38, and Panzer IV/70(V) tank destroyers scavenged from the remnants of various units.

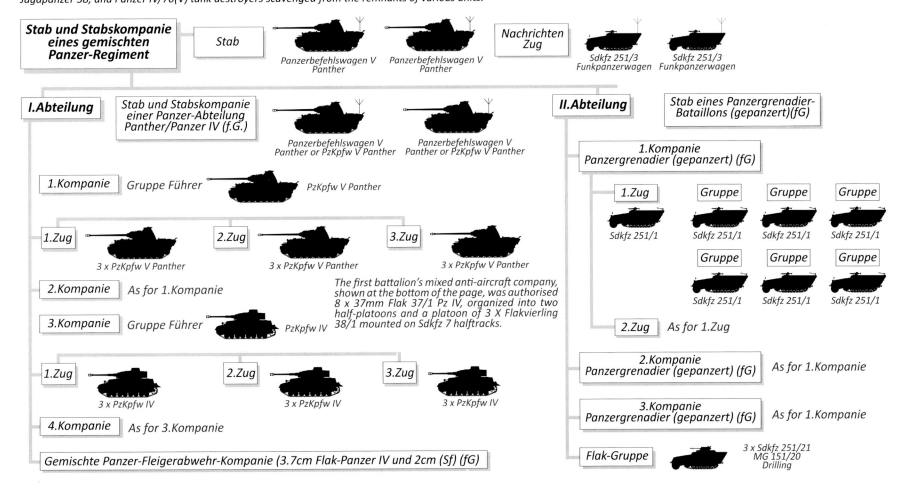

PANZERS IN THE WEST, MARCH–APRIL 1945

	MARCH													APRIL													
Unit	Stug III	Stug IV	StuH 42	JagdPz IV	Jagdpanther	Jagdtiger	Tiger II	Tiger I	Panther	Pz IV/70(V)	Pz IV/70(A)	PzKfpw IV	PzKfw III	Stug III	Stug IV	StuH 42	JagdPz IV	Jagdpanther	Jagdtiger	Tiger II	Tiger I	Panther	Pz IV/70(V)	Pz IV/70(A)	PzKfpw IV	PzKfw III	Notes
2.Panzer-Division	22*								35*			16*															* Reported March 15, 1945.
II/Panzer-Regiment 3		10																									
9.Panzer-Division	2*								18*	8*		5*															* Reported March 15, 1945.
II/Panzer-Regiment 33														9										10			
11.Panzer-Division	6*								33*			17*															* Reported March 15, 1945.
116.Panzer-Division	11*								32*	7*		6*															* Reported March 15, 1945.
I/Panzer-Regiment 16				15																							
Panzer-Lehr-Division									29*	14*		6*															* Reported March 15, 1945.
I/Panzer-Lehr-Regiment 130									10																		
II/Panzer-Lehr-Regiment 130				35																							
3.Panzergrenadier-Division	9*								20*			1*															* Reported March 15, 1945.
15.Panzergrenadier-Division	14*								21*			3*															* Reported March 15, 1945.
Panzer-Abteilung 115												19															
25.Panzergrenadier-Division																											
Panzerjäger-Abteilung 25														6													
17.SS-Panzergrenadier-Division	62*											2*															* Reported March 15, 1945.
Panzer-Brigade 106									5*	7*		3*															* Reported March 15, 1945.
Schwere-Panzer-Abteilung 424							3	1		1																	* 3.Kompanie only
Schwere-Panzer-Abteilung 506							7*													6							* 15 tanks reported on March 15, 1945
Schwere-Panzer-Abteilung 507		3				21*																		2			* 2.Kompanie and 3.Kompanie
Schwere-Panzer-Abteilung 508																				3*	1*	6*					* 1.Kompanie only
Schwere-Panzer-Abteilung 510																				6*							* 3.Kompanie only
Schwere-Panzer-Abteilung 511																				8*							* 3.Kompanie only
Panzer-Abteilung (Fkl) 301								13*																			* Reported March 15, 1945.
Schwere-Panzerjäger-Abteilung 512						17													14								
Schwere-Panzerjäger-Abteilung 559				5														19									
Schwere-Panzerjäger-Abteilung 655																		10									
Sturmgeschütz-Brigade 667																							3				
Panzer-Lehr-Abteilung Putlos														1		1				2	10		11				
Kampfgruppe Grosan														2						2	1						
Panzer-Kompanie Kummersdorf														1		1					1*	4		2		1	* Tiger I (Porsche) as static defense
Panzergruppe Paderborn																				3	5	4			4		
Tigergruppe Fehrmann																					6	5*					* Kampfgruppe Schulze
Kampfgruppe Wiking					7																						
OB West	53	17							15					40	17	2											

Accurate records from this period are scarce and this chart was compiled from several sources, including personal accounts. As with the other charts in this book, the armored vehicles allocated to the Panzerjäger battalions of Grenadier, Volksgrenadier, and other infantry formations are not included. During this period, the Jagdpanzer 38(t) Hetzer tank destroyer was the most numerous armored vehicle at the front, with 256 reported on hand in the last three months of the war. Many of these vehicles were allocated to newly raised infantry formations, such as the RAD and Marine-Infanterie divisions. By the end of 1944, all the independent Panzer brigades, with the exception of Panzer-Brigade 106 Feldherrnhalle, had been disbanded with their personnel and material absorbed by rebuilt Panzer and Panzergrenadier divisions. The Tiger (P) of Panzer-Kompanie Kummersdorf was one of only two completed Porsche prototypes and although immobile, could still fire its gun. The tank was supported by a Volkssturm unit in the defense of the Wehrmacht's weapons testing facility at Kummersdorf. Kampfgruppe Wiking refers to the 150 men from SS-Panzer-Regiment 5, under the command of Hauptsturmführer Nicolussi-Leck, who had been sent to Germany to pick up new tanks in early April 1945. After some searching, they took control of seven Jagdpanthers from the MNH factory at Hannover-Laatzen. Nicolussi-Leck's Kampfgruppe spent the next weeks fighting against American armored units in the area between Celle and Wolfsburg until April 16, when they surrendered. This was the only unit of the SS-Wiking division to fight on the Western Front.

PANZER-DIVISION CLAUSEWITZ, APRIL 1945

Typical of the ad-hoc formations created in the last months of the conflict, Panzer-Division Clausewitz was ordered into existence on Wednesday April 4, 1945, barely five weeks before the end of the war, with the stipulation that the division was to be ready for operations by the following Sunday. Panzer-Division Clausewitz was originally to be formed from elements of a Panzer replacement and training unit and the anti-tank battalion from Panzergrenadier-Division Grossdeutschland and elements of 325.Infanterie-Division. However, the infantry units were heavily engaged at the front and could not be spared. Panzerjäger-Abteilung Grossdeutschland had lost all its new Panzer IV/70(V) tank destroyers in East Prussia and had to be refitted with Sturmgeschütz III assault guns before the battalion could join the division. On April 6, new orders were issued stating that Panzer-Division Clausewitz would be organized from remnants of various units. These would eventually include Panzer-Division Holstein (which had been largely destroyed in the fighting for Kolberg), parts of 233.Reserve-Panzer-Division, and the tanks of the Schiess-Schule Putlos, the German army's tank gunnery school. Although the new division lacked transport and a full complement of armored vehicles, many of its personnel were combat veterans or instructors and the division's commander, Generalleutnant Martin Unrein, was a highly experienced and competent officer who had led 14.Panzer-Division in Russia and, briefly, the III.(germanisches) SS-Panzerkorps. The division's original complement of armored infantry was provided by Panzergrenadier-Ersatz und Ausbildungs-Regiment Feldherrnhalle, a training and replacement unit consisting of three battalions and totalling 3,321 men. Although strong in numbers of personnel, the regiment had no transport for its Panzergrenadier companies, which were in effect ordinary infantry units. Soon after joining the division, the regiment was reduced from three to two battalions. The surplus personnel formed a second regiment and the two formations were then referred to as Feldherrnhalle 1 and Feldherrnhalle 2. This is first noted in a report of April 12, 1945. Confusingly, reports for April 17 and April 28 both show Feldherrnhalle 1 as having three battalions, the latter report referring to "III/Panzergrenadier Ers u Aus Regt Feldherrnhalle." Attached to the division on April 6, 1945, Panzergrenadier-Regiment 42 was formed from the remnants of 233.Panzer-Division. This unit also lacked most of its authorized motor transport, with just the Panzerjäger Kompanie having its full complement.

Divisions-Stab

Formed from the headquarters staff of Panzer-Division Holstein, which had been almost completely destroyed in the fighting in Prussia and Pomerania in March 1945.

Begleit-Kompanie (mot) Clausewitz

This company, a headquarters security unit, is first mentioned in the April 9, 1945, report.

Nachrichten-Kompanie (mot)

Formed from signals personnel seconded from Heeresgruppe H. First referred to as Panzer-Nachricten-Kompanie Clausewitz on April 12, 1945.

Panzer-Aufklärungs-Abteilung Elbe

Stabs Begleit-Kompanie (mot)

Panzerspähwagen-Kompanie

Panzer-Aufklärungs-Kompanie (gep)

On April 17, 1945 this Abteilung reported that 2 x Sdkfz 234/1, 2 x Sdkfz 234/4, 29 x Sdkfz 250/8, 24 x Sdkfz 250/9, 6 x Sdkfz 221, and 2 x Sdkfz 222 were on hand.

Panzer-Aufklärungs-Abteilung Döring

Possibly raised from Panzer-Aufklärungs-Abteilung 16, this battalion joined the division on April 13, 1945.

6 x Sdkfz 234/4

Panzerjäger-Abteilung Grossdeutschland

Panzerjäger-Kompanie

Stug III

Panzerjäger-Kompanie

Stug III

Panzerjäger-Kompanie

Stug III

Versorgungs-Kompanie

Panzerjäger-Abteilung 661

Formed from two companies of the Grossdeutschland division and one company from Panzer-Abteilung Potsdam. All companies were equipped with Sturmgeschütz III assault guns and at one time the battalion had a motorized Begleit-Kompanie attached to the headquarters. On April 6, 1945, the battalion reported that thirty-one assault guns were on hand.

Sources differ here, with at least one account suggesting that the battalion was attached to the division from April 9, 1945 with three Panzerjäger companies. Other records state that the battalion was disbanded on February 19 and used to rebuild Panzerjäger-Abteilungen 682, 683, and 686.

Panzer Pionier Bataillon

Formed from Panzer-Pionier-Bataillon 144 of Panzer-Division Holstein.

Pionier-Ersatz und Ausbildung-Regiment Fredericia

Made up of two Pionier companies, this unit is first mentioned as en route on April 14, 1945 and may have never arrived.

Heeres-Flak-Artillerie-Abteilung 321

It is probable that only the headquarters troops of this unit reached the division.

Panzer-Artillerie Abteilung 144

This unit was formed from the remnants of the artillery assets of Panzer-Division Holstein and one battery of light field howitzers seconded from 233. Panzer-Division. On April 15, the battalion was reported as still being in transit to the division.

Panzergrenadier-Regiment Feldherrnhalle 1

Regiments Stab | **Begleit-Kompanie** | **Pionier-Kompanie**

I Abteilung | **II Abteilung** | **III Abteilung**

Each Abteilung contained a Stabs-Begleit-Kompanie and four Panzergrenadier companies.

Panzergrenadier-Regiment Feldherrnhalle 2

Regiments Stab

I Abteilung | **II Abteilung**

Each Abteilung contained a Stabs-Kompanie and five Panzergrenadier companies.

Panzergrenadier-Regiment 42

Regiments Stab | **Panzerjäger-Kompanie**

I Abteilung | **II Abteilung**

Each Abteilung contained a Stabs-Kompanie and four Panzergrenadier companies.

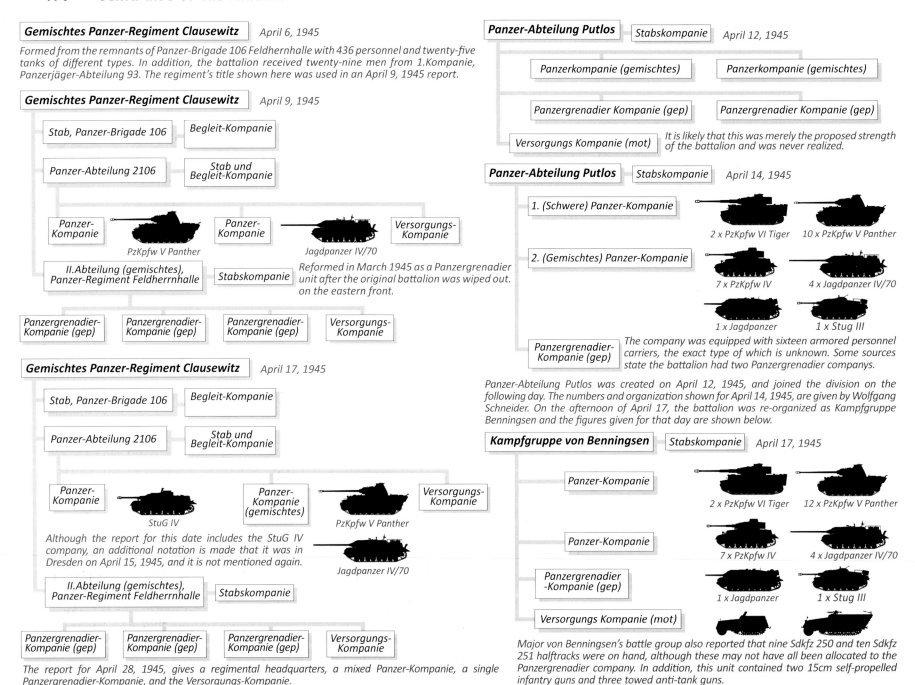

Gemischtes Panzer-Regiment Clausewitz   *April 6, 1945*

Formed from the remnants of Panzer-Brigade 106 Feldhernhalle with 436 personnel and twenty-five tanks of different types. In addition, the battalion received twenty-nine men from 1.Kompanie, Panzerjäger-Abteilung 93. The regiment's title shown here was used in an April 9, 1945 report.

Gemischtes Panzer-Regiment Clausewitz   *April 9, 1945*

Stab, Panzer-Brigade 106 — Begleit-Kompanie

Panzer-Abteilung 2106 — Stab und Begleit-Kompanie

Panzer-Kompanie — *PzKpfw V Panther*

Panzer-Kompanie — *Jagdpanzer IV/70*

Versorgungs-Kompanie

II.Abteilung (gemischtes), Panzer-Regiment Feldherrnhalle — Stabskompanie   *Reformed in March 1945 as a Panzergrenadier unit after the original battalion was wiped out. on the eastern front.*

Panzergrenadier-Kompanie (gep)

Panzergrenadier-Kompanie (gep)

Panzergrenadier-Kompanie (gep)

Versorgungs-Kompanie

Gemischtes Panzer-Regiment Clausewitz   *April 17, 1945*

Stab, Panzer-Brigade 106 — Begleit-Kompanie

Panzer-Abteilung 2106 — Stab und Begleit-Kompanie

Panzer-Kompanie — *StuG IV*

Panzer-Kompanie (gemischtes) — *PzKpfw V Panther* / *Jagdpanzer IV/70*

Versorgungs-Kompanie

Although the report for this date includes the StuG IV company, an additional notation is made that it was in Dresden on April 15, 1945, and it is not mentioned again.

II.Abteilung (gemischtes), Panzer-Regiment Feldherrnhalle — Stabskompanie

Panzergrenadier-Kompanie (gep)

Panzergrenadier-Kompanie (gep)

Panzergrenadier-Kompanie (gep)

Versorgungs-Kompanie

The report for April 28, 1945, gives a regimental headquarters, a mixed Panzer-Kompanie, a single Panzergrenadier-Kompanie, and the Versorgungs-Kompanie.

Panzer-Abteilung Putlos   Stabskompanie   *April 12, 1945*

Panzerkompanie (gemischtes)

Panzerkompanie (gemischtes)

Panzergrenadier Kompanie (gep)

Panzergrenadier Kompanie (gep)

Versorgungs Kompanie (mot)   *It is likely that this was merely the proposed strength of the battalion and was never realized.*

Panzer-Abteilung Putlos   Stabskompanie   *April 14, 1945*

1. (Schwere) Panzer-Kompanie — *2 x PzKpfw VI Tiger* / *10 x PzKpfw V Panther*

2. (Gemischtes) Panzer-Kompanie — *7 x PzKpfw IV* / *4 x Jagdpanzer IV/70* / *1 x Jagdpanzer* / *1 x Stug III*

Panzergrenadier-Kompanie (gep)   *The company was equipped with sixteen armored personnel carriers, the exact type of which is unknown. Some sources state the battalion had two Panzergrenadier companys.*

Panzer-Abteilung Putlos was created on April 12, 1945, and joined the division on the following day. The numbers and organization shown for April 14, 1945, are given by Wolfgang Schneider. On the afternoon of April 17, the battalion was re-organized as Kampfgruppe Benningsen and the figures given for that day are shown below.

Kampfgruppe von Benningsen   Stabskompanie   *April 17, 1945*

Panzer-Kompanie — *2 x PzKpfw VI Tiger* / *12 x PzKpfw V Panther*

Panzer-Kompanie — *7 x PzKpfw IV* / *4 x Jagdpanzer IV/70*

Panzergrenadier-Kompanie (gep) — *1 x Jagdpanzer* / *1 x Stug III*

Versorgungs Kompanie (mot)

Major von Benningsen's battle group also reported that nine Sdkfz 250 and ten Sdkfz 251 halftracks were on hand, although these may not have all been allocated to the Panzergrenadier company. In addition, this unit contained two 15cm self-propelled infantry guns and three towed anti-tank guns.

5.01. Captured after the fighting for Ostheim north of Colmar on January 31,1945 by US 75th Infantry Division, which had been attached to the French First Army for the capture of Neuf-Brisach near Colmar, this Hotchkiss H-39 light tank or Panzerkampfwagen 39-H 735 (f) must have been a rare sight by this time.

5.02. Photographed in Clervaux on January 25, 1945 this Panther ausf G of 3.Kompanie, Panzer-Regiment 2 was abandoned by its crew due to a mechanical failure. In early 1945, most of the Panthers of this battalion were November 1944 production models identified by the self-cleaning rear idler, raised housing for the crew compartment heater, and the Flammvernichcter exhaust mufflers. The company number of 301 is visible on the turret side.

5.03. Abandoned in the streets of the small town of Mittlewihr, just north of Colmar in France, this Panzer IV/70(A) was knocked out when 7.Kompanie, Panzer Regiment 2, which had been attached to Panzer-Brigade 106 Feldherrnhalle, attempted to take the town in December 1944. The fighting here continued well into January 1945 and damaged the town so completely that it was never rebuilt. Parts of a medieval church and a wall at the entry of the village are all that remain today.

5.04. Although no identifying markings are visible on either of these Sturmgeschütz III assault guns except the Balkenkreuz on the rear of the nearest vehicle, both Panzerjäger-Abteilung 38 of 2.Panzer-Division and Panzerjäger-Abteilung 212 of 212. Volks-Grenadier-Division were both involved in the fighting for Wallendorf on the Luxembourg-German border, where this photograph was taken, and both were equipped with a number of these vehicles. Note the pattern impressed into the Zimmerit on the nearest assault gun indicative of vehicles manufactured by the firm of Alkett at their Berlin plant.

5.05. Photographed in February 1945 after the surrender of the German units defending the area around Castle Rath at Düren, south-west of Cologne, this Sturmgeschütz III assault gun has a stylized mouth and eyes painted onto the Topfblende gun mantlet. Neither the US Army or OKW situation maps for this period show any units equipped with these vehicles in the area, although it is possible that Sturmgeschütz-Abteilung 1363 of 363.Volksgrenadier-Division, equipped with Hetzer tank destroyers, may have had a small number of Sturmgeschütz III from another unit temporarily attached.

5.06. A Tiger I of Panzer-Kompanie Hummel photographed in Elsdorf in February 1945 shortly after the company was detached from schwere Panzer-Abteilung 506. German sources insist that this tank was caught in the debris of the house in the background as it reversed during a fire fight with Pershing tanks of US 3rd Armored Division, while American accounts state it was hit and disabled by a Pershing. This vehicle, number 201, is also show in the illustration section on page 138.

5.07. Abandoned in one of the open fields around Hargarten, some 25 kilometers north of Bitburg, this Panzerjäger V Jagdpanther of schwere Panzerjäger-Abteilung 654 is one of a number the battalion lost here. Commanded by Major Karl-Heinz Noak, this formation was under the direct control of Heeresgruppe G during the Nordwind operation and suffered heavy casualties. By February 1945, the battalion had been reduced to just six serviceable tank destroyers.

5.08. Photographed in March 1945, this Jagdtiger is one of two vehicles of schwere-Panzerjäger-Abteilung 653 that were abandoned by their crews near Morsbronn-les-Bains after both suffered mechanical failures. In his authoritative history of the battalion, author Karlheinz Münch states that this vehicle's commander, Feldwebel Heinz Telgmann, destroyed this Jagdtiger with a demolition charge. Although badly damaged, the vehicle's company number and Balkenkreuz insignia are still visible on the side of the fighting compartment and photographs of other Jagdtigers of this battalion suggest that the numbers all the company numbers were painted in solid black.

5.09. The official caption of this image states that these soldiers of the US 4th Cavalry Group were photographed in Flesch on March 2, 1945 taking cover behind this abandoned German tank. The correct location, however, is almost certainly Frechen just outside Cologne, which was, according to the published US 12th Army Group situation map, right on the front line on that date. Both the US Army and OKW situation maps for early March 1945 confirm German dispositions in the area and this Panther ausf A is probably from Panzer Regiment 33 of 9.Panzer-Division.

5.10. Disabled near the fortress town of Bitche, some 40 kilometers south-east of Saarbrücken in early March 1945, this Jagdpanzer 38(t) Hetzer tank destroyer may be from Panzerjäger-Abteilung(mot) 1316 of 16.Volks-Grenadier-Division, the only unit close to the town at that time equipped with these vehicles. The style of factory-applied camouflage is an identifying feature of the Hetzers manufactured by the Bömisch-Märische Maschinenfabrik (BMM) in occupied Czechoslovakia. Just visible to the left of the gun mantlet is a matte black rectangle, which was painted onto the hull from October 1944 in an effort to decoy enemy gunners away from the prominent drivers visor and vision block.

5.11. This Pzkpfw V Panther ausf G was photographed in the town of Kelberg, approximately 30 kilometers west of Koblenz on March 11, 1945, shortly after the town was captured by units of the US 11th Armored Division. According to the American account, Kelberg was defended by six German tanks including at least one Tiger II. In early March, 5.Panzerarmee was retreating through this area and it is likely that this Panther belonged to either 2.Panzer-Division or 9.Panzer-Division. The only unit on the Western Front equipped with the Tiger II at this time, schwere Panzer-Abteilung 506, was fighting much further to the north.

5.12. The Jagdpanther G2 depicted here of 1.Kompanie, schwere Panzerjäger-Abteilung 654 took part in the fighting around the village of Ginsterhahn, south of Cologne in the Ruhr pocket, in March 1945, when the company was attached to Kampfgruppe Paffrath. Commanded by Oberleutnant Waldemar Paffrath, this battle group consisted of the first and fourth companies of schwere Panzerjäger-Abteilung 654, the latter made up of the surviving Nashorn 88mm self-propelled anti-tank guns of 1.Kompanie, schwere Panzerjäger-Abteilung 525, and elements of 11.Panzer-Division.

5.13. Photographed in Dörgerstrasse in the town of Osterode am Harz, north-east of Kassel in Germany, on April 12, 1945 this Tiger II was allocated to schwere Panzer-Abteilung 507 and may be one of the tanks of the battalion's 3.Kompanie, which was attached to SS-Panzer Brigade Westfalen between March 30 and April 11, 1945. In his exhaustive works on the Tiger battalions, Wolfgang Schneider states that this vehicle had broken down outside the Gasthof, visible in the background, due to track damage and was abandoned there. However, in the following days the tank was photographed from several angles and in all photos the tracks appear intact. The official caption suggests that this vehicle was knocked out by a 90mm round and towed into the town by the battalion's Werkstatt-Kompanie and a point of impact can be discerned on the turret side just behind the spare tracks. This vehicle is also depicted in the colored illustration section on page 146.

5.14. The scene at Aschaffenburg in northwest Bavaria after the heavy fighting which took place here in late March and early April 1945. This was one of the few German towns where the civilian population took an active part in the defense, with both local Volkssturm and Hitler Youth members attempting to halt the American advance. It is entirely possible that these tanks did not in fact take part in the battle and may have been left in this open space outside the town awaiting repair or cannibalization. A detailed US Army account of the fighting mentions the use of a single tank by the Germans and that was a captured M4 Sherman.

5.15. The railway yards at Aschaffenburg photographed after the town's capture by units of the US Army in April 1945. These complete Panther turrets were probably destined to be converted to Pantherstellung, a static fortification made up of a concrete bunker or the purpose-built OT-Stahlunterstand, which was a metal box capable of accommodating a crew of three, topped by the turret of a tank. A special low-profile cupola was designed for the Pantherstellung turrets but photographic evidence confirms that many were standard Panther turrets and a number of installations were complete tanks, buried up to the top edge of the hull. The camouflage pattern on the nearest turret is an interesting variation on the factory-applied schemes.

5.16. An Sdkfz 11 HKL Abschlussausführung half-track abandoned by the roadside. The German term translates literally as final version, however it was probably applied to vehicles to indicate a simplified model. These late production, cargo carrying vehicles were produced by converting Sdkfz 11/3 half-tracks, which had originally been designed to deploy poison gas.

5.17. Photographed in April 1945 outside the Krupp- owned Grusonwerk Magdeburg-Buckau factory, south-west of Berlin, the vehicles shown here are all obsolete Pzkpfw III tanks, probably ausf F or early ausf G models, with some later features retro-fitted such as the additional mantlet armor on the tanks second from the left and at far right. At the end of the war the factory was assembling the Sturmgeschütz IV but was also involved in other projects including the development of new torpedoes. I can offer no explanation as to why the tanks shown here would have been sent to the Magdeburg plant. It is entirely possible that they were part of a scratch unit made up of older training vehicles sent to defend the plant, a common practice at this stage of the war. However, a report compiled by the headquarters of US 30th Infantry Division, which was responsible for the city's capture, makes no mention of any German armored vehicles despite describing many of the weapons employed in the town's defense in some detail.

5.18. Shown here is the very heavily damaged interior of the workshop of Panzer- Ersatz und Ausbildungs-Abteilung 35 located at Bamberg, south-east of Schweinfurt on the river Main, after its capture. This formation was a training and replacement unit that provided tank crews for, amongst others, Panzer-Regiment 25, Panzer-Regiment 35, and Panzer-Regiment 36. The tank closest to the camera is an early Pzkpfw III fitted with a turret from a Tauchpanzer, a vehicle modified to run underwater, identified by the flange around the bottom edge of the turret. The other tanks are a Pzkpfw IV ausf G and a Panther ausf D identified by the early drum-style commander's cupola. In March 1945 many of the officers and men of this battalion were transferred to Denmark and in April the remainder were absorbed by Panzer-Ausbildungs-Verband Franken and Kampfgruppe Massenebach.

5.18a. Although we cannot be certain this Pzkpfw V ausf D may be one of the seven such tanks of Panzer- Ersatz und Ausbildungs-Abteilung 35 attached to Kampfgruppe Massenebach during the defense of Bamberg. Commanded by Oberst Dietrich Freiherr von Massenbach this battle group also contained a number of assault guns drawn from Panzerjäger-Ersatz-Abteilung 10 and as many as nine additional Panthers of Panzerlehrgang Erlangen, both training establishments. Of note is the very rough application of Zimmerit paste on the turret, not uncommon on these early Panthers, and the prominent Balkenkreuz. This tank was manufactured sometime prior to August 1943 when the communications port on the left hand side of the turret was dropped from production.

5.19. Photographed near Fernegierscheid, approximately 20 kilometers northeast of Remagen, in early April 1945 this Pzkpfw V Panther ausf G is from Panzer Regiment 15 of 11.Panzer-Division. This regiment took part in the counterattacks against the Remagen bridgehead which began on March 23. It had been reduced to a strength of thirty-three Panthers and seventeen Pzkpfw IV tanks by that time. Just visible on the spare track links is a company number rendered in small white numbers which may be 311.

5.20. Probably photographed in the Saar region sometime in the spring of 1945, this Sdkfz 7/1 2cm Flakvierling 38 was attached to the anti-aircraft company of the Panzerjäger battalion of 256.Volksgrenadier-Division. On the side of the cab be seen the division's unit insignia above the notation 'Pzkpfw.Jg.Abt.256' with the tactical symbol identifying an anti-aircraft gun company and the company number below that.

5.21. Commanded by Leutnant Sepp Tarlach this Jagdtiger of 1.Kompanie, schwere Panzerjäger-Abteilung 512 was disabled in the streets of Obernetphen near Siegen in early April 1945 by German infantrymen armed with Panzerfausts who apparently mistook it for an enemy tank. All ten of the first company's vehicles were marked from 1 to 10. The large white numbers are evident here with the letter X identifying the company. The second company used Y and it is usually assumed that 3.Kompanie numbers began with a Z, although no photographs have survived.

5.22. The next three photographs document the surrender of 1.Kompanie, schwere Panzerjäger-Abteilung 512 to units of the US 99th Infantry Division on 16 April 1945 at Iserlohn, south-east of Dortmund in Germany. Equipped with the Panzerjäger Tiger ausf B, perhaps better known as the Jagdtiger, this company had taken part in the attack on the Remagen bridgehead on March 24, 1945, having only completed firing trials on their new vehicles just two weeks previously. This image shows the company's last three Jagdtigers together with a number of support vehicles drawn up on the Schillerplatz in Iserlohn.

5.22a. Commanded by Hauptmann Albert Ernst, an experienced soldier who had been awarded the Knight's Cross as a platoon leader on the Russian Front, the company had been ordered to defend Iserlohn. However, Ernst took it upon himself to surrender both his command and the town despite the potential danger to his family, who were still living in Dresden. The German defenders were well equipped with fuel and ammunition, unusually at this stage of the war, including 128mm rounds for the main guns of the Jagdtigers. This photograph shows rifles and boxes of machine gun ammunition piled up in front of the company's transport vehicles. As can be seen here, the Jagdtiger crews wore the black Panzer uniform and the battalion was sometimes referred to in official documents of the period as Jagd-Tiger-Abteilung 512, the number following the logical sequence of army Tiger battalions.

5.22b. A partial view of a captured US M3A1 White Scout Car which may have been used by schwere Panzerjäger-Abteilung 512, although it is almost certain that elements of other units were present in Iserlohn. Repainted and conspicuously marked with the white outline of the Balkenkreuz national insignia on both the front and sides, this vehicle was, in parts, badly worn and the original US Olive Drab could be seen as a decidedly darker shade.

5.23. This Tiger II of schwere Panzer-Abteilung 506 was lost on April 11, 1945 near the village of Mahmecke, where the battalion was supporting 338.Infanterie-Division north of Schmallenberg in the Ruhr pocket. After this action, the battalion was left with just eleven serviceable tanks and very little fuel and most of the crews were serving as infantrymen. On April 14, Hauptmann Jobst-Christoph von Römer, who had assumed command on February 9 when Hauptmann Heiligenstadt was captured, gathered the survivors together in the forest of Iserlohn and formally disbanded the battalion.

5.24. The following three images depict the surrender of 11.Panzer-Division to units of US XII Corps on May 4, 1945. This photograph shows a convoy of transport vehicles passing through the village of Neumark, today know as Všeruby in the Czech Republic north-west of Pilsen, as they drive into captivity. The vehicle parked by the side of the road is a Jagdpanzer IV/70 (V) and must have been from another unit operating in the same area as neither the division's Panzer-Regiment 15 nor Panzerjäger-Abteilung 61 were ever allocated any of these tank destroyers. The hard-edged camouflage pattern may be the scheme introduced in late 1944, where swathes of Dunkelgelb RAL 7028 and Rotbraun RAL 8017 were applied over a base coat of Dunkelgrün RAL 6003 before the vehicle left the assembly plant.

5.24a. A Jagdpanzer IV/70 (V) and Pzkpfw IV ausf J of photographed after the surrender of May 4, 1945. This is not the same vehicle shown in the first image in this series but is probably from the same unidentified unit and is painted in the same factory-applied camouflage scheme. Both vehicles are very late production models, identified by the solid gun travel lock, the steering and brake access panels without armored air intakes on the hull front, and the small camouflage loops around the top of the superstructure. The first two road wheels are the metal versions designed to compensate for the added weight of the main gun. The vehicle's number may indicate that this tank destroyer was allocated to a Panzer battalion, but that is merely speculation without any further information. The Pzkpfw IV ausf J in the background is another Panzer-Regiment 15 tank and has the large company number on the turret Schürzen which is, however, largely illegible.

5.24b. Taken at the same time as the previous photographs, this image depicts a late production Pzkpfw IV ausf J of Panzer-Regiment 15, 11.Panzer-Division. Note the three steel return rollers introduced in December 1944 in place of the previous four and the lack of any form of bracket which could have held the hull Schürzen. Another Pzkpfw IV of this battalion is shown in the illustration section and the black, two-digit company numbers were an identifying feature of these II.Abteilung tanks late in the war. I can, however, offer no explanation as to their exact meaning and they may have simply been numbered sequentially throughout the battalion. Accurate figures for May are not available, and probably do not exist, although it is known that the regiment reported thirteen serviceable Pzkpfw IV tanks on hand in January 1945.

5.25. An Opel Blitz 3 ton lorry of 3.SS-Panzer-Division Totenkopf photographed on May 9, 1945 as survivors of the division entered the American lines in western Czechoslovakia. Just over 1,000 men of this formation managed to escape from the Russians after attempting to defend Vienna and they were all handed back to the Soviets. The division's famous unit insignia can be seen on the right-hand side front fender and also on the side of the wooden body.

5.26. Photographed in Norway in May 1945 this assortment of elderly Pzkpfw III tanks, including three ausf N models closest to the camera, are from Panzer-Abteilung Norwegen. This unit was originally formed from the 2nd and 3rd companies of I Abteilung, Panzer Regiment 9 of 25.Panzer-Division in September 1943 and according to the official caption to this photograph, the battalion had seventy-one tanks on hand at the time of the German surrender. All appear to be in good condition and all are coated with Zimmerit anti-magnetic mine paste. Post-war photographs also depict a number of Sturmgeschütz III assault guns operating with this unit in mine clearing actions.

APPENDIX

Glossary

Many German words or expressions, particularly those related to the military, are difficult to translate directly into English and throughout this book I have chosen to use the original form were I felt it was appropriate. The terms listed below are commonly encountered in most works on the German Army of the 1939-1945 period and although some are not used in the period covered by this book I have included them here for the reader who may want to carry out their own research or further reading. I have avoided any anglicized spellings with the exception of the scharfes S which is rendered as ß and is common in older German language publications. For example Großdeutschland, is written here as Grossdeutschland.

Abteilung. In civilian usage this word usually refers a department but its military meaning is a detachment or a battalion. In Panzer, Kavallerie and Artillerie regiments the battalions were referred to as Abteilungen. Units titled Armee-Abteilung and Korps-Abteilung were much larger formations, most of which were raised to meet the fluid conditions of the Russian front.

Abwehr. Generally referring to a defensive action or weapon. Sometimes abbreviated to Abw. The German military intelligence service was also known as the Abwehr.

Abzeichen. A badge or sign. Unit signs painted onto vehicles or signposts were known as Truppenkennzeichen.

Alarmeinheiten. This term, which translates as Alarm Unit, was commonly used to denote an ad hoc formation, usually assembled from rear area or training units to respond to local emergencies. Panzer-Kompanie Hummel, formed to aid the defense of Arnhem, was one such unit.

Allgemeines Heeresamt. The General Army Directorate which administered the various Inspectorates such as the Inspekteur der Panzertruppen. Abbreviated to AHA.

Alter Art. Older version or model.

Arko. An abbreviation of Artilleriekommandeur or Artillery Commander. These were usually the commands of corps or army level artillery units.

Armee. An organizational formation made up of two or more Korps units such as Armeekorps, Gebirgs-Armeekorps or Panzerkorps. Also referred to as an Armeeoberkommando, or AOK, it was usually commanded by a Generaloberst.

Armee-Abteilung. See Abteilung.

Armeegruppe. A formation made up of two or more Armies and usually intended as a more temporary arrangement than a Heeresgruppe. By the late war period the term had become somewhat more elastic and could refer to an Armee sized formation or the equivalent of a Korps. See also Heeresgruppe.

Armeekorps. A corps, usually containing two or more divisions in addition to attached independent units and formations, such as Sturmgeschütz or heavy tank battalions, reserves, and organic artillery and signals units. Usually commanded by a General.

Armeeoberkommando. See Armee.

Ausbildungs. Education, or in the military context, training. For example, Panzer-Ausbildungs-Verband Böhmen, a unit raised from training establishments for the defense of Prague.

Ausführung. A model designation , as in PzKpfw IV ausführung J. Usually abbreviated to ausf.

Balkenkreuz. The familiar straight-armed cross used by all branches of the Wehrmacht as a national recognition marking. It evolved from the simplified markings applied to military aircraft from early 1918.

Bataillon. A battalion usually made up of three or four companies. The term was used in the infantry and engineer branches while a battalion of an artillery, cavalry or tank was referred to as an Abteilung, as was a signals battalion. Certain independent formations were also referred to as Bataillonen. See also Abteilung

Batterie. An artillery unit of about company size. An Artillerie-Abteilung was made up of three or four Artillerie-Batterien.

Baupionier. Construction engineers.

Befehlshaber. A commander, usually with authority over a considerable area such as the Militärbefehlshaber in Belgien und Nordfrankreich, the military commander of Belgium and northern France. See also Oberbefehlshaber West.

Befehlspanzer. Command tank, sometimes Befehlspanzerwagen is used.

Begleit. An escort. For example, Führer-Begleit-Batallion, Hitler's escort battalion.

Beobachtungs. Observation. For example, Panzerbeobachtungswagen IV, an armored observation vehicle built based on a Panzer IV tank.

Berge. Recovery. Most Panzer battalions had a number recovery vehicles that were conversions built on the chassis of the tanks they were intended to tow, for example the Bergepanther.

Beute-Panzer. A Captured tank. Literally a booty tank.

Bezirkskommando. A district command.

Bodenständige. Meaning grounded or static, this term was used to describe a formation with limited mobility, in effect a garrison unit. In June 1944 approximately half the divisions defending the Normandy area were classed as Bodenständige.

Brigade. A brigade, as in English. During the early war period divisions contained brigades, usually made up of two regiments. This structure was, however, abandoned as the war progressed and the term was most often used to describe an independent formation. Some Sturmgeschütz battalions were referred to as brigades.

Brückenbau. Literally bridge construction, however, the word is almost always used to describe the bridging element of an engineer unit.

Chef. Literally, the boss. The word was also used to describe a commander, for example Kompanie chef. Hitler's staff privately referred to him as Der Chef.

Chef des Generalstabes des Heeres. Chief of the general staff of the army. The Luftwaffe and Kriegsmarine had similar appointments. Generaloberst Heinz Guderian held the position from July 21, 1944 until March 28, 1945.

Dienstgrad. Service grade, usually used in connection with rank although Rang is also correct.

Division. As in English, a division. An administrative and organizational unit generally made up of two or three regiments with support battalions and companies. Usually commanded by a Generalleutnant.

Einheit. A general term for unit or formation.

Einsatz. Employment or service.

Eisenbahn. Railroad or railway.

Eisern Kreuz. Iron Cross. Awarded for acts of bravery the second class medal was worn on the day of award only and thereafter as a ribbon while the first class medal was correctly worn on left breast of the uniform tunic. Thousands were awarded during the war, one of the last to 12 year old Hitlerjugend Alfred Zeck who was personally decorated by Hitler.

Ergängzug. Replacement. For example, Ergängzug-Einheit or replacement unit.

Ersatz. Replacement. For example, Panzer-Ersatz-Abteilung 18 , a replacement unit based at Böblingen in Germany. The Ersatzheer was the replacement Army.

Fahrer. Driver or private of a horse-drawn unit. A driver in a mechanized formation was referred to as a Kraftsfahrer.

Fahrgestell. Chassis. Each tank received a unique Fahrgestellnummer or chassis number.

Fallschirmjäger. A paratrooper. The word is also used in the titles of paratroop units, for example 3.Fallschirmjäger-Division and Fallschirm-Panzer-Jäger-Abteilung 3.

Faustpatrone. The forerunner of the Panzerfaust to which it was visually similar. The overall length, and importantly the warhead, of the Faustpatrone was, however, considerably smaller and therefore less effective.

Feld. Literally field, although in the military context the word's meaning would be the same as when it was used in the US or British armies, that is, an area of operations.

Feldausbildungseinheit. An operational training unit.

Feldgendarmerie. The military field police. Referred to within the Waffen-SS as SS-Feldgendarmerie.

Feldgrau. Field grey. The word was also a colloquialism used to describe German soldiers.

Feldheer. The active field Army, as opposed the Ersatzheer.

Feldherrnhalle. An honor title inherited from the Nazi SA or Sturm Abteilung and originally bestowed on units recruited from SA personnel. As the war progressed other units, notably 13.Panzer-Division and schwere Panzer-Abteilung 503, also received the title.

Feldjägerkorps. A military police organization formed in 1943 separate from the Feldgendarmerie and Geheime Feldpolizei and concerned mainly with apprehending deserters and preventing panic during a withdrawal, often by the harshest methods. After the surrender of Germany units of the Feldjägerkorps were rearmed and employed by the Western Allies as a police force to maintain discipline amongst German prisoners of war and civilians.

Feldlazarett. A military field hospital.

Festung. Literally a fortress. A number of depleted formations that were capable of defensive operations only were designated as Festungs-Divisionen or Festungs-Brigaden and certain locations were declared fortress cities, for example Festung Breslau.

Fliegerabwehrkanone. An anti-aircraft gun, abbreviated to Flak. Most army divisions contained a Heeres-Flak-Artillerie-Abteilung.

Flakpanzer. A tracked vehicle armed with an anti-aircraft weapon.

Flakvierling. A mounting made up of four anti-aircraft guns.

Flammenwerfer. A flamethrower.

Flammpanzer. A tracked vehicle fitted with a flamethrower.

Freiherr. A title of nobility roughly equivalent to a baron. In many regiments officers were addressed by their titles rather their rank. Major Bernd Freiherr Freytag von Loringhoven, who served on the Russian front and as adjutant to General Guderian, recalled that almost all his fellow officers of Panzer-Regiment 2 were the sons of aristocratic families.

Freiwillige. A volunteer. During the Second World War this term usually referred to a foreigner who had volunteered to serve with the German armed forces.

Führer. Literally a leader. This term was used in a number of rank titles, particularly those of the Waffen-SS, but could also be used as a general term, such as Kompanieführer. When used in the form of a proper noun, Der Führer, it invariably meant Hitler.

Funk. Radio, usually abbreviated to Fu. The term Funkgerät, of FuG, refers to a radio set.

Funklenk. Radio controlled. Abbreviated to F.L. or, more often, Fkl.

Fusilier. On 15 October 1942 infantry regiments were renamed Grenadier-Regiment except for the regiments numbered 22, 26, 27, 34, 68, 202, 230, and 334 which received the honor title Fusilier-regiment. There were also Panzer-Fusilier regiments. See also Grenadier.

Graf. A title of nobility roughly equivalent to a count.

Granatenwerfer. A mortar. Literally, a grenade thrower.

Gebirgsjäger. Mountain troops or units specially trained to operate in mountainous regions.

Geheime Feldpolizei. The German Army's plain-clothes field police. Recruited from men who had been detectives in civilian life they were mainly employed against resistance and subversive organizations.

Gemischte. Mixed. A tank company equipped with mix of tanks and assault guns was referred to as a Panzer-Kompanie (gemischte).

Gepanzerte. Armored. Mechanized infantry battalions were referred to as Panzergrenadier-Bataillon (gepanzerte). Usually abbreviated to gep or gp.

Geschütz. A gun.

Gliederung. Organisation. The term Kreigsgliederung is also encountered.

Grenadier. On 15 October 1942 infantry regiments were renamed Grenadier-Regiment. The change did not affect the title of the parent division, as is sometimes stated, which continued to be referred to as Infanterie-Division. A certain number of divisions were, however, raised as or rebuilt as Grenadier-Divisionen.

Generalkommando. A general headquarters.

Grossdeutschland. Literally Greater Germany. Most often encountered as the honor title of Panzergrenadier-Division Grossdeutschland.

Hakenkreuz. Literally a hooked cross. An ancient symbol appropriated by the Nazis and almost universally known outside Germany as a swastika.

Haubitze. Howitzer.

Höherer Artillerie-Kommandeur. Literally the higher artillery commander. The officer holding this appointment was responsible for the coordination of all Armee command level artillery assets. It was term usually encountered late in the war.

Heer. The regular German Army. Began formation in 1933, announced to the world in 1935, disbanded in August of 1946 by the Allies.

Heeresgruppe. An Army Group was a formation made up of a number of Armies. This was a large and complex organisation and consisted of many support elements. For example in June 1944 Heeresgruppe B had control of 7.Armee, 15.Armee, Panzergruppe West and the Wehrmachtbefehlshaber Niederlande. An Army Group was usually commanded by a Generalfeldmarschall.

Heeresmitteilung. An army general order. These were issued on a regular basis and covered all aspects of the army life from the award of decorations to the introduction of new camouflage paints. When organizational changes were introduced the order was accompanied by a Kriegsstärkenachweisungen.

Heeres-Zeugamt. Army ordnance depot, abbreviated to H.Za.

Heimat. Homeland, Germany.

Hilfswillige. Usually abbreviated to Hiwis, these were Soviet citizens, most often prisoners, who served the Wehrmacht in non-combat roles. They are rarely encountered in the west.

Hoheitsabzeichen. The national emblem. The familiar eagle and swastika insignia worn on the right breast by Wehrmacht personnel. The units of the Waffen-SS employed a similar version which was worn on the upper left shoulder.

Infanterie. Infantry.

Inspekteur. Literally inspector. Each branch of the army was overseen by an Inspector-General, for example the Inspekteur der Panzertruppen.

Instandsetzung. Repair

Jäger. Literally a hunter. This term was traditionally used by the German military to describe a light infantryman or unit. As a rank it was the equivalent to private within Jäger, Gebirgsjäger, Skijäger Fallschirmjäger, and Luftwaffe ground formations. Anti-tank units were usually referred to as Panzerjäger battalions or companies.

Jagd. Literally hunt or hunting. The word is often used in conjunction with another term to describe anti-tank units or weapons. For example, the Jagdtiger which was the self-propelled anti-tank gun variant of the Tiger II tank.

Jagdpanzer. A tank destroyer.

Kampfgruppe. A battle group, usually of an ad-hoc and temporary nature. They were often, but not always, named for the commander, for example Kampfgruppe Peiper.

Kampfstaffel. A small mixed, combat unit.

Kanonier. A private of an artillery unit. A senior private was an Oberkanonier.

Kaserne. A barracks.

Kavallerie. Cavalry.

Kolonne. A column. In the military sense it was used for bridging or transport services.

Kommando. Command, abbreviated to Kdo. Not to be confused with the English commando.

Kompanie. A company. Usually 100-120 men organized into Züge or platoons.

Kompanie-Trupp. A company headquarters.

Korps. A corps. During the war the army raised a number of Armeekorps, Gebirgs- Armeekorps, Panzerkorps, Kavalleriekorps and Reservekorps. Usually made up of two or more divisions and support elements they were, however, highly flexible. Waffen -SS units were organized identically with the prefix SS.

Korps-Truppen. Independent units directly under Corps control.

Korps-Abteilung. A term used predominantly on the Eastern front where depleted divisions were into a detachment which, it was hoped, would be rebuilt into a full-strength Korps.

Kradschützen. A motorcycle unit or motorcycle infantry.

Kreigsgliederung. See Gliederung.

Kriegsmarine. The German navy.

Kriegsstärkenachweisungen. A wartime organisation table, usually abbreviated to K.St.N or simply KStN.

Kriegstagebuch. A unit war diary. Many survived the war and are an invaluable source of information.

Kübelwagen. Literally a bucket car. The familiar Volkswagen Type 82 car.

Kurz. Short.

KwK. Fully, Kampfwagenkanone. Any type of main gun mounted in an armored fighting vehicle. For example, 8.8cm KwK L/56, the gun used to arm the Tiger I.

Landespolizei. The German state police.

Lastkraftwagen. A truck.

Lehr. Literally, teaching. Military training establishments were made up of Lehr-Abteilungen for example the Artillerie-Schiess -Schule at Thorn in Germany which contained Lehr-Abteilungen 1-5 and Lehrstäbe I and II. In December 1943 the Panzer-Lehr-Division was formed from personnel drafted from various schools and instructional establishments throughout Germany.

Lehrgang. A training course.

Leichte. Light. Can refer to either weight or a type of unit as in leichte Infanterie-Division.

Legion. As in English, a legion. Often used by both the Heer and Waffen-SS to describe a unit made up of foreigners in German service. A Legion was of no fixed size and could vary from battalion to brigade strength. See also Osttruppen.

Luftwaffe. The German air force. The Luftwaffe also controlled a number of paratroop and ground units as well as independent Sturmgeschütz battalions. The largest formation under its control were the Hermann Göring Panzer and Panzergrenadier divisions which served on the Eastern front.

Marine-Infanterie-Division. In 1945, three divisions were raised from surplus Kriegsmarine personnel and two further divisions were in the process of formation when the war ended, although the latter may have been fictitious titles invented to camouflage the movements of other formations. They were commanded by a mixture of navy and army officers and fought as regular infantry formations.

Maschinengewehr. Machinegun, abbreviated to MG.

Minenraumen. Mine clearing.

Mitte. The center, as in Heeresgruppe Mitte.

Mittlere. Medium.

Motorisiert. Motorized. Used to indicate a unit equipped with wheeled transport.

Musketier. An honor title granted to a regiment of the Grossdeutschland division late in the war. It was probably formed personnel of the division's Panzer-Fusilier regiment and tanks crews fighting as infantry. See also Fusilier.

Nachricten. Signals.

Nachschub. Supply service.

Nahkampfwaffen. Close defense weapon.

Nebel. Literally meaning fog, the word is used in the military context in connection with smoke or chemical weapons. For example, Nebelgranate or smoke shell.

Nebelkerzen. Smoke candles. Early models of some German tanks, including the Tiger I, were fitted with smoke candle dischargers. It was found that stray rounds could ignite the candle inside the discharger and they were dropped from production during 1943 although some could be seen in combat for some time.

Neu. New.

Nebelwerfer. Usually used in reference to rocket artillery. To circumvent the restrictions of the Versailles Treaty, early versions of these weapons were name Nebelwerfer, literally smoke projector, to hide their true purpose.

Oberbefehlshaber West. Abbreviated to OB West, the high command of the armed forces on the Western front was directly subordinated to Oberkommando der Wehrmacht. In June 1944 Feldmarschall Gerd von Rundstedt held this position. By May 1945 OB West was reduced to the command of units fighting in Bavaria.

Oberkommando des Heeres. The high command of the army. Abbreviated to OKH.

Oberkommando der Wehrmacht. The high command of the armed forces. Abbreviated to OKW.

Ostheeres. A general term for the German army on the Eastern front.

Osttruppen. A generic term used to describe Soviet citizens who had volunteered to with the Germans. From early 1942 Armenians, Azeris, Georgians, North Caucasians, Turkestanis and Volga Tartars were formed into Ostlegionen while the battalions raised from Estonians, Russians, Byelorussians and Ukrainians were referred to as Osbataillonen. The many Hilfswillige, or volunteer helpers, recruited on a semi-official basis from Soviet prisoners of war were not considered part of the Ostruppen.

Panzerabwehrkanone. An anti-tank gun. Abbreviated to Pak or PaK.

Panzer. Literally armor, however, in the military context the word refers to German tanks and tank units. The term was incorporated into the titles of formations which had a similar function, for example Panzerjäger, or were organic elements of Panzer divisions, such as Panzer-Artillerie or Panzer-Pionier. Engineers attached to a Panzer division.

Panzerbefehlswagen. A command tank.

Panzerbeobachtungswagen. A tank converted for artillery observation. A total of 262 vehicles based on the Panzer III and a further 133 on the Panzer IV were built during the war. The proposed conversion based on the Panther tank was abandoned.

Panzerfaust. A single shot rocket-propelled anti-tank weapon. The culmination of the Faustpatrone program. The Panzerfaust was produced in five versions with the last model, the Panzerfaust 150, going into service just weeks before the end of the war. Prototypes of the proposed Panzerfaust 250 influenced the development of the Soviet RPG.

Panzergranate. An armor-piercing shell. Abbreviated to Pzgr. There were several different types produced during the war including shells with a ballistic cap and also solid high-density core rounds.

Panzergrenadier. Armored Infantry. Contrary to popular belief not all Panzergrenadiers travelled to the battlefield in armored halftracks and, by the late war period, many consid-

ered themselves fortunate to be equipped with trucks.

Panzerjäger. Literally, a tank hunter. Most anti-tank units were referred to as Panzerjäger, for example schwere Panzerjäger-Abteilung 512 which was equipped with the Jagdtiger tank destroyer. Regardless of their equipment, Panzerjäger units were administered by the Inspekteur der Panzertruppen.

Panzerschreck. The popular name for the Raketenpanzerbüchse, a man-portable anti-tank rocket launcher similar to the US Army's Bazooka.

Panzerzerstörer. Literally mean tank destroyer. Some late war units were given this title.

Panzer-Jagd-Kommando. Formed almost at the end of the war, these units were made up primarily of boys from the Hitler Youth and Volkssturm men equipped with bicycles, if available, and armed with Panzerfausts. They were later renamed Panzer-Jagd-Verbände.

Panzerkampfwagen. Literally an armored fighting vehicle, but specifically a tank.

Panzer-Kompanie. A tank company, usually commanded by a Hauptmann.

Panzer-Regiment. A tank regiment, usually made up of two Abteilungen and commanded by a Oberst or Oberstleutnant.

Pionier. Engineer. The engineer battalion of a Panzer division was referred to as Panzer-Pionier-Bataillon.

Pionierpanzerwagen. An armored engineer

vehicle, specifically an SdKfz 251/7 halftrack equipped with the bridging sections.

RAL. Formed in 1925, the Reichs-Ausschuss für Lieferbedingungen und Gütesicherung was the German national quality assurance organization which gave its name to the RAL color system which is still in operation today. Army and Kreigsmarine vehicles and ships were painted in colors based on the RAL classifications, for example RAL 7028 Dunkelgelb, while the Luftwaffe maintained its own system.

Radfahr. A bicycle. Some infantry formations contained a mobile reconnaissance unit equipped with bicycles.

Reiter. Literally a rider. In the military sense, a cavalryman. The rank was equivalent to private in mounted units.

Reiter-Regiment. A cavalry regiment.

Ritterkreuz. Commonly referred to as the Knight's Cross, the correct title is Ritterkreuz des Eisernen Kreuzes, or Knight's Cross of the Iron Cross. Instituted in 1939, the Ritterkreuz and its grades were the highest awards that German military personnel could receive. It cannot, however, be compared to the Victoria Cross or the Congressional Medal of Honor, both of which can only be earned for acts of uncommon valor in the face of the enemy. Many senior German commanders were awarded the Ritterkreuz for the successful conduct of an operation while U-Boat commanders were decorated for sinking 100,000 tons of shipping and a points system operated for Luftwaffe fighter pilots.

Ritterkreuzträger. Someone awarded the Knight's Cross.

Rollbahn. The main route of advance.

Sanitäts. Medical services.

Schlacht. Battle.

Schiesschule. Gunnery school. Armored training establishments were all under the command of the Kommandeur der Schuler der Panzertruppen.

Schnell. Literally, fast or hurry. Administratively, Panzer, Panzergenadier and Panzerjäger units were referred to as Schnelltruppen.

Schürzen. Removable armor plates fitted to the hull side, and sometimes the turret, of German tanks.

Schützenpanzerwagen. An armored infantry carrier, abbreviated to SPW. Usually refers to the SdKfz 250 and 251 halftracks.

Schwadron. A Squadron. A term used in the cavalry, a squadron was basically a company-sized unit. The companies of Panzer-Regiment 24, which had been raised from a cavalry unit, continued to be referred to as Schwadronen.

Schwere. Heavy. Could be used when referring to a weight class or to the equipment of a specific unit, for example schwere Panzer-Abteilung, a Tiger tank battalion.

Selbsfahrlafette. Self-propelled.

Sicherung. Security.

Sicherungseinheit. Security unit or detachment.

Sonderkraftfahrzeug. A special purpose vehicle, usually abbreviated to Sd.Kfz. or SdKfz. All German armored fighting vehicle were identified by a Sonderkraftfahrzeug inventory number, for example SdKfz 181 Panzerkampfwagen VI Tiger Ausf. E.

Sonderverband. A special unit. This term could refer to a special operations formation, for example Sonderverband 288, or it could be applied to a temporary unit organized for a special purpose.

Stab. A headquarters or staff.

Stahlhelm. A steel helmet. Probably the most distinctive feature of the German soldier.

Standarte. Prior to 1940 a regiment of the Waffen-SS was referred to as a Standarte, hence the rank Standartenführer. After the French campaign the standard Wehrmacht unit designations were adopted.

Stellung. A fighting position.

Strassenbau. Road building or construction. Road engineer unit.

Stummel. Literally a stump, this was the unofficial name given to the SdKfz 251/9 halftrack armed with the short-barreled 75mm gun.

Sturm. Literally storm but more often assault.

Sturmartillerie. Literally assault artillery. This term was used during the early-war period to describe the assault gun units as they were controlled by the Inspekteur der Artillerie. The term came back into use in 1944 when some assault gun battalions were renamed as Heeres-Sturmartillerie-Brigaden.

Sturmbann. A term used to describe a battalion by Waffen-SS units until 1940.

Sturmgeschütz. Assault gun. Initially referred to the self-propelled guns built on the chassis of the Panzer III and later Panzer IV tanks, this term was also used later in the war for the companies of Panzerjäger battalions equipped with armored vehicles.

Sturmhaubitze. The howitzer armed version of the Sturmgeschütz III.

Sturm-Mörser. The 38cm armed assault gun built on the chassis of the Tiger I. Just nineteen of these vehicles were built, including the mild steel prototype, and saw action with three Sturm-Mörser -Kompanien before the end of the war.

Sturmpionier. A assault engineer.

Tauchpanzer. A tank specially equipped to run under water. These are rarely encountered in the period covered by this book.

Teile. A part or portion of a unit. This expression is often seen on contemporary situation maps and is sometimes abbreviated as Tle.

Totenkopf. Literally a death's head. As a form of uniform insignia the Totenkopf was used by the cavalry of Frederick the Great and possibly earlier. The version worn by the Panzer units is significantly different to the Waffen-SS model.

Tropen. Tropical. A term which could be applied to everything from uniform items to vehicle modifications.

Truppenkennzeichen. Unit signs painted onto vehicles or signposts to identify a particular formation. Although these were necessarily approved by division or corps level command, many unofficial versions existed.

Truppenübungsplatz. A military training area. The German army controlled ninety-five main training centers within Germany and the annexed territories of Poland and Czechoslovakia. Most of these establishments had smaller satellites. The military facilities of the occupied countries were also appropriated and the Waffen-SS had six of its own major training grounds.

Umbenannt. Reformed or reorganized.

Verband. A unit.

Versorgung. Supply.

Veterinär. Veterinarian.

Volksgrenadier. Literally, people's grenadier or infantry. A number of infantry division's formed or rebuilt from August 1944 were named Volksgrenadier as a morale building exercise. They were organized along the same lines as regular infantry formations although they were allocated a greater number of automatic weapons. These formations should not be confused with Volkssturm.

Volkssturm. The German national militia formed from October 1944. All males between the ages of 16 and 60, who were not already serving in the armed forces, were eligible for conscription into the Volkssturm.

Waffenamt. Ordnance department.

Waffen-SS. The armed units of the SS or Schutzstaffel.

Werfer. Literally a projector or thrower. See also Nebelwerfer and Granatenwerfer.

Wehrmacht. The German armed forces was made up of the Heer, Luftwaffe and Kriegsmarine. The Waffen-SS, while under the authority of the Reichsführer-SS and the Nazi Party, was tactically subordinated to the Wehrmacht.

Wehrmachtsgefolge. A cover-all term used to refer to organizations that were part of the armed forces but served outside Germany supporting units of the Wehrmacht such the Reichsarbeitsdienst, Deutsche Rote Kreuz, and Organization Todt. Working under the authority of the Wehrmacht also provided these groups with some protection under the Geneva Convention.

Werkstatt-Kompanie. A maintenance company.

Wirtschaft. Administration.

z.b.V. (zur besonderen Verwendung). For special use.

Zimmerit. A thick past applied to the horizontal surfaces of armored vehicles, most often tanks, for roughly a year until September 1944. Once applied the paste was softened with a blow torch and scored with a trowel or special roller to produce a pattern of ridges or grids. The resulting uneven surface was intended to minimize the ability of magnetic mines to stick to the vehicle.

Zug. A platoon. Several Züge formed a company.

Zugkraftwagen. A three-quarter tracked towing vehicle.

COMPARATIVE RANK TABLE

Heer	Waffen-SS	Luftwaffe	Reichsarbeitsdienst (RAD)	Deutscher Volkssturm	British Army	US Army
Schütze (1)	SS-Schütze (1)	Flieger (5)	Arbeitsmann	Volkssturmmann	Private	Private
Oberschütze	SS-Oberschütze					Private 1st Class
Gefreiter	SS-Sturmmann	Gefreiter	Vormann		Lance Corporal	
Obergefreiter	SS-Rottenführer	Obergefreiter	Obervormann			
Stabsgefreiter		Hauptgefreiter (6)	Hauptvormann			
Fahnenjunker (2)	SS-Junker (2)	Fahnenjunker (2)				
Unteroffizier	SS-Unterscharführer	Unteroffizier	Untertruppführer	Gruppenführer	Corporal	Corpoal
Unterfeldwebel	SS-Scharführer	Unterfeldwebel			Sergeant	Sergeant
Fähnrich (2)	SS-Oberjunker (2)	Fähnrich				
Feldwebel	SS-Oberscharführer	Feldwebel	Truppführer			Staff Sergeant
Oberfeldwebel	SS-Hauptscharführer	Oberfeldwebel	Obertruppführer		Company Sergeant Major	Master Sergeant
Hauptfeldwebel						
Oberfähnrich (2)	SS-Standartenoberjunker (2)	Oberfähnrich (2)				
Stabsfeldwebel	SS-Sturmscharführer	Stabsfeldwebel	Unterfeldmeister		Regimental Sergeant Major	Warrant Officer
Leutnant	SS-Untersturmführer	Leutnant	Feldmeister	Zugführer	Second-Lieutenant	Second-Lieutenant
Oberleutnant	SS-Obersturmführer	Oberleutnant	Oberfeldmeister		First-Lieutenant	First-Lieutenant
Hauptmann (3)	SS-Hauptsturmführer	Hauptmann	Obserstfeldmeister	Kompanieführer	Captain	Captain
Major	SS-Sturmbannführer	Major	Arbeitsführer	Bataillonsführer	Major	Major
Oberstleutnant	SS-Obersturmbannführer	Oberstleutnant	Oberarbeitsführer	Kreisstabsführer (7)	Lieutenant-Colonel	Lieutenant-Colonel
Oberst	SS-Standartenführer	Oberst	Oberstarbeitsführer		Colonel	Colonel
	SS-Oberführer (4)					
Generalmajor	SS-Brigadeführer	Generalmajor	Generalarbeitsführer	Gaustabsführer (7)	Brigadier	Brigadier-General
Generalleutnant	SS-Gruppenführer	Generalleutnant	Obergeneralarbeitsführer	Gauleiter (7)	Major General	Major General
General	SS-Obergruppenführer	General	Generalfeldmeister	Stabsführer (8)	Lieutenant General	Lieutenant General
Generaloberst	SS-Oberstgruppenführer	Generaloberst	Generaloberstfeldmeister		General	General
Generalfeldmarschall	Reichsführer-SS	Generalfeldmarschall	Reichsarbeitsführer		Field Marshal	General of the Army

Within German military and paramilitary organizations, rank is known as Dienstgrad or service grade. The rank of Schütze (1) indicated a private of an infantry regiment. In the cavalry, a private soldier was referred to as a Reiter, a Kanonier in the artillery, a Pionier for engineers, Funker for signals, Panzerschütze in a tank unit, and Jäger for light infantry or a mountain unit. Somewhat confusingly, an Oberjäger was the equivalent of an Unteroffizier. In late 1942, in an effort to boost morale, infantry regiments were renamed Grenadier-Regimenter and the rank of Schütze became Grenadier while a private of an armored infantry regiment was a Panzergrenadier. Certain infantry regiments received the honor titles of Fusilier and Musketier and their soldiers were renamed accordingly. The ranks of Fähnrich and Junker (2) signified an NCO who had been accepted as an officer candidate. A Captain or Hauptmann (3) was referred to as a Rittmeister in the cavalry or any mounted branch. Similarly, the rank of Feldwebel was replaced by Wachtmeister in cavalry, artillery, signals, and any horse-drawn formations. In fact, the non-commissioned officer rank structure was quite complex, with titles such as Oberbeschlagmeister identifying a battalion Farrier sergeant major, but it need not be detailed here. It should be noted that battalions or regiments which had been raised from cavalry formations, such as Panzer-Regiment 24, continued to use the cavalry rank titles. In addition, many German officers were from aristocratic families and, in some regiments at least, were addressed by their titles rather than rank. The Waffen-SS rank of Oberführer (4) had no direct equivalent and was a holdover from the early days of the Nazi Party. It should be thought of as a senior Colonel. The Luftwaffe rank of Flieger (5) only applied to flying units and due to the meddling of Reichsmarschall Göring, the air force controlled a large number of infantry and armored formations, which used a rank structure similar to the Heer. Within paratroop and Luftwaffe ground units, Schütze was replaced by Jäger with the rank of Oberjäger being the equivalent of an Unteroffizier, as it was in the army. The specialized ranks such as Kanonier, Pionier, Funker, and Panzergrenadier were also used. The rank of Hauptgefreiter (6) was abolished in May 1944 and replaced by Stabsgefreiter, which had been introduced earlier in the year. The units of the Volkssturm, which first went into combat in October 1944, were never employed in greater than battalion strength. The upper ranks shown here (7), although officially in control of these militia units, were in fact functionaries of the Nazi regime and are included here as a matter of interest only. Interestingly, the rank of Stabsführer (8) was a Hitlerjugend grade, although it is uncertain if this indicates any connection with that organization. During the last weeks of the war, four divisions and two mountain brigades were raised from men of the Reichsarbeitsdienst or RAD, the official state labor service. Personnel of RAD units had in fact fought in the front line during the war, famously reinforcing 9.SS-Panzer-Division in the battles around Arnhem in Holland. The RAD combat units raised in 1945 contained a high proportion of army officers among their commanders, although at least Infanterie-Division Schlageter, the first RAD division, was initially commanded by an RAD Generalarbeitsführer. In 1945, three divisions were raised from Kriegsmarine personnel and two further divisions were in the process of formation when the war ended, although the latter may have been fictitious titles invented to camouflage the movements of other formations. They were commanded by a mixture of navy and army officers. Within the army and air force, the rank of General was formally given with the officer's branch—for example, General der Panzertruppen or General der Fallschirmtruppe. General officers of the Waffen-SS were formally referred to by their Schutzstaffel title and its army equivalent—for example, SS-Oberstgruppenführer und Generaloberst der Waffen-SS. In the field, there was a tendency for Waffen-SS personnel to adopt the simpler Heer ranks—for instance, Major instead of SS-Sturmbannführer—and the office of the Reichsführer-SS was forced to issue a number of directives during the war forbidding the practice.